FOR WINDOWS & MACINT

SHOCKWAVE!

breathe new Life
into your
web pages

FOR WINDOWS & MACINTOSH

SHOCKWAVE!

breathe new life into your web pages

DARREL **PLANT**

A **VENTANA** Production

Library of Congress Cataloging-in-Publication Data

Plant, Darrel.
Shockwave! : breathe new life into your Web pages / Darrel Plant.
p.   cm.
Includes index.
ISBN 1-56604-441-3
1. Multimedia systems. 2. Macromedia director. 3. Shockwave   (Computer file) 4. World Wide Web (Information retrieval system)
I. Title
QA76.575.P58 1996
006.75—dc20   96-12645
CIP

First Edition 9 8 7 6 5 4 3 2 1
Printed in the United States of America

Ventana Communications Group, Inc.
P.O. Box 13964
Research Triangle Park, NC 27709-3964
919/544-9404
FAX 919/544-9472

President/CEO
Josef Woodman

Vice President of Content Development
Karen A. Bluestein

Production Manager
John Cotterman

Technology Operations Manager
Kerry L. B. Foster

Product Marketing Manager
Diane Lennox

Art Director
Marcia Webb

Product Manager
Cheri Robinson

Developmental Editor
Tim Huddleston

Project Editor
Jessica A. Ryan

Copy Editor
Marion Laird

Assistant Editor
JJ Hohn

Cover Designer
Laura A. Stalzer

Desktop Publisher
Jaimie Livingston

Proofreader
Angela Anderson

Indexer
Stephen Bach

Dedication

This book is dedicated to my wife, Barbara, and my parents, JoAnn and David.

About the Author

Darrel Plant is a multimedia producer for Moshofsky/Plant Creative Services in Portland, Oregon, where he has specialized in the production of compact disk-based multimedia presentations and World Wide Web site design. Plant teaches Macromedia Director for the Portland (Oregon) State University Multimedia Professional Certificate Program. He published and edited the quarterly *Plant's Review of Books* and has written for *Step-by-Step Graphics* and *WIRED* magazines. Plant currently edits the newsletter of the Oregon chapter of the International Interactive Communications Society and is Vice President of the chapter for the year 1996.

Acknowledgments

My most profuse thanks go to my wife and partner, Barbara Moshofsky, without whose encouragement and understanding I would not have (a) even tried to undertake a project such as this or (b) been able to finish it.

Extreme thanks are also due the following:

My agent, David Rogelberg of Studio B, for floating the idea in the first place and for doing a fantastic job of coordinating everything on the business end.

Cheri, Jessica, JJ, Eric, and everyone else at Ventana for their hard, hard work getting everything together for the book.

David Duddleston of Violet Arcana, who provided invaluable advice and samples for the chapter on sound.

the-guys@moshplant.com: Eric Rewitzer, Peter Sylwester, and Brian "No, not Brain" Wry, who all deserve oodles of credit for their support throughout the process.

Praise be to Brad Hicks of Hicks Design Group and Dale Ott of Design Studio 2, who for two months had to shift the portions of their production schedules for which they relied on me in order to accommodate the creation of this book.

And last—but far from least—thanks to my family: my parents, JoAnn and David Plant, for all of the support they've given over many years, and my grandmothers, Grace Danton and Margaret Baker, for their interest—and therefore my interest—in books and writing.

Contents

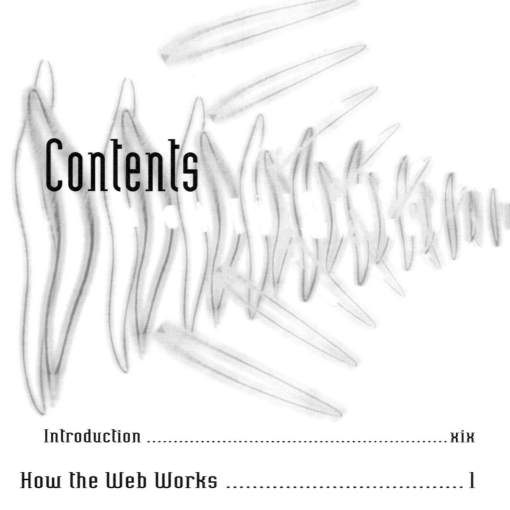

Introduction

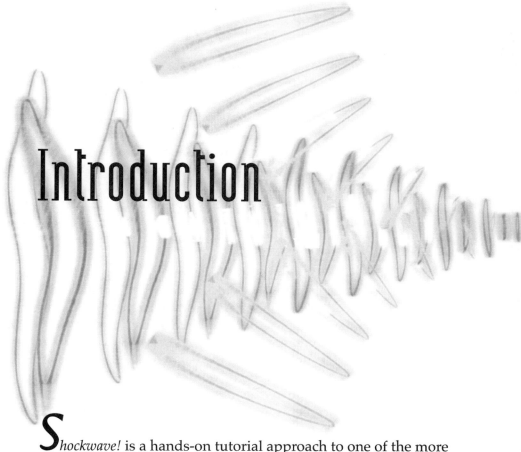

*S*hockwave! is a hands-on tutorial approach to one of the more interesting things to come down the information turnpike: Macromedia's Shockwave for Director. Shockwave for Director lets users—over 200,000 of them—of Macromedia's premiere multimedia authoring tool create truly interactive presentations, with animation and sound, for the World Wide Web.

This book focuses on how to optimize graphics and sound for your Shockwave movies, and emphasizes the new Shockwave Lingo commands and functions through the use of exercises specifically created to highlight a particular ability of this new technology.

Shockwave allows you to create complex and attractive multimedia presentations for the Internet using a tool far simpler to learn and/or use than other technologies with the same capabilities (can you say "Java"?). While somewhat limited in scope in its first releases, Shockwave has already been incorporated by many companies and organizations into their World Wide Web sites.

Because Macromedia allows free downloading of the Shockwave viewer (a plug-in for Web browsers) and Afterburner (the tool that creates Shockwave movies from Director files), it's possible for anyone with a browser capable of supporting the plug-in to view Shockwave movies. And anyone with Director 4.04 on Windows or Mac OS platforms can create Shockwave movies.

It was early in 1995, just after we at Moshofsky / Plant set up our own World Wide Web server, that I started to worry about the direction my own skills were taking. I'd gotten into multimedia because of the promise it showed for integrating graphics and sound with the power of the computer to control the entire experience.

As I spent more and more time working in HTML, coding pages, converting graphics to GIFs, optimizing our Web server, and collecting tools that would make the tedious tasks easier, I was spending less and less time using Director. "The Web is the future," everyone was saying. "Learn HTML and CGI or die." Indeed, I spent more of the year working on Web sites than I did on more "conventional" multimedia.

Then in the middle of the year, Macromedia began making announcements about how they were meeting the challenge of online communications, and the word "Shockwave" began to be bandied about. A light began to glimmer at the end of the tunnel.

The Shockwave seminars at the Macromedia Users Conference in October were jammed, almost as if the plan was to create a pressure cooker atmosphere. Many of the people I talked to said a deciding factor in their decision to attend the 1995 conference was to get their first look at Shockwave.

On December 4, 1995, the floodgates opened, with the release of the public beta test of the Shockwave plug-in (for Windows—the Mac OS plug wouldn't be ready for two more months) and Afterburner tool (for both platforms). Shockwave sites began to multiply.

For me, a happy convergence was occurring. The Internet and the World Wide Web, which had threatened to drag me away from the type of responsive, synchronized work that had attracted me to multimedia in the first place, was becoming a place where—with a little planning and good craftsmanship—I could create work that appealed to those original sensibilities.

1996 looks good.

Who Needs This Book?

Shockwave! is intended for anyone interested in creating interactive multimedia for the World Wide Web using Macromedia Director and Shockwave for Director.

The exercises in this book are constructed so that a beginning Director user should be able to follow the instructions. But because our central focus has been on demonstrating the techniques of preparing graphics and sound for Internet delivery and the use of Shockwave Lingo commands, experienced Director users who have been more focused on other areas apart from the Web will be able to get something out of them as well.

What's Inside?

Each of the eight chapters of this book deals with a specific area of knowledge necessary for using Shockwave for Director.

Chapter 1, "How the Web Works," provides some background on the Internet and the World Wide Web, focusing on the URL addressing schemes used in HTML and Shockwave.

Chapter 2, "Into the Shockwave," focuses on how Shockwave fits into the scheme of things on the Web, how it works, and its capabilities.

Chapter 3, "Eine Kleine Shockwave," takes you through the procedure to create your first Shockwave movie using the Afterburner. Then it moves on to showing how interactivity using Shockwave differs from the standard Web page, and guides you through the process of creating a set of pages and movies using Shockwave Lingo.

Chapter 4, "Preparing Graphics for Shockwave," details how to squeeze the most from your bitmap and object graphics for use in Shockwave movies, as well as how to convert an existing Web design into something Shockwave.

Chapter 5, "Asynchronous Text," introduces another series of Shockwave Lingo commands and functions that allow you to read text files from Web servers and use them to control and modify your Shockwave movies.

Chapter 6, "Other Asynchronous Operations," completes the introduction of Shockwave Lingo commands and functions, with exercises that focus on how to manage multiple Shockwave Lingo operations.

Chapter 7, "The Sounds of Shockwave," shows how to prepare sounds for Shockwave so that they don't hog Internet bandwidth, and details how to use several short, repeatable sound loops to vary the user experience.

Chapter 8, "Shockwave Tricks," brings many of the previously discussed techniques together to do things like keeping the screen from being blank while your movies are loading, testing the speed of your connection with the user, using Shockwave movies as button bars, and using tiled objects in graphics.

Finally, visit the Gallery, which highlights 14 movies created by some very talented Shockwave artists and programmers.

In addition to the eight chapters and gallery that comprise the book proper, you'll find six appendices: Appendix A, "About the Online Companion"; Appendix B, "About the Companion CD-ROM"; Appendix C, "Shockwave Lingo," provides a useful reference for all of the Shockwave Lingo terms; Appendix D, "What You Can't Do With Shockwave," lists the features of Director that are disabled or unavailable in Shockwave; Appendix E, "File Size Estimates," is a chart of approximate final file sizes for Director movies and Shockwave movies made from them; and Appendix F, "Configuring Your Web Server for Shockwave," concerns the MIME type information needed for your World Wide Web server to properly serve Shockwave files.

Hardware & Software Requirements

To follow the exercises in this book, you will need a computer running the Windows 3.1, Windows 95, or Mac OS operating system. Software needs include Macromedia Director and Afterburner and a plug-in-capable Web browser with the Shockwave for Director plug-in installed. Some exercises in Chapter 4 require an image-editing program such as Adobe Photoshop, and an exercise in Chapter 7 details the use of Macromedia SoundEdit 16.

Many of the Shockwave Lingo commands in Chapters 5 and later require that the files you create be served through a World Wide Web server, so Internet access to a server configured for serving Shockwave movies is necessary for those exercises.

Keep On Shockin'

The world of Shockwave is new and evolving. This book will give you your first set of Shockwave lungs and get you onto dry land, but it's up to you to grow legs and run with it. Shockwave for Director is truly the most accessible tool available for bringing to the Web the type of interactive multimedia that people have come to expect from computer presentations.

At Moshofsky/Plant we are always interested in comments and examples of what's being done in the world of multimedia. Feel free to send any such contributions you may have to us at shockwave@moshplant.com.

1
How the Web Works

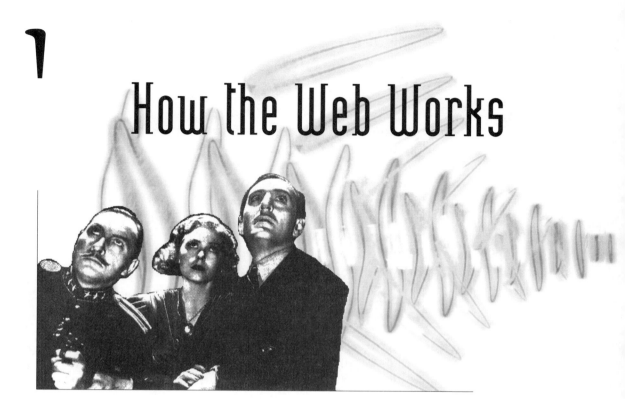

Multimedia projects created for use with Macromedia's Shockwave for Director are delivered via World Wide Web browsers. At the time of this writing, the only browser which supported the Shockwave technology was Netscape Navigator 2.0 (and plug-ins were available only for Microsoft Windows and Windows 95, and the Apple Mac OS), but Macromedia has future compatibility plans for the Microsoft Internet Explorer, Navisoft Navipress, and SGI's WebForce, among others.

The World Wide Web is just a part (although for the past year or two, it's been the most *talked about* part) of the international network of computer systems we call the Internet. The focus of this book will be entirely on the World Wide Web, but many of the underpinnings of the Web are dependent on the larger supporting structure of the Internet.

The Internet

An internet (lowercase *i*) is simply a term referring to a number of connected local-area or wide-area networks (LANs and WANs). *The Internet* (uppercase *I*) that's been making all the headlines lately is simply the biggest collection of connected networks in the world. The Internet grew out of work begun nearly thirty years ago to link military research computer systems together. As time went on, other networks sprang up and gradually, around the early 1980s, began connecting together—in effect creating the underpinnings of the Internet as we know it . . . this year.

Internet Growth

Increasingly, private networks developed, owned, and operated by companies and institutions have linked their systems to the larger—and now worldwide—network. By doing so, all or part of those private networks effectively have become parts of *the* Internet. Despite a wide variety of internal network protocols and a huge variety of computer types connected to those networks— everything from dumb terminals on legacy systems, to home computers dialing up online services, to workstations on a LAN— virtually any machine attached to the Internet can communicate with any other, directly or indirectly.

The Internet is largely based on what is known as a *client-server* relationship between computers. One computer, the *client*, makes a request of some sort, and the other computer, usually one dedicated to a particular task (or tasks), responds to the request as the *server*. Generally, the requests are relatively short—in part by necessity—because until recent years most connections to the Internet have been comparatively limited. Recent years have seen an amazing amount of progress in data communication technology, and it's now possible to have a digital phone line installed in your home that's many times faster than the connections available to most companies and organizations only a decade ago.

Internet Addresses

Addresses on the Internet (for the time being) are composed of four numbers ranging from 0 to 255, separated by periods. Every computer directly attached to the network through a dial-up or dedicated connection is assigned an IP (Internet Protocol) address. The IP address, in turn, is usually given an alphanumeric name in a DNS (Domain Name Server), so that when you send some sort of request to, for instance, moshplant.com, you don't need to know that the actual address is 38.248.92.3. The name is called a *domain* and is much easier to remember than the numerical sequence. Additionally, the domain can be assigned to a different set of numbers, should there be a need to change the server to another machine on the network or should the organization change its ISP (Internet Service Provider). Through a fairly complex updating scheme, DNS systems can allow information about the addresses they maintain to percolate into the rest of the Internet, so that when changes to the numerical address occur, those addresses can still be found by someone referring to the domain name.

There are a number of top-level domains, the .com and .edu domains probably being the most well known. Most countries now have their own two-letter codes for domains (.ca is Canada and .mx is Mexico).

Within each of the top-level domains is a variety of second-level (and third-level) domains. In the United States, which started off with most of the addresses in the first place, it's gotten to the point that the San Francisco area has its own domain (.sf.ca.us). Most companies that have affiliated with the Internet have registered their own second-level domain within .com (as if you hadn't already figured that out), schools within .edu, nonprofit organizations within .org, etc.

Masters of Their Own Domains

Each domain administrator can assign subdomain names within the domain they're in charge of, and large companies or organizations may have several levels of subdomains. Additionally, each computer within a domain may be assigned an individual named address. Administrators can assign different names to the same computer—or even the same name to different computers. When you see a Web address for www.moshplant.com (which would be a subdomain of moshplant.com), that could be the same computer as ftp.moshplant.com or another machine altogether. The address *hueylong.studio.moshplant.com* would most likely refer to an individual machine named hueylong within the studio subdomain of the moshplant.com second-level domain.

Serving the Net

As recently as two years ago, books introducing the Internet to the general public usually described four major services: e-mail (electronic mail), Usenet news, Telnet, and FTP (File Transfer Protocol), along with other, lesser services such as Archie, Gopher, WAIS (Wide Area Information Servers), and—oh, yeah—something called the World Wide Web. Internet sites may run one or more of these services, with one or more computers devoted to each service, or even one computer running all services. The first incarnation of my site—moshplant.com—was a Macintosh with a modem on a dedicated phone line, running just a World Wide Web server and an e-mail server.

A Packet Full of Data

Data is passed around on the Internet in a series of small chunks of information called *packets*. When data is sent from one computer to another, it travels as one or more (depending on its size) individual packets, each bearing some information about itself, not the least of which is destination. Depending on the ever-changing network conditions, packets from the same transmission may travel different paths from origin to destination.

I Link, Therefore I Am

To use Macromedia Shockwave to its full extent, you will need to know how to use URLs (Uniform Resource Locators), the addressing scheme for finding files on the Web. Most often, a reference to a URL will create a link to another file, which can be used to move among documents on the Web. The specifics are a little more complex than that, but you'll get the idea before long. In the following examples, I'll refer to HTML (which stands for HyperText Markup Language) files, but most of this information is exactly the same for any file type you can deliver on the Web, including images in GIF (Graphic Interchange Format), QuickTime video, or Shockwave movies. You've seen addresses such as this:

```
http://machine.subdomain.topdomain
```

And you've probably already figured out what the various parts of the name mean. The *http* (HyperText Transfer Protocol) at the beginning is the *method*, which tells the receiving computer that this request should be routed to an http (World Wide Web or HyperText Transfer Protocol) server. The :// separates the method header from the address. The address, *machine.domain.topdomain*, is simply the Internet address of the server. (See the "World Wide Web" section coming up soon in this chapter.)

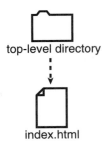

top-level directory

index.html

Figure 1-1: *The default page is served indirectly by a URL pointing to the server.*

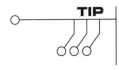

TIP

You can use the numeric IP address rather than the alpha-numeric domain name if you wish. But by doing so, your link will become invalid if the server changes to another machine that is assigned a different numeric address.

The example above will return only the default document for the top-level directory of the Web server. This is usually a file named "index.html" (or "index.htm"), a name specified by the server administrator and commonly referred to as the "home page." The same file could be accessed by the following URL:

```
http://machine.subdomain.topdomain/index.html
```

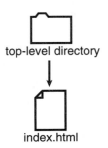

top-level directory

index.html

Figure 1-2: *The default page is served by a URL pointing directly to the file.*

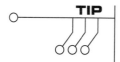

TIP Server administrators have varying methods of dealing with default pages, and not all will use "index" as the default file name for their directories.

Instead of just grouping all of the files accessible on a server in one directory, most administrators will create subdirectories in the top-level directory, for reasons of both organization and efficiency. On the server machine, a directory will hold the files to be accessed by the server, and this directory may itself be the following:

```
http://machine.subdomain.topdomain/subdirectory/file.html
```

Where *subdirectory* is inside the top-level directory, and *file.html* is inside *subdirectory*. Slashes are used to separate directories and file names (the domain name by itself is considered a reference to the top-level directory of the server).

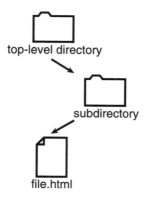

top-level directory

subdirectory

file.html

Figure 1-3: *A URL indicates a file in a subdirectory of the top-level directory.*

Close Relatives

An important thing to remember is that the URLs above are *complete* URLs, and if you're making references to files on your own server, it may be best not to use them. Relative URLs, which leave off most of the address, can be used to reference other files up or down the directory structure from the originating page (or *referrer*). Using relative URLs means that the entire file structure of a site can be moved from one place to another, allowing development to occur on one machine, with the actual serving being done on another.

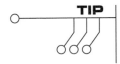

TIP

URLs are relative to the *page* or movie they are called from. Because a Shockwave movie need not be in the same directory as the page in which it's placed, references made relative from the page may not be correct.

A relative URL which specifies a file on the same server and within the same directory as the referring page can be as simple as the following:

```
otherfile.html
```

If there's no http method prefix, browser programs automatically know that the URL is relative, and they add the server and directory information of the current page.

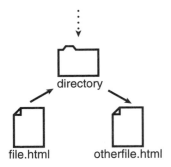

Figure 1-4: *A simple relative URL in* file.html *references another file of the same directory.*

A file in a subdirectory of the current directory is easily referenced by using the subdirectory and the file name, separated by a slash:

```
subdirectory/otherfile.html
```

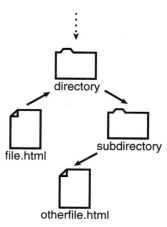

Figure 1-5: *A relative URL references another file in a subdirectory of the current directory.*

A file in a directory above the current level can also be referenced, by using two periods (dots, as they're usually called) instead of a directory name for each level up the directory structure you need to go. A file one level above the referring document would be as follows:

```
../otherfile.html
```

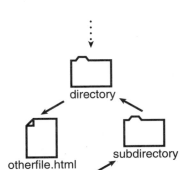

Figure 1-6: *A relative URL references a file higher in the directory structure than itself.*

Finally, by combining these techniques, you could refer to a file in a different subdirectory of a directory two levels up:

```
../../othersubdirectory/otherfile.html
```

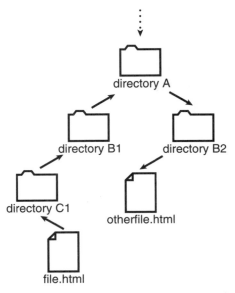

Figure 1-7: *A relative URL is used to reference a file in directory B2 from a file in directory C1.*

Absolutely Not So Fabulous

Another type of URL, used by many large organizations, lies somewhere between the complete and relative URL styles and is known as an *absolute* URL. The absolute URL contains everything the complete URL does, except for the http:// header and the domain name. An absolute URL for the file located at http://machine.subdomain.topdomain/subdirectory/file.html would be the following:

```
/subdirectory/file.html
```

Note that there is a slash preceding the absolute URL. Generally, absolute URLs are used on Web servers located behind "firewalls," which are computers and programs that protect an organization and its data from outside intrusion. They can make development difficult for Web developers who don't have their own servers, because most browsers will not open the files locally. It's necessary to mount the files on a Web server (with a duplicate of the final directory structure) to test them out, which can slow development.

Portal Call, Anchors Sway

Internet servers of all types listen to requests on *ports*, and the default port for Web servers is port 80. For various reasons, administrators may set up a server to run on a different port, and URLs pointing at that server will need to have the port explicit in the address, just after the server name, separated from it by a colon:

```
http://moshplant.com:1080
```

One type of URL that's been specific to HTML pages up until now has been the *anchor*. This is a URL that references not just a file but a specific place within a file. Normally used to identify a link to a point in a long text file, it can also be used to refer to a named marker in a Shockwave movie. It can be either a relative or full URL to the file, followed by a pound sign and the name of the anchor:

```
http://moshplant.com/moshplant.html#otherlinks
```

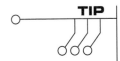

TIP

See Chapter 8, "Shockwave Tricks," for more on using links to anchors in HTML pages and Shockwave movies.

Locals Only

All that said, I just want to point out that a World Wide Web server doesn't absolutely need to be connected to the Internet at large. Many Web servers are not only unavailable to the wide world, the computer systems they're on aren't even connected to an outside system. Companies and organizations have discovered the value of electronic document distribution and information retrieval, and they're using Web servers and HTTP protocols for everything from technical support documentation to database interfacing. So be aware that while most of the time you'll be developing for situations in which your links could potentially go anywhere in the world, there might be times when you need to restrict your world view for a bit, and focus on a closed site.

The World Wide Web

The Web, as I'll call it from now on, isn't some special network. In actuality, it's simply a method of communicating across the same connections that carry your e-mail, FTP, and other Internet services. It has its own transfer standard, HTTP, to which data is attached for routing information and specific request information.

The Web is a new phenomenon, even as computer-related phenomena go. The original HTTP specifications were developed in about 1990 by Tim Berners-Lee at CERN, the European Laboratory for Particle Physics in Switzerland, as a method of linking documents to related items. They included the ability to incorporate other types of protocol requests, including FTP, Gopher, and e-mail, among others.

By using URLs embedded in documents, HTTP is able to simply link one document to a multitude of others, each of which, in turn, can link to many others—including the original. In its simplest implementation, as text with links to other text, it enabled its users to link concept to concept, idea to idea, or what is known as *hypertext*. The term hypertext is generally attributed to Ted Nelson, who developed the view that if all of the world's information could be linked together, concepts could then be connected to similar concepts, making it possible to jump from one idea to another in a rather free-ranging method. It took about thirty years to get from that original vision to the Web, the fulfillment of Nelson's dream—sort-of.

Just Browsing

To view this new phenomenon, special programs called *browsers* were developed. Early Web browsers were mostly text-based, with the ability to display images or graphics in a separate window included as an option on some platforms. What has really driven the explosion of the Web—and by extension the Internet—was the development of graphical browsers, which could view text and graphics simultaneously. The first such browser to enjoy widespread usage was Mosaic, a project developed at the National

Center for Supercomputer Applications (NCSA) by a team of programmers, many of whom went on to form Netscape Communications Corporation. A number of other browsers were developed concurrently with Mosaic.

Figure 1-8: *A page from moshplant.com displayed with NCSA Mosaic for the Macintosh.*

Sur la Page

The ability to display text and graphics together on the screen, apart from leading to the widespread designation of an HTML file as a "Web page," also sparked interest in making more attractive and configurable pages. The earliest pages consisted of text and graphics aligned along the left side of the screen, with formatting limited to several sizes of headlines and a few types of lists; variations in type styles were concept-based (for emphasis or citation purposes) rather than explicit (using bold or italic). The formatting codes used then and now (the HTML *tags* described in the next section) also include the ability to create links from the page to other pages, images, and files—even to programs and databases. Perhaps most important—and this is the big difference between the Web and other forms of electronic multimedia—the items that the links refer to don't need to be on the same server or even the same site. In fact, it's generally considered better to put in as many links as possible, to make surfing the Web a more exciting experience.

Figure 1-9: *The same page as shown in Figure 1-8, displayed in Netscape Navigator for the Macintosh, showing how HTML tags ignored by one browser make a great difference in appearance.*

HyperText Markup Language

The basic unit of the Web is a text file, containing simple character combinations called *tags*, which indicate, in a very general way, the type of information that is to follow. The various tags are known collectively as HTML (HyperText Markup Language).

Tag, You're It

The hard part is over. If you've got a grasp on how URLs are formed, then you can handle the small amount of HTML you *need* to know for showing Shockwave movies on the Internet. At its most basic, an HTML document or page is a text file that looks like this:

```
<HTML>
<HEAD>
<TITLE>Bland HTML Document</TITLE>
</HEAD>
<BODY>
</BODY>
</HTML>
```

Most HTML tags (<BODY>, for instance) are closed— or *delimited*—by the same tag, with a slash added just before the tag identifier (</BODY>). The tag affects whatever is placed between itself and its delimiter. The above document would show up in a Web browser as an empty page with the words "Bland HTML Document" appearing in the title bar. Information between the <HEAD> tag and its delimiter is used to provide general data about the document (such as the title); information between <BODY> and </BODY> constitutes the main portion of the page. It's not necessary to put the tags on different lines; the example above typed out on a single horizontal line would produce identical results. The difference is that it would be much more difficult to read the HTML.

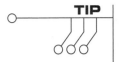

TIP

It's not necessary to put the <HTML>, <HEAD>, or <BODY> tags into a document if it is your intention to simply place Shockwave movies into the page, but it is generally considered good form, and use of the <TITLE> tag to name the document in the title bar requires by extension the use of <HEAD> and <BODY>.

The tag that's most important to Shockwave is a relatively new one: <EMBED>. Unlike the examples shown above, <EMBED> does not use a delimiter, so there is no </EMBED> tag.

<EMBED> is used to place a nonstandard resource into an HTML document, usually one which requires a plug-in extension to the browser. The resource could be a Java applet, an Adobe Acrobat document, or a Shockwave movie. All of these file types—when viewed within the context of a browser—require special plug-ins to properly display or execute.

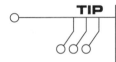

TIP

A browser *plug-in* works differently from a *helper application*. Most browsers can be configured to open a document with another application, based on information sent from the server to the browser. Adobe Acrobat files, for instance, can be downloaded from the server, permanently or temporarily saved to the client's hard drive, and viewed with the Acrobat Reader. The Acrobat plug-in for Web browsers, called Amber, displays Acrobat documents *within the browser page*, allowing HTML and Acrobat to be mixed together on the screen. The same is true of Shockwave.

In all cases, the <EMBED> tag stores information about the location of the resource on the Web, and it may contain other parameter information specific to the resource type (the value of which is a URL pointing to the location of the movie), WIDTH, and HEIGHT (assigned values reserving the appropriate amount of space within the browser window for the movie to play).

```
<HTML>
<HEAD>
<TITLE>No Longer Bland HTML Document</TITLE>
</HEAD>
<BODY>
<EMBED SRC="http://www.server.domain/shockwave.dcr"
WIDTH="448" HEIGHT="300">
</BODY>
</HTML>
```

The HTML page above, slightly modified from the earlier Bland HTML Document, makes only one change apart from the title. An <EMBED> tag has been added between <BODY> and </BODY> (it can't be used in the <HEAD> section). The URL of a Shockwave movie is defined in quotes as the SRC, and the movie's width and height are defined by the WIDTH and HEIGHT fields (quotes here are not necessary).

Moving On

This chapter has introduced the basic concepts of how the Internet works and how it grew, focusing on the hypertext system called the World Wide Web. The Internet, as we have seen, works on a client-server system in which many individual client computers may make requests of a single server computer, to which the server responds.

I've also described the two types of Internet addresses: IP addresses (which identify a particular machine on the Internet) and URLs (which identify files on machines). And we've covered complete and relative URL addressing.

We've also delved briefly into the HyperText Markup Language (HTML)—the coding used to create documents on the World Wide Web, which contains styling information for text, links to other documents, and information on embedded objects like Shockwave movies. And we have seen that there are display differences between Web browsers, even when viewing the same documents.

There's much more to come. In the next chapter we'll move ahead to the real focus of this book—we'll turn the spotlight on Shockwave. We'll see how this exciting phenomenon evolved from Web technology and explore its potential for interactive computing.

2

Into the Shockwave

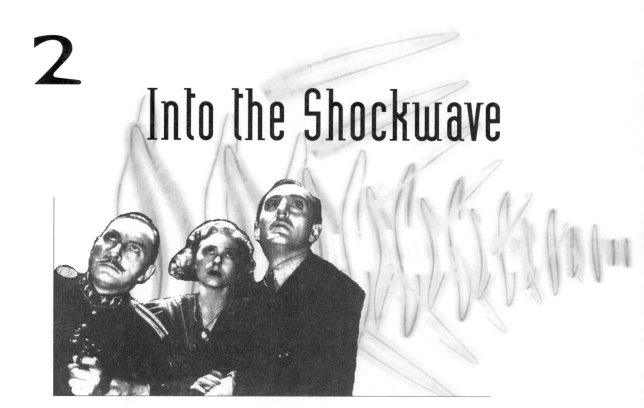

Static on the Web

Despite the fact that it's been lumped in with the rest of the world of "multimedia," most of what's been available for the past couple of years on the World Wide Web has been immobile text and images, without any of the interactivity that's part of what most of us think of as multimedia. Sure, it's *hypertext-linked* immobile text and images, but the basic vanilla flavor of the Web doesn't have much in the way of motion or sound. And as far as real-time interactivity, well . . . .

Most Web browsers can download sound, video, and other types of media files, and can be configured to open the appropriate helper applications to play or display the files after the download. *Streaming* technologies begin display or playback of media files (including sound or video) before the entire file has been transferred from the server to the client. (Web browsers themselves are actually examples of this, as they receive data and begin interpreting it—displaying it onscreen and sending requests for linked items before the entire HTML document has been completely received.) RealAudio, a streaming technology developed by Progressive Networks, allows real-time delivery of compressed sound across the Web, and other schemes exist for Web delivery of video and audio transmissions.

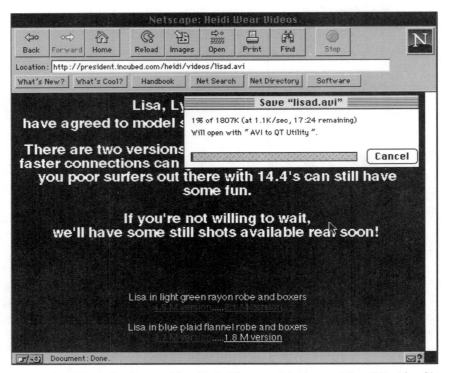

Figure 2-1: *Downloading a video file in Netscape Navigator. The AVI video file* lisad.avi *will be opened by the helper application* AVI to QT Utility.

Helper applications, streaming or no, don't allow integration of other media types into the static text and images on the page. When you click on a hypertext link to download a video or sound file from a Web server, it simply starts to play when it's ready, it plays in a separate window (really a separate application), and when it's done it's done. The only interaction you can have is to stop it or start it.

Like everything else about the Web, though, all that has changed in the past few months.

Embedded to You

1995 was the year intractive multimedia came to the Web, with the introduction or widespread acknowledgment of several important technologies which greatly expanded the capabilities of the Web. While some, such as the Virtual Reality Modeling Language (VRML), are initially reliant on independent helper applications and viewers, most of the new technologies are being incorporated into Web browsers by means of plug-ins that extend the functionality of the browsers themselves and allow the display of multimedia objects alongside the text and graphics of standard Web pages. Among those new technologies are the Java programming language from Sun Microsystems, the Acrobat portable document format from Adobe Systems, and Shockwave, from Macromedia.

Director: Shocking the Web

One of the most widely used tools in the multimedia world over the past several years has been *Macromedia Director*, a general-purpose, high-powered, extremely extensible program used in the production of everything from diskette-based portfolio pieces to CD-ROM games. Director isn't (usually) used to create graphics, video, or sound, but it is a resource where all of these media can be brought together and made to interact with each other.

Director can be used to combine text, animation, QuickTime video, and sound into exciting multilayered, branching presentations that provide an enormous potential for true user interaction. Its built-in scripting language, known as Lingo, enables even nonprogrammers to put together simple interactive productions, yet it's complex enough to provide a great amount of control and flexibility for advanced multimedia producers. With its support for external code segments called XObjects, which can add the ability to do things the program itself wasn't designed for, Director has proven to be an incredibly powerful program.

Figure 2-2: *A Director presentation can combine graphics, sound, animation, and video with user interaction.*

There are at least a couple of hundred thousand Director users in the world, on both the Apple Mac OS and IBM PC-compatibles running Microsoft Windows. Director was one of the first cross-platform multimedia authoring programs and can share program files between the most common operating systems. Its capacity to create stand-alone multimedia applications for both Windows and Mac OS platforms has contributed to its success.

That widespread, heterogeneous usage by multimedia professionals—ranging from graphic designers to computer programmers—seems to have made it inevitable that Macromedia would find a way to put Director movies on the Web.

In mid-1995, Macromedia announced that it would create a plug-in extension to Web browsers called *Shockwave* that would enable Director movies to be viewed on the Web. The plug-in contains code that can play back Director movies compressed with a utility called Afterburner and placed into an HTML page. Shockwave supports most—but not all—of the standard Director capabilities, and includes support for a number of Lingo commands added specifically for interaction with Web browsers and the Internet.

The Shockwave for Director plug-in was publicly released in February, 1996 for Windows 3.1, Windows 95, and Mac OS versions of the Netscape browser. Macromedia has promised to extend the Shockwave technology to other platforms (Windows NT, UNIX, SGI, etc.) as well as to other browsers (Navisoft Navipress, Microsoft Internet Explorer, and more) in the near future. Macromedia has also announced plans to distribute a Shockwave plug-in for their drawing program, Freehand, which will enable vector graphics to be embedded into HTML documents. Like the Amber plug-in for Adobe's Acrobat PDF files, Shockwave for Freehand will allow you to zoom in on portions of an image which, being vector-based, maintain their resolution at any level of magnification, unlike bitmap graphics which become rasterized when magnified.

Other plug-ins currently available or in the works for Netscape and other browsers include VRML viewers for 3D models, video, audio, and a number of other file formats of new and existing programs which allow you to include these types of documents as an integral part of your HTML pages.

Why Shockwave?

What sets the Shockwave/Director combination apart from other Internet-capable multimedia technologies? One factor in its widespread acceptance throughout the multimedia community has been ease of use. When supplied with basic graphic elements to work with, a novice user can quickly learn to create simple animations and, with a little more instruction, write Lingo scripts that add interactivity. Director features a timeline-oriented sequencer called the *Score,* which gives users flexibility and speed by means of direct visual feedback for prototyping and production of multimedia presentations.

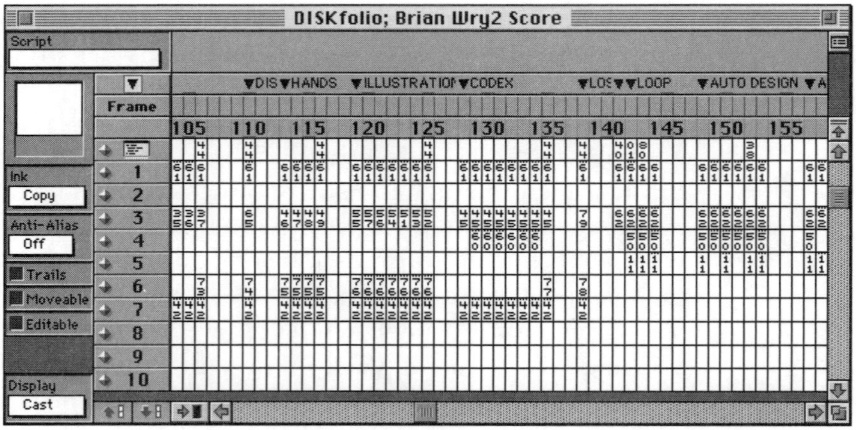

Figure 2-3: *Director's* Score, *a timeline-based sequencer for coordination of graphics, sound, and visual effects.*

Another advantage of Director is its support for a number of media types, and its ability to make them work together using Lingo. The capability for creating frame-based animations that can be controlled or modified by user interaction (through the use of Lingo), capabilities for including sound, editable text fields for data entry, etc., make Director and Shockwave far more attractive to many developers as an Internet multimedia vehicle than Adobe Acrobat—which is oriented toward simple hyperlinked document production—or Java, which is a powerful but complex programming language without the visual feedback that Director employs. There are purposes for which Acrobat, Java, and other multimedia schemes are better suited, but Director combines much of the power of a true programming language with a shorter learning curve than any other program with the same range of capabilities.

Figure 2-4: *The Cast window, showing several types of media, including bitmaps, text, Lingo scripts, and QuickTime video.*

That said, there are a few things Director can do that aren't possible yet with Shockwave. Leading the list is QuickTime video, MIAW (movie in a window), and input/output-related functions and commands (for a complete list, see Appendix D, "What You Can't Do With Shockwave"). In the ever-changing world of the Web, though, what's impossible today is old hat tomorrow, so don't write *anything* off for the future.

What You Need to Get Shocked

To *see* a Shockwave movie, you need to have a browser capable of using the Shockwave plug-in. As of early March 1996, the only browser officially able to do so was Netscape Navigator 2.0 (available free from the Netscape site at http://www.netscape.com). You also need to have the Shockwave plug-in itself (available from Macromedia—also free—from their site: http://www.macromedia.com). It's a good idea to put links to these sites somewhere on your Web pages leading to your Shockwave movies.

To create a Shockwave movie, you need Director first of all. All of the animation and scripting of interaction of a Shockwave movie is created in Director. You'll also need a utility from Macromedia called *Afterburner* (again, available free from their site at http://www.macromedia.com or on the Companion CD-ROM packaged with this book). Afterburner takes a Director file and compresses it to create a Shockwave movie. Once it's been compressed, it can't be reopened with Director, so it's typically saved with the filename extension ".dcr" to distinguish it from the original Director file.

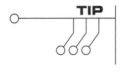

TIP

While filename length isn't a problem, the HTTP protocols used on the Web aren't friendly to spaces in filenames. If you're a Macintosh user who's addicted to spaces in your filenames, get used to using underscores "_" or dashes "-" to separate words instead.

Serving Shockwave movies on the Web requires access to an HTTP server that has been properly configured to serve up Shockwave (see Appendix F, "Configuring Your Server for Shockwave").

A Site of Something Shocking

Once you've got your Shockwave-capable browser up and running, and made your connection to the Internet, why not take a look at some of the things people have been using Shockwave for? A good place to start is—of course—Macromedia's own site, where they've put up galleries of sites developed by the Shockwave Vanguard: corporate early adopters of their technology. Use your browser to open this URL:

```
http://www.macromedia.com/Tools/Shockwave/Gallery/Vanguard/
```

Figure 2-5: *The Shockwave Vanguard Gallery page.*

There you'll find several pages of links to companies that have Shocked some portion of their site. Use the "More Vanguard" links to move to the last of the Vanguard pages and you'll find a name that's probably very familiar: Yahoo.

The Shocked version of the Yahoo site (http://shocked. yahoo.com) animates the familiar Yahoo cartoon logo, giving it a funky, happy feel, and adding a little bit of visual feedback to a user as the mouse is rolled over the buttons. This is a typical use of a Shockwave movie as a replacement for the standard navigation bar.

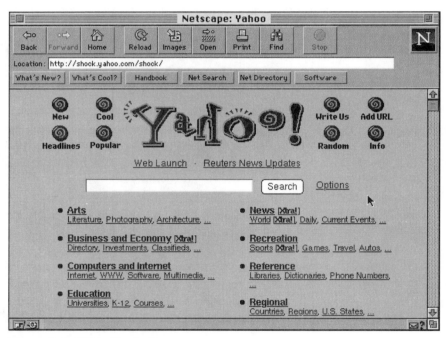

Figure 2-6: *Yahoo Shocked.*

United Airlines put a spinning globe and some lush mood music on their Shocked home page. Use your browser's Reload command to hear the music again.

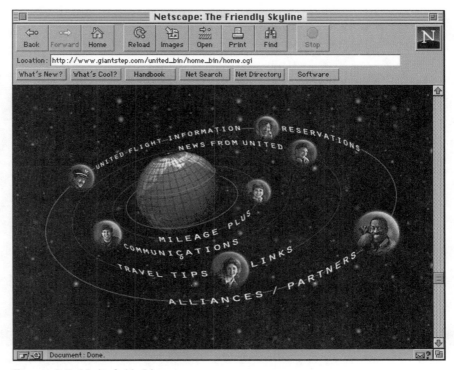

Figure 2-7: *United Air Lines.*

For elaborate graphics, nobody does it like MTV. There are two Shockwave movies on the page below, adding up to over 220K of files, just to give you an animated interface.

Figure 2-8: *MTV Rocks and Shocks.*

A corporate site that's not on the Vanguard list is Valvoline, which uses Shockwave to offer an Internet driving game, as a draw to entice people to their site.

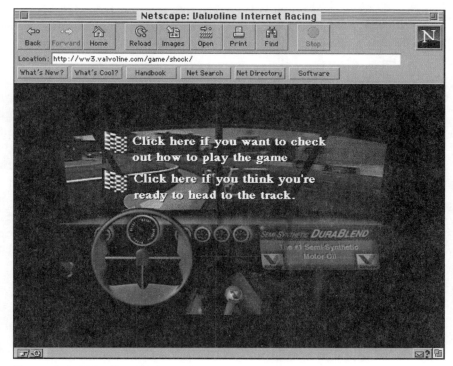

Figure 2-9: *Valvoline driving game.*

There are, of course, many, many more Shockwave sites to see out there. The Macromedia site lists quite a few, and there are other compilations as well. One of the most extensive (and most useful) is Director Web's (http://www.mcli.maricopa.edu/ director/), which is just part of a larger multimedia information site maintained by Alan Levine at Arizona's Maricopa Community Colleges (it's also where you can find indexed archives of the Direct-L mailing list). Another extensive listing is at the Shocker site (http://www.shocker.com), the keepers of a mailing list dedicated to Shockwave itself. And there are innumerable private lists of Shockwave sites, like the one at Violet Arcana (http://www.teleport.com/~arcana/). Surf and enjoy!

Moving On

This chapter dips its toes into the Shockwave phenomenon. You should know that Shockwave is an additional capability for your Web browser that's added by installing a plug-in module. It is freely available to anyone who wants it (that's important if anyone's going to see your movies). You might have picked up that although Shockwave is a bit short on public history, it has nonetheless been adopted by some large organizations (can you say "Vanguard"?). You've even seen some of the major sites that have incorporated Shockwave. Now that you've seen it, it's time to do it.

3

Eine Kleine Shockwave

It's incredibly easy to make a Shockwave movie and watch it play—you don't even need to have access to a World Wide Web server! All you need is a copy of Macromedia Director to make your movie, the Afterburner program to prepare the movie, a simple text editor to add the movie to an HTML page, and a Shockwave-capable Web browser to view your handiwork. In this chapter, you'll make some Shockwave movies, put them into HTML pages, make a simple interactive movie, and learn how to navigate around on the Web using two Shockwave Lingo commands: *GotoNetMovie* and *GotoNetPage*.

Burning Your Movies

A Shockwave movie can do almost anything you want without your having to know any of the special Lingo extensions developed for the Web. You can include graphics, animation, sound, interactivity—just about everything that can be done in a Director movie except playing QuickTime video—so long as there are no references to external files. That means no linked images, sounds, or movies, and no *play movie, go to movie* or other Lingo commands that draw on resources outside of the Shockwave movie itself.

To convert a Director movie for viewing with Shockwave, use the Afterburner program, which compresses the file in addition to *protecting* the movie (removing editable information about cast members). Depending on the content of the movie, Afterburner will compress the file by 50 to 75 percent. If you're familiar with making projectors from Director movies, this is equivalent to creating a projector without the playback engine. One advantage of this is that because the playback engine is contained in the Shockwave extension, movies created with the Afterburner extension should play back on any platform with a properly configured browser.

To use Afterburner, start the program by double-clicking on its icon. A dialog box will appear asking you which movie you want to convert to the Shockwave format. After choosing a Director movie in the dialog box, a Save File dialog will appear, asking where you want to save the Shockwave file (Afterburner will automatically append a *.dcr* extension to the file name). You can either accept this name or save it under another, keeping the extension. Afterburner will automatically quit after converting the movie. It's as simple as that.

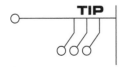

TIP

It's a good idea to use lowercase letters in your filenames for Shockwave movies as well as other files for Web distribution. Some UNIX file servers do not recognize uppercase characters in filenames, which can necessitate a burdensome amount of recoding if you develop on a machine that uses a different operating system.

Exercise 3-1: Feel the burn.

This exercise shows you exactly how to use Afterburner to create a Shockwave for Director movie. The files for this exercise are in the EXER0301 directory in the *Shockwave!* Companion CD-ROM.

Step 1. Double-click on the Afterburner icon to start the program.

Afterburner   Afterbur.exe

Figure 3-1: *Afterburner icons for the Macintosh and Windows.*

Step 2. Using the Open File dialog box that automatically comes up, navigate to the TUTORIAL directory on the Companion CD-ROM.

Step 3. Open the EXER0301 directory.

Step 4. Select the file *simple.dir*.

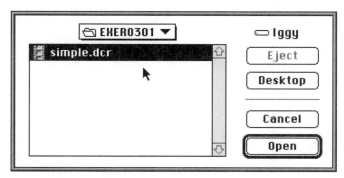

Figure 3-2: *The Afterburner Open File dialog box.*

Step 5. Using the Save File dialog box that comes up, save *simple.dcr* to your hard drive (Afterburner will automatically add or change the file extension to dcr). An indicator will show you the progress as the movie's being burned, and Afterburner will automatically quit when it's done.

Figure 3-3: *The Afterburner Save File dialog box.*

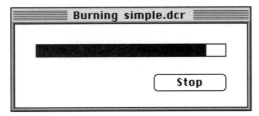

Figure 3-4: *Afterburner's progress bar.*

That's it. Your Shockwave movie is ready to be placed into an HTML page.

Figure 3-5: *Shockwave movie file icons.*

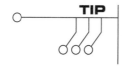

TIP

On the Mac OS, you can drag one or more Director movie files you wish to convert on top of the Afterburner icon to start the program. Each movie will trigger a new Save File dialog box, giving you control over the Shockwave movie's name and location.

Shocking Web Pages

The ability to add Director movies to Web pages is made possible by a new HTML tag: EMBED. The EMBED tag is used not just for Shockwave movies but also for other types of data objects which can be viewed inside Web pages with the aid of browser plug-ins. The EMBED tag is easy to use and takes the following form:

```
<EMBED SRC="movieURL" WIDTH="movieWidth"
HEIGHT="movieHeight">
```

movieURL is a reference to the location of the Shockwave movie on the World Wide Web. It can be either a full or a relative URL to the HTML page that contains the movie (see Chapter 1, "How the Web Works," for a discussion of URLs—or just wander on through the rest of this chapter). *movieWidth* and *movieHeight* are, respectively, values representing the width and height of the Director movie's Stage.

If you want to substitute an image or text in the place of an embedded Shockwave movie for viewers with browsers that can't display the movie, you can use a NOEMBED tag either before or after the EMBED tag. Any text or HTML used between a <NOEMBED> and its delimiter </NOEMBED> won't be displayed by browsers with the appropriate plug-in.

Exercise 3-2: Placing EMBED.

In this exercise, the Shockwave movie you made in Exercise 3-1—simple.dcr—is EMBEDded into an HTML page, where you can view it with a Shockwave-capable Web browser.

Step 1. Fire up the text-editing program of your choice. Anything that will save a simple text file will do.

Step 2. Open the file *htmltemp.txt* in the TUTORIAL directory. This is a template file containing a skeleton HTML document that resembles the "No Longer Bland HTML Document" from Chapter 1.

Step 3. Replace the words *title goes here* between the <TITLE> and </TITLE> tags with a title of your own choosing. These words will be displayed in the browser window title bar.

Step 4. Replace the word *shockwavemoviefile* between the quotes with simple.dcr (be sure to leave the quotes in place).

Step 5. The Director movie simple.dcr is 464 pixels wide by 300 pixels tall. Put those values in for *xxx* after WIDTH and *yyy* after HEIGHT.

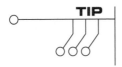

TIP

The quotes around the values for WIDTH and HEIGHT aren't necessary—although they are part of the HTML specification—but if you use them, you need to make sure of two things. First, make sure that you always have pairs of them; just one before or after will cause problems. Second, if you're using a word processor or text editor with a "curly" or "smart" quotes option, be sure to turn it off, because typesetter's quotes are not legal characters in HTML files.

You should now have a text document which looks something like this:

```
<HTML>
<HEAD>
<TITLE>Simple Shockwave Movie</TITLE>
</HEAD>
<BODY>
<EMBED SRC="simple.dcr" WIDTH="464" HEIGHT="300">
</BODY>
</HTML>
```

Step 6. Save your file with the name *simple.htm* in the same directory as the file *simple.dcr*.

Step 7. Quit your text editor and start up a Shockwave-capable Web browser.

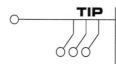

TIP

Leaving the HTML text file open in some text editors may keep the browser from accessing the file due to permission conflicts. Be sure that the file is saved and closed.

Step 8. Use the Open File or Open Local menu command of your browser (most browsers use the Command+O or Ctrl+O key combination) to open the file *simple.htm*.

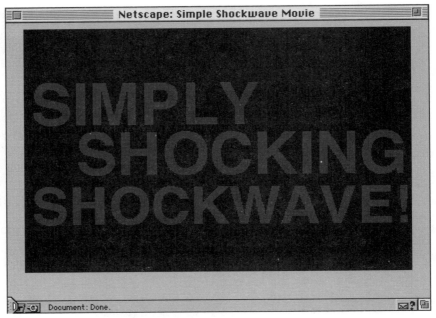

Figure 3-6: *Your first, simple Shockwave movie.*

This movie doesn't do much; it just blinks the color of the word "Shockwave!" But it didn't take you much time to make it, either.

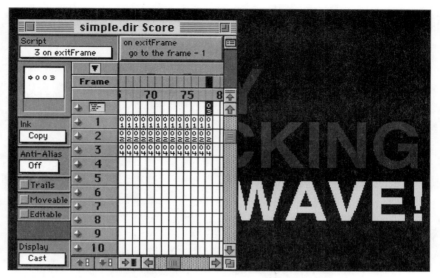

Figure 3-7: *The Stage and last frames of the Score for* simple.dir.

Exercise 3-3: Not just another pretty interface.

The most attractive aspect of Shockwave is its ability to add user interaction to the normally quiescent Web. *Interactive* multimedia isn't about spinning logos and canned sounds: it's about a human and a computer in a sort of Newtonian action-reaction kind of thing. Not really equal, not necessarily opposite, but something's got to happen above and beyond animation, or you've simply added extra time and cost to your Web page projects. The first step toward interaction is knowing what the viewer is doing. This exercise does just that, providing visual feedback as the viewer moves the mouse.

Step 1. Start the Macromedia Director program.

Step 2. Open the *mousetrk.dir* file in the EXER0303 directory.

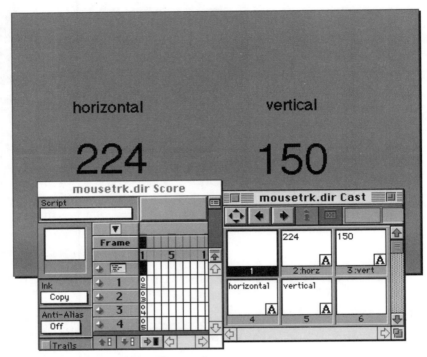

Figure 3-8: *mousetrk.dir: The movie.*

This movie contains four text fields. You'll use the two fields named *horz* and *vert* to show the position of the mouse on the screen within the Web browser.

Step 3. Open the Score window and double-click in frame 1 of the Script channel, or click in the script entry area. Enter the following script:

Listing 3-1.

```
on exitFrame
  put the mouseV into cast "vert"
  put the mouseH into cast "horz"
  go the frame
end
```

This script tells the movie that at the end of the frame it should put the x and y coordinates of the mouse into the appropriate fields, then loop back to the beginning of the frame. No new Lingo here.

Step 4. Close the Script window by pressing Enter. Open the menu item File | Preferences and take note of the size of the movie's Stage. Use File | Save As to save the movie to your hard drive. Quit Director.

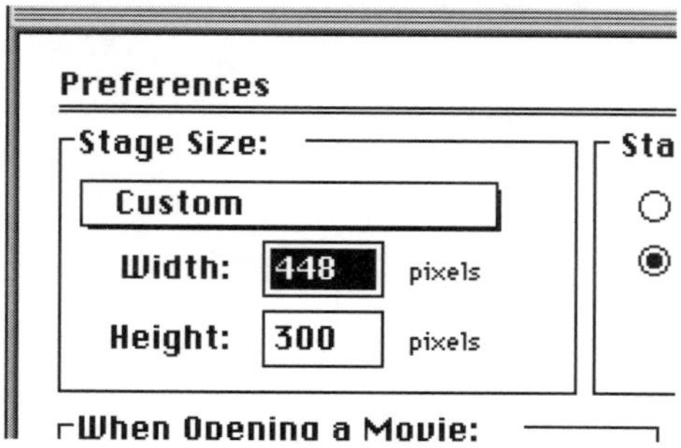

Preferences

Stage Size:

Custom

Width: **448** pixels

Height: 300 pixels

When Opening a Movie:

Figure 3-9: *Stage Size in the Preferences dialog box for the* mousetrk.dir *movie.*

Step 5. Use Afterburner to create a file called *mousetrk.dcr* on your hard drive.

Step 6. Create a new HTML file from the *htmltemp.txt* file as you did in Exercise 3-2, give it a title (between <TITLE> and </TITLE>), and insert *mousetrk.dcr*, *448*, and *300* for the file name, width, and height. Save the file as *mousetrk.htm*.

Step 7. Open *mousetrk.htm* with your Web browser.

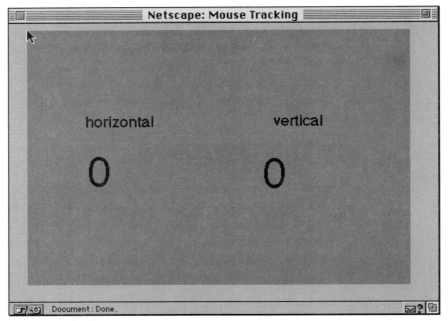

Figure 3-10: *The cursor is at the origin (upper left corner) of the Shockwave movie.*

Notice as you move the mouse around on the screen that new numbers appear for the horizontal and vertical coordinates of the mouse. The coordinates will be updated when you move outside the edges of the movie—even when you move outside of the browser window!

Self-contained Shockwave movies—those that don't need to interact with the Web once they're loaded—can be made with what you've learned so far. Animations, games, painting programs, or anything else that can be made small enough to transmit across the Internet needs just two simple steps to put it on the Web. Burn it and embed it.

From here on out, it's new Lingo, and the *real* potential for interactive multimedia on the Web.

Learning the Lingo

Essentially, what the first version of Shockwave allows you to do is create Director movies for placement in HTML pages which can change HTML pages, change Shockwave movies, and retrieve data from HTTP servers. There are also a number of commands for managing those requests. That's in addition to nearly the complete feature set of Director, which can be used to create everything from training presentations to arcade-style games. This means that a Shockwave movie can be used to present an attractive, entertaining addition to static HTML pages, with the ability to incorporate nearly instantaneous response to the user—something that ordinary Web documents can't supply.

Ordinarily, when a hypertext link on a Web document is activated by pressing on it with the mouse, a request for the linked document is sent out across the Internet, the request is processed by the appropriate server, and the server returns data across the Internet. Depending on the speed of the Internet connections at both ends (the server's and the user's), and conditions in between their locations, the response can be almost instantaneous, a matter of seconds, or even minutes. With Shockwave (and other technologies, including Java, VRML, and others), an embedded file is transmitted to the user just like any other file, but once there, it can interact in real-time with the user. The response time can be far superior to a simple hypertext link, because most of the necessary data is contained within the movie—which has already been completely downloaded to the user's computer.

A number of games have been written for the Web with Shockwave—games that can store high scores from players all around the world because of the Internet connection. The Director Web site at Maricopa Community Colleges in Arizona (http://www.mcli.dist.maricopa.edu/director) can provide an up-to-the-minute listing of Shockwave sites through interaction with programs on the server. With Shockwave, you can write order forms that change to meet the requirements of the user as entries are made, then send the order to your server for processing. Of course, the whole thing can be just as animated and chockful of gee-whiz graphics as you think necessary to make your viewers want to download it. That's typical of Director. But what Shockwave really adds to the Director environment are some new Lingo commands.

Shockwave Lingo can be divided into two basic types: *asynchronous*—commands which can be executed simultaneously with others—and *synchronous*, which can't be simultaneously executed. Since the synchronous commands are easier to use—and since there are only two of them—we'll start there.

GotoNetMovie

This command loads in a new Shockwave movie and replaces the current movie (the one containing the GotoNetMovie command) with the new movie, in the current HTML page. The new movie will begin execution immediately upon loading. The form it takes is as follows:

```
GotoNetMovie "URL"
```

The URL can be either a full or a relative URL, and it should reference a Shockwave movie with Stage dimensions which are the same as the original movie.

GotoNetPage

This command loads a new Web object, which may include an HTML page, an image, or even a Shockwave movie. The object is viewed in a new browser window. GotoNetPage is invoked this way:

```
GotoNetPage "URL"
```

The URL can be either a full or a relative URL.

Exercise 3-4: Using GotoNetMovie.

This exercise and the ones which follow will demonstrate the usage of—and the differences between—the two synchronous commands. The first step is to make a single HTML page that will switch between two Shockwave movies.

Step 1. Open the file *pageone.dir* in the EXER0304 directory in TUTORIAL with Director.

Step 2. Open the Cast window and select cast member 3, the button with the label "go to second movie." Press the script button in the cast window and type in the following script:

```
on mouseUp
  GotoNetMovie "pagetwo.dcr"
end
```

Step 3. Close the Script window by pressing Enter. Open the Score window and double-click on frame 1 of the Script channel. Type in the following script:

```
on exitFrame
  go the frame
end
```

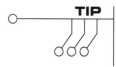

TIP You might be tempted to use the Tempo channel's Wait for Mouse Click or Key option instead of a *go the frame* loop, but the Wait function of the Tempo channel is among the Director features unavailable in Shockwave.

Step 4. Close the Script window by pressing Enter, and use File | Save As to save the movie to your hard drive.

Step 5. Use File | Open to open the Director movie *pagetwo.dir* from the EXER0304 directory.

Step 6. Open the Cast window and select cast member 3, the button with the label "go to first movie." Press the script button in the cast window and type in the following script:

```
on mouseUp
  GotoNetMovie "pageone.dcr"
end
```

Step 7. Close the Script window by pressing Enter. Open the Score window and double-click on frame 1 of the Script channel. Type in the following script:

```
on exitFrame
  go the frame
end
```

Step 8. Close the Script window by pressing Enter, and use File | Save As to save the movie to your hard drive.

Step 9. Use Afterburner to create Shockwave movies from the versions of *pageone.dir* and *pagetwo.dir* on your hard drive. Name them *pageone.dcr* and *pagetwo.dcr*, and save them in the same directory.

Step 10. Use your text editor to create a new HTML document from the *htmltemp.txt* file.

Step 11. Make the page's title *Changing NetMovies*.

Step 12. Change the SRC in the EMBED tag to *pageone.dcr*, change WIDTH to *448*, and change HEIGHT to *300*.

The new HTML document should look like this:

```
<HTML>
<HEAD>
<TITLE>Changing NetMovies</TITLE>
</HEAD>
<BODY>
<EMBED SRC="pageone.dcr" WIDTH="448" HEIGHT="300">
</BODY>
</HTML>
```

Save the file (in the same directory as the Shockwave files you just made) as *pageone.htm*.

Step 13. Open *pageone.htm* with your Web browser and press the button labeled "go to second movie." *pagetwo.dcr* will be loaded in place of *pageone.dcr*.

Step 14. Press the button labeled "go to first movie." *pageone.dcr* will be returned to its original position.

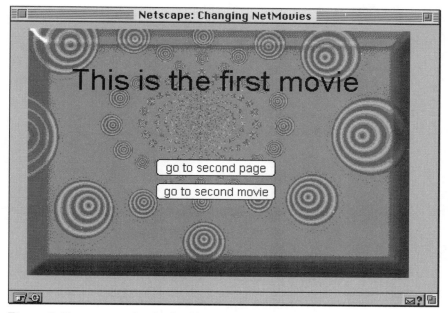

Figure 3-11: pageone.dcr *in the Changing NetMovies version of* pageone.htm.

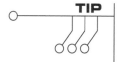

TIP

Any of the movies we've created in the exercises above will work equally well if you view them from the Web instead of opening them locally from your hard drive. Put the page and Shockwave file in a directory on your Web server and enter the appropriate full URL into your Web browser.

That's GotoNetMovie. Now let's explore the differences between GotoNetMovie and GotoNetPage.

Exercise 3-5: 2 x 2 = 4.

This exercise will utilize the files you created in Exercise 3-4.

Step 1. Open your version of the HTML file *pageone.htm* with a text editor and make the following modifications (changes in bold).

```
<HTML>
<HEAD>
<TITLE>First Page</TITLE>
</HEAD>
<BODY>
<H1>This is the first page</H1>
<EMBED SRC="pageone.dcr" WIDTH="448" HEIGHT="300">
</BODY>
</HTML>
```

The <H1> tag means that the text following it will be in the largest headline style.

Step 2. Save the file.

Step 3. Modify the file again, so that it now reads as follows:

```
<HTML>
<HEAD>
<TITLE>Second Page</TITLE>
</HEAD>
<BODY>
<H1>This is the second page</H1>
<EMBED SRC="pagetwo.dcr" WIDTH="448" HEIGHT="300">
</BODY>
</HTML>
```

Step 4. Save this file with a new name: *pagetwo.htm*, in the same directory as the other files.

Step 5. In Director, open the version of *pageone.dir* that you added scripts to in Exercise 3-4.

Step 6. Open the Cast window, select cast member 2 (the button cast member labeled "go to second page"), and press the Script button. Enter the following script:

```
on mouseUp
  GotoNetPage "pagetwo.htm"
end
```

Step 7. Close the Script window by pressing Enter, and save the movie.

Step 8. Open the version of *pagetwo.dir* that you modified in Exercise 3-4.

Step 9. Open the Cast window, select cast member 2 (the button cast member labeled "go to first page"), and press the Script button. Enter the following script:

```
on mouseUp
  GotoNetPage "pageone.htm"
end
```

Step 10. Close the Script window by pressing Enter, and save the movie.

Step 11. Use Afterburner to update the Shockwave movies *pageone.dcr* and *pagetwo.dcr*. Save over the older versions.

You should now have the following files in the same directory on your hard drive:
pageone.dcr
pageone.htm
pagetwo.dcr
pagetwo.htm

(You should also have modified versions of *pageone.dir* and *pagetwo.dir* somewhere on your hard drive, but they don't necessarily need to be in the same directory as the others.)

Step 12. Open *pageone.htm* with your Web browser and click on the button "go to second page." Note that *pagetwo.htm* is loaded in, along with *pagetwo.dcr* (because of the EMBED tag in *pagetwo.htm*). If you click on the button labeled "go to first page," *pageone.htm* and *pageone.dcr* should be reloaded into the browser.

Experiment with the different buttons. You'll find that there are four possible combinations of pages and movies.

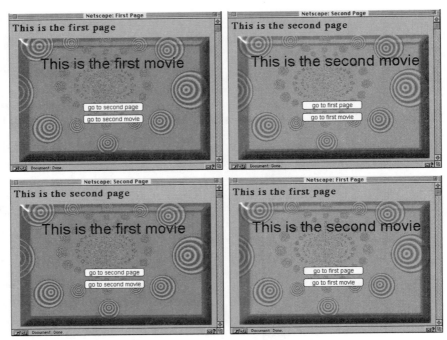

Figure 3-12: *The four variations possible as a result of Exercise 3-5.*

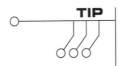

TIP

It is possible to use GotoNetPage to load in a Shockwave movie, without an accompanying HTML page. It's one way to potentially counteract the spacious border some browsers put around their graphics. Doing so prevents you from displaying other objects or giving a title to the page, of course.

Figure 3-13: *A freestanding Shockwave movie referenced by the GotoNetPage command instead of GotoNetMovie.*

Exercise 3-6: Directing Shockwave.

So far, we've referenced and moved between files that are all in the same directory. This exercise examines how to reference files in a local directory structure which aren't at the same level.

Step 1. Copy the directory *levela* from the directory EXER0306 to your hard drive. This directory contains three subdirectories—*levelb1*, *levelb2*, and *levelc* (inside *levelb1*)—HTML pages, and Director files for the exercise. The HTML pages have already been created with the proper EMBED tags.

Step 2. Open the Director file *navi-a.dir* inside the directory *levela*. Play the movie and press the twirling donuts. Note that while the donuts twirl faster while the mouse is over them, and the text highlights when you press the donut, nothing else happens yet.

The four movies in this exercise each have one donut in a fixed position, next to a dimmed label which indicates the current position in the directory structure. By the time we're done, pressing on a donut will take you to the corresponding page, navigating through the local directory structure as we go.

Figure 3-14: *The* navi-a.dir *movie—with donuts.*

Step 3. Bring up the Script window for Score Script 27. This is the mouseDown event handler for the active donut button sprites in each movie. **Note:** Ordinarily some of these actions would be accomplished through the use of the mouseUp handler, but in the early releases of Shockwave, the mouseUp event is not always passed correctly to the movie from the browser.

Add the text in boldface below to the mouseDown script. (The
¬ symbol (option+L or alt+return) can be used after a space to
break a Lingo statement.)

Listing 3-2.

```
on mouseDown
    put the clickon into thisDonut
    put thisDonut - 4 into thisLabel
    put the castNum of sprite thisLabel ¬
      into blueLabel
    repeat while the mouseDown
      starttimer
      --the timer is used to keep
      --the donuts from turning too fast
      if rollover(thisDonut) then
        set the castNum of sprite ¬
          thisLabel to blueLabel + 1
        puppetsOff
       if thisDonut = 6 then
          GotoNetPage "/levelb1/navi-b1.htm"
          else
            if thisDonut = 7 then
              GotoNetPage "/levelb2/navi-b2.htm"
            else
              if thisDonut = 8 then
                GotoNetPage ¬
                  "/levelb1/levelc/navi-c.htm"
              end if
            end if
          end if
      else
        set the castNum of sprite ¬
          thisLabel to blueLabel
      end if
      rotate
      repeat while the timer < 7
        nothing
      end repeat
      updateStage
```

```
    end repeat
    set the castNum of sprite thisLabel to blueLabel
    updateStage
end
```

These new lines test to see if the sprite that was clicked on (thisDonut) is one of the active sprites (6, 7, or 8), and uses the GotoNetPage command to branch to the appropriate HTML page. Because the current HTML page is in the *levela* directory, the first GotoNetPage, which branches to the document *navi-b1.htm*, is preceded by the subdirectory that *navi-b1.htm* is in. The subdirectory and the file name are separated by the standard slash ("/") used for Web (and UNIX) directory structures. The slash is used regardless of the platform the movie is served from or developed on. The URL (in this case a relative URL) is enclosed in straight quotes.

The next reference is almost identical, with *b2* substituted for *b1*.

The third URL is a reference to a file two levels down in the file structure, so the file name is preceded by both of the subdirectories on the path: *levelb1* and *levelc* (and, of course, the ubiquitous slash marks).

Close the Script window by pressing Enter, and save the file.

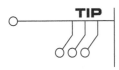

TIP If you're feeling adventurous, use Afterburner to make Shockwave movies out of each of the four Director files now, and open *navi-a.htm* with your Web browser. You should be able to branch to any of the other pages from the Level A page (you still need to add the scripts for the other movies). If you have problems, check to see that each of the four directories has a Director movie, a Shockwave movie, and an HTML page (plus any subdirectories).

Step 4. Next you'll need to modify the scripts for the other movies. Open *navi-b1.dir* and add this to its mouseDown score script (be sure to place it directly after the statement *set the castNum of sprite thisLabel to bluelabel + 1* in the repeat loop).

Listing 3-3.

```
puppetsOff
if thisDonut = 5 then
  GotoNetPage "../navi-a.htm"
else
  if thisDonut = 7 then
    GotoNetPage "../levelb2/navi-b2.htm"
  else
    if thisDonut = 8 then
      GotoNetPage "levelc/navi-c.htm"
    end if
  end if
end if
```

Notice that a reference to a file *up* the directory structure from the current HTML page (this movie will be called by an HTML page in the *levelb1* subdirectory) in the first GotoNetPage is preceded by two periods (".."). To get to *navi-b2.htm* from *navi-b1.htm*, it's necessary to go up one level to *levela* ("..") and then down into subdirectory *levelb2*. The path to *navi-c.htm* from *navi-b1.htm* is simply a reference to a subdirectory in *levelb1* and the file itself.

Close the Script window by pressing Enter, save the file, and open *navi-b2.dir*.

Step 5. Modify Score Script 27 of *navi-b2.dir* to include the following:

Listing 3-4.

```
puppetsOff
if thisDonut = 5 then
  GotoNetPage "../navi-a.htm"
else
  if thisDonut = 6 then
    GotoNetPage "../levelb1/navi-b1.htm"
  else
    if thisDonut = 8 then
      GotoNetPage ¬
        "../levelb1/levelc/navi-c.htm"
    end if
  end if
end if
```

As you can see, this almost perfectly mirrors the script for *navi-b1.dir*, with the only real change being that to get to *navi-c.htm*, it's necessary to traverse up the directory tree (".."), then back down through *levelb1* and *levelc*.

Close the Script window with the Enter key, save, and open *navi-c.dir*.

Step 6. Our final script modification for this exercise is to do yet another variation of Score Script 27—this time for the movie at Level C. It should look like this:

Listing 3-5.

```
puppetsOff
if thisDonut = 5 then
  GotoNetPage "../../navi-a.htm"
else
  if thisDonut = 6 then
    GotoNetPage "../navi-b1.htm"
  else
    if thisDonut = 7 then
      GotoNetPage ¬
        "../../levelb2/navi-b2.htm"
    end if
  end if
end if
```

This script shows two instances where a local URL refers to directories two levels *above* the referring HTML document in the hierarchy. Remember that to get from the Level C subdirectory to the Level B2 directory, a reference is made to Level B1 (the first ".."), then Level A (second ".."), and then to Level B2 (by name, as *levelb2*).

Step 7. Use Afterburner to make Shockwave files out of all four Director files (overwrite any versions you might have already made). Be sure that each of the four directories has a Director file, a Shockwave file, and an HTML page. You should be able to open any of the pages with your Web browser and freely navigate from there to any other movie in the exercise.

Once you've mastered the art of relative URLs, full URLs are a snap. Just stick the complete URL (including the "http://" header and domain name) between the quote marks.

Moving On

In this chapter you've done a number of exercises related to Web file access using the EMBED tag, the GotoNetMovie command, and the GotoNetPage command. These are the basics of navigation on the Web, and they underlie the process of moving from one place to another via HTTP links. Now that you've seen a little bit of what's under the Shockwave hood, let's take a look at some fancy stuff—preparing graphics for Shockwave.

4

Preparing Graphics for Shockwave

Nothing has driven the development of the Web over the past couple of years more than the ability to include graphics. Much as other forms of multimedia have inspired enhancements to home and business computer systems (who needs a sound card, a 24-bit color monitor, and a mouse for small business accounting? but just try to buy a new computer without them nowadays), the progression of graphics on the Web—from small GIF (Graphic Interchange Format) icons to larger page headers, and the addition of JPEG (Joint Photographic Experts Group) graphic support to many browsers—has been a primary focus. Over the past year, as more and more commercial enterprises have gone online, and fast Internet connections have become *de rigeur*, large image map graphics have become almost mandatory. (If you're wondering how image maps work, the browser simply sends the coordinates of a mouse click to a program running on the server computer—which determines the appropriate action based on those coordinates.)

Figure 4-1: *Apple Computer, Inc. home page GIF image map.*

In such a world, it would be amiss for multimedia types like us to simply whack a few simple buttons onto the Director Stage, 'Shock the movie, and call it interactive Web content. No, if you're going to make Web pages with truly cool content, you're going to need to include graphics. And that means knowing some things about color—color palettes, graphics file formats, and compression. Chances are, if you've been developing Web sites or Director movies already, you know some of this. But there are a few peculiarities associated with embedding Shockwave movies in Web pages.

This chapter examines how to get the most out of the graphics you include in your Shockwave movies—both in terms of keeping file sizes small and maintaining as much quality as possible. That means intimate knowledge about what monitor depth is; how images are stored in memory; what color palettes are; something about file compression; and when to substitute object-oriented graphics for bitmaps. Keeping all of these things in mind when designing and creating Shockwave movies will allow you to get the most quality out of your work and make it travel the highways and byways of the Web as fast as possible.

Figure 4-2: *Apple Computer home page Shockwave movie in action.*

Monitoring Depth

Most computers capable of viewing Shockwave movies have monitors and video cards capable of either 8-bit (256-color) or 32-bit (16 million-color) display. In many cases, depending on the size of the monitor and the *pitch* (pixels per inch on the display—often a user-selectable option), it's possible to switch between the two. It's often assumed that monitors are 72 *ppi* (*pixels per inch*, also frequently referred to as *dpi* or *dots per inch*), but 80 ppi monitors are fairly common, and many monitors can be set to 90-100 ppi.

Pixellated Memory

Every pixel in a bitmap image requires a certain amount of memory to store information about the color of the pixel. An 8-bit image stored on disk or video memory in Shockwave movies requires only a third as much memory as a 32-bit RGB image does (32-bit images are composed of 8 bits each for Red, Green, and Blue components, plus another 8 bits for an alpha channel, but Director stores only the color information). Most important for Shockwave movies, smaller images mean smaller movies and shorter transmission times across the Internet. While movie size is always a concern in Director presentations (size affects initial load time from disk and playback speed, among other things), it's far more important with regard to Shockwave, because a double-speed CD-ROM (considered the lowest common denominator for most current multimedia titles) is about 300 times faster than the average 14.4 kb modem connection—at its best.

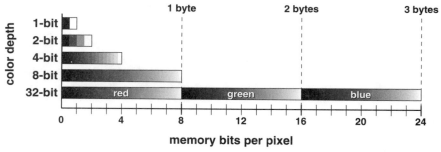

Figure 4-3: *Memory storage required for different pixel depths.*

Quantity Versus Quality

8-bit color is pretty much a standard for multimedia productions today. It's a minimum requirement for the MPC (Multimedia PC) specification on Windows machines, and it's standard on all current color Mac OS computers. A computer running in 8-bit color can display 1-bit movies (black-and-white with no levels of gray), 2-bit movies (usually black, white, and two other colors), and 4-bit movies (16 colors) as well as 8-bit movies.

While there is an increasing base of computers that can display full 32-bit RGB color, they can't necessarily do it quickly. So multimedia presentations that incorporate a lot of movement will usually rely on 8-bit color for display. And since you can store at least three times the amount of visual data in a movie composed with 8-bit as opposed to 24-bit color, there are storage advantages as well.

The tradeoff, then, is quality over size, with size affecting speed and transportability. A fast-moving 8-bit image may be more effective than a barely crawling 32-bit image, particularly if the reason you're using Shockwave is to create animation in your Web pages.

Even more so than in the general world of multimedia, multimedia design for the Web involves an intelligent choice of trade-offs. If you design for CD-ROM, you make decisions based on the assumed CD-ROM player speed of your expected viewer, as well as other decisions based on total storage capacity of the medium, assumed CPU capabilities, and assumed monitor size. When designing and creating graphics (and sound) for Shockwave for Director, you not only don't know how fast your viewer will be receiving your movie but you don't even know what platform your movie will be playing on.

By knowing the trade-offs involved in creating graphics ranging from beautiful, high-resolution images to less-colorful but functional indexed color and 1-bit images, you can take charge of the process and determine what's best for your own situation—and for your viewers.

Cleansing Your Palettes

While a 32-bit RGB image stores information about the color of every single pixel—keeping track of its Red, Green, and Blue components by referring to a number from 0 to 255 for each color—the lowly 8-bit image has no such luxury. With only a third as much allocated memory as an RGB image—just a single byte

(8 bits equals 1 byte)—there's only enough room to store one number between 0 and 255. So 8-bit images use what is called a *palette* or *color lookup table* (*CLUT*, for short). A palette is just what it sounds like, a selection of colors to choose from—and for an 8-bit image, using a single byte of memory, that's 254 colors plus black-and-white.

CLUTtering Your Field of Vision

To make a distinction, 8-bit images don't keep track of *what* the color of the pixel is, they keep track of *which* color the pixel is. Since 8-bit images have only a limited selection of colors to choose from, less memory is required than would be needed to keep track of color values for each individual pixel. On the other hand, the total number of colors available is restricted.

The 256 colors in a palette each have their own Red, Green, and Blue component values. The colors themselves are each assigned an *index* number from 0 (normally reserved for white) to 255 (reserved for black), which is why an 8-bit image is referred to as an *indexed-color* type of image. (8-bit images are only one type of indexed-color format.) Keeping the number of colors small means that the image needs only one-third of the memory normally required, plus a small amount of overhead for palette information (a Director palette takes up less than 2K of memory). Multiple images can refer to the same palette without the palette having to be duplicated.

By using ever smaller chunks of memory to keep track of which palette color a pixel is using, images can be made even more compact. An 8-bit image uses a whole memory byte to store a pixel's color index value; a 4-bit (16-color) image uses half a byte; and 2-bit (4-color) images store four pixels worth of information in a byte. A 1-bit image is sort of a special case: it can store only information that relates to whether a pixel is turned on or off—but then again, it can store enough information for eight pixels in a single byte. (1-bit images are commonly called *bitmap images*, although technically every image discussed in this section is a bitmap.) Again, with economy of memory comes a compromise: less memory means less variety of color.

"Is That Vermilion in Your Palette, or Are You Happy Just to See Me?"

Depending on which colors you want to use to show an image, it's possible to create a variety of palettes. A scan of a black-and-white photograph, for instance, would best be shown with a *grayscale* palette, one in which each color has an equal amount of Red, Green, and Blue components. A picture of a famous painting is going to look more like the real thing with a custom palette made especially for the occasion. But on the Web it's another case of "pretty" meeting a hard wall.

In a traditional multimedia production, you control the horizontal, you control the vertical, and—most important—you control the color palette. When you're in the Web environment, though, you surrender much of that control.

On a monitor set to 8-bit color, the entire screen uses the current palette, and changing palettes in a Director movie changes the colors of screen items outside the movie, including menus and other windows—that means other elements on the same Web page, such as backgrounds, text, images, and other Shockwave movies.

So what's a Shockwave designer to do? With no control over the platform (Windows and the Mac OS use different standard lookup palettes), potential problems with other graphic elements on the same page, and the possibility that the viewer might just decide to jump from your page to another (with a totally different palette), there doesn't seem to be any safe ground. The answer, as with most things Internet, is a compromise.

One Palette to Bind Them

Currently, your safest bet is to convert Shockwave graphics to a palette independently developed by a number of people on the Internet. Because it's derived from the default palette for the Netscape Navigator Web browser, this palette is usually referred to as "the Netscape palette." It includes 216 colors, with the remaining 40 positions left unspecified.

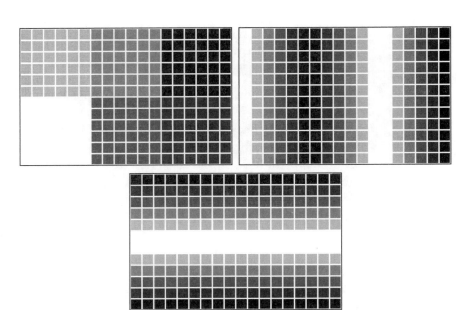

Figure 4-4: *Red (top left), Green (top right), and Blue(bottom) components of "the Netscape palette" from the MetaTools, Inc. Web site's "webtips" pages (http://www.metatools.com/webtips/webtip5.html).*

As you can see from Figure 4-4, there's some order to the way this palette is constructed. The Red component is made up of six 6 x 6 regions, with values at 0 (black in the diagram), 51, 102, 153, 204, and 255 (white). The Green component, with vertical bands of color, uses the same values for its part, and the horizontal striping of the Blue component does the same. (The placement of the squares is irrelevant; I've used this illustration simply because it's the best graphic representation of them that I've seen.) By distributing the colors in this way, this palette includes as much of the RGB color space as possible, as evenly as possible, which guarantees not the best image possible in each case but still a better general palette for overall usage.

Exercise 4-1: Using "the Netscape palette" in Adobe Photoshop.

A PCX-format image and a Photoshop palette are included on the Companion CD-ROM, which you can use in any image editor that can read those formats. This exercise will show you how to convert images to the Netscape palette in Photoshop 3.0 (the process is very similar in Photoshop 2.5). Photoshop (or some other image-editing program) is usually preferred over Director for image conversion, because it generally provides the user with more control of the process. Since Photoshop is an image-editing program, and Director is a multimedia authoring program, that is only to be expected.

Step 1. Open the file *flood.tif* (in the EXER0401 directory of the TUTORIAL directory on the Companion CD-ROM) with Photoshop. The *flood.tif* image has already been converted to an 8-bit indexed-color image for other multimedia usage, but we now want to use it in a Shockwave movie with the Netscape palette.

Figure 4-5: *The* flood.tif *image.*

Step 2. Convert the image to RGB by choosing the RGB selection from the Mode menu. Whenever possible, convert to the Netscape palette from an original, preindexed version of an image; but if you must convert an image that has already been indexed, changing the image to RGB rather than simply switching palettes will usually cause less color shifting.

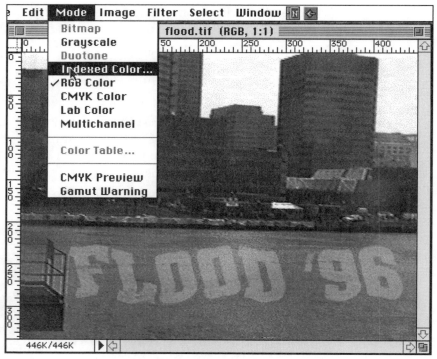

Figure 4-6: *Changing the Mode in Photoshop.*

Step 3. Now switch the image back to indexed mode by selecting Indexed Color from the Mode menu. A dialog box will appear offering you a number of options for the conversion.

Step 4. Choose Custom from the Palette section of the Indexed Color dialog box.

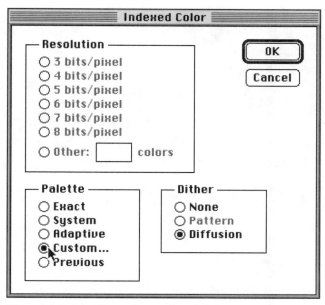

Figure 4-7: *The Photoshop Indexed Color dialog box.*

Step 5. The choice you make under the Dither section makes a great difference in the final appearance of your image and—important in Shockwave—the size of the image. You should have two choices at this point: None and Diffusion. When you choose None, the image is converted to the new palette by choosing the closest color in the palette to each individual pixel. The Diffusion option analyzes a small area of the image a few pixels square, and creates a pattern of pixels of varying colors which best approximates the overall color of the area. The two methods can produce vastly different results on the same image.

Figure 4-8: flood.tif *converted with a Dither setting of None.*

Because it simply chooses the closest match for any particular pixel in an image, the None option usually produces the best conversion for images with large areas containing the same shade (a posterized effect, in conventional art terms). For much line art and cartoon-style artwork, no dithering is not only acceptable but preferred over diffusion dithering, because it prevents fills from looking grainy and irregular. In graduated fills and blends, the None option will create banding, which pretty much ruins the effect of a smooth gradation. Nevertheless, whenever possible an unditherered conversion should be the option of choice for Shockwave graphics, because, as we will discuss later, it produces images that can be compressed more readily than diffusion-dithered images.

The diffusion dither generally produces better results on photo-graphic images and smoothly blended artwork. In these cases, the None option often degrades image quality significantly, while the irregularity of diffusion dithering maintains at least the illusion that much of the original subtle range of colors remains.

Choose Diffusion for now, and press the OK button.

Step 6. Another window—the Color Table window—opens up, allowing you to choose the Custom palette to convert to. Press the Load button, and open the Photoshop palette file *netswin.pal* from the TUTORIAL directory. This will load the palette into Photoshop as the Custom palette.

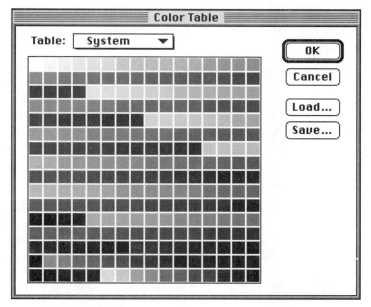

Figure 4-9: *The Color Table dialog.*

Step 7. Press OK in the Color Table dialog, and the image will be converted.

Step 8. Choose Save As from the File menu, and save the file in PICT format as *palconv.pct* (or one of the many other formats supported in Director for Windows) for import into Director.

Step 9. Start Director, and Import the image into the Cast of a new movie. You should get a Palette Mismatch dialog box which will allow you to import a Palette cast member into the movie.

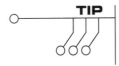

TIP

To import the image and palette into Director for the Macintosh, be sure that your Monitors Control Panel (under the Apple menu) is set to 256 colors. If the Monitors setting is for Thousands or Millions of colors, the image will be imported as either 16-bit or 32-bit, and the palette will not be imported.

Exercise 4-2: Combining flat & diffusion dithering in Adobe Photoshop.

Inevitably there will be cases where an image contains areas with both smooth gradations suitable for diffusion dithering and solid color areas that might work better with no dithering. In this exercise, we'll use both techniques on the same image.

Step 1. Use Photoshop to open the image *mixed.tif* in the directory EXER0402. This RGB image includes a smooth, graduated fill on the left and several flat areas of color fill on the right.

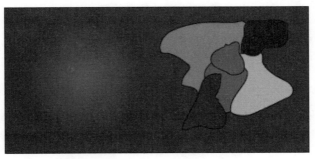

Figure 4-10: *The original image for* mixed.tif.

Step 2. Select the entire image with the Select | All menu command (Command+A on Mac OS machines or Ctrl+A under Windows).

Step 3. Copy the image with the menu command Edit | Copy.

Step 4. Create a new Photoshop file with the menu command File | New. A dialog box will appear with the size of the image you just copied already entered in the Height and Width. Check to make sure that the Mode pop-up menu is set to RGB, name the image *undither.pct,* and press the OK button.

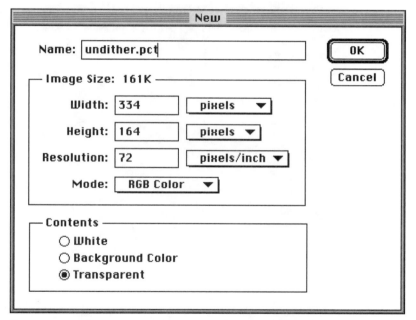

Figure 4-11: *Creating a new image in Photoshop after a File | Copy command.*

Step 5. Paste the image into the new image window with the menu command Edit | Paste.

Step 6. Repeat Steps 4 and 5, naming the new image *dithered.pct.* You should now have three versions of the same image: the original and two copies.

Step 7. Convert *dithered.pct* to indexed color by selecting Indexed in the Mode menu. Use the Diffusion dither option and the *netswin.pal* palette, as in Exercise 4-1. Save *dithered.pct* as a PICT file.

Step 8. Convert the image *ubdither.pct* to indexed color with a dither setting of None and the *netwin.pal* palette. Save the image as a PICT file.

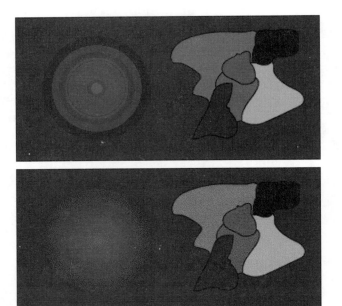

Figure 4-12: undither.pct *(at left) and* dither.pct *(at right).*

Step 9. Compare the dithered image to the undithered image. The blend on the undithered image has become several concentric circles of color. The background, however, is a solid color, and the outlined shapes on the right are filled with solid color as well. The blend on the dithered version, while not perfect, more closely approximates a blend, but the background is splotchy, as are the fills of the outlined shapes.

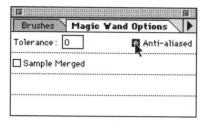

Figure 4-13: *The Magic Wand Options palette in Photoshop.*

Double-click the Magic Wand tool in the toolbar and set the Magic Wand Options Tolerance to 0. Uncheck the Anti-aliased check box if it is checked.

Use the Magic Wand tool to select the outermost ring of the blend in the undithered version.

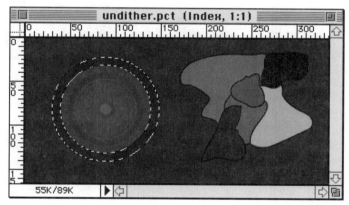

Figure 4-14: *The outermost ring of the undithered blend is selected.*

Step 10. With the Shift key held down, use the Lasso tool, or any other selection tool you choose, to add the rest of the blend area to the selection. This will create the mask you will use to blend the two copies of the original image.

While cases exist where the dithered shape cannot be as easily separated from its background, it should be relatively easy to create this kind of mask, due to the nature of the undithered indexed color image.

Step 11. Use the menu item Selection│Save Selection to create a new channel for this selection.

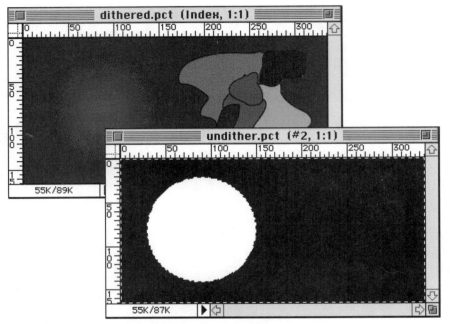

Figure 4-15: *The selection saved in channel 2 of* undither.pct.

Step 12. In the dithered image, choose the menu item Selection | Load
Selection, and load channel #2 from the image *undither.pct.*

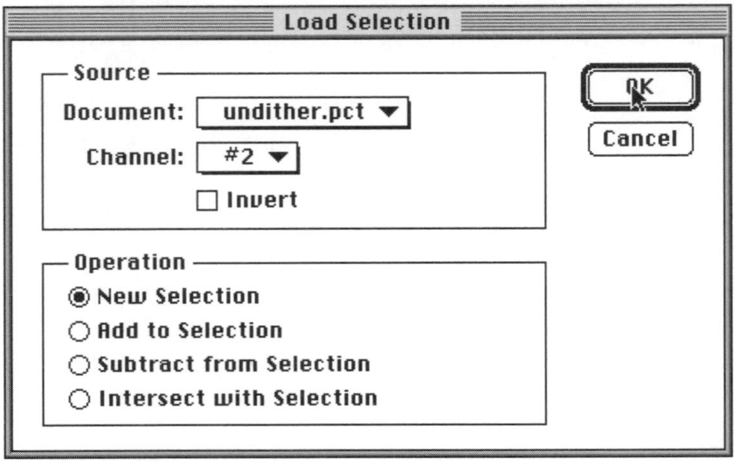

Figure 4-16: *Loading the selection into* dithered.pct.

Step 13. Choose Edit I Copy from the menu bar to copy the dithered blend from the image.

Step 14. Switch to the *undither.pct* image, and choose menu item Selection I Load Selection to load channel #2 of *undither.pct*.

Step 15. Use the menu item Edit I Paste to incorporate the dithered blend into the image with an undithered backgound and flat-colored shapes. Use the menu item File I Save As to save this image as *mixed.pct*.

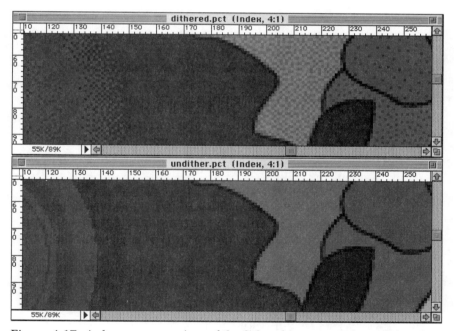

Figure 4-17: *A close-up comparison of the dithered image and the undithered image with the dithered blend inserted. Notice the patterning in the background and the shapes in the top image.*

Because the images have been indexed with the same palette, there will be no color shift during the process of combining the dithered blend with the undithered image.

Cold Compress

Now that you have experience in maintaining flat colors in images, you may be wondering exactly why that's important. The answer, as usual with regard to the Internet, is bandwidth, or how fast your Shockwave movies will be able to fly across the Web. The Macromedia Shockwave Afterburner is a compressor that can shrink a Director file to just over a quarter of its original size in some cases. Those cases are determined by how you put together your movie's graphics.

In uncompressed form, an 8-bit indexed-color image—for example—stores each pixel's color value in a single byte of memory. For an image that's 150 x 150 pixels square, that's 22,500 bytes (or over 22K) of memory for the color data. An RGB image of the same dimensions would require three times that: over 67K uncompressed.

Data compressors work by looking for patterns of information in the data they're compressing. Most image formats store pixel data from left to right, top to bottom, so that images with long horizontal stretches of similar pixels tend to compress more than images with lots of variation in color.

Exercise 4-3: Comparing compression.

This exercise shows you the difference flat color values make in Director files compressed with Afterburner.

Step 1. Open Director and create a new movie. Be sure that your monitor is set to 256-color mode.

Step 2. Use the menu item File | Import to add the PICT file *red.pct* to the cast (*red.pct* can be found in the EXER0403 directory). This should open the Cast window if it is closed.

Step 3. Save the Director movie as *red1.dir*.

Step 4. Save another copy of the file as *red2.dir* with the menu selection File | Save As.

Step 5. Double-click on cast member 1, the red square, to bring up the Paint window.

Figure 4-18: *Detail of the dithered red square.*

Step 6. Double-click on the Pencil tool to shift into magnified view. Here you can see that far from being flat the red square has been dithered. Virtually every other pixel is a different color.

Step 7. Use the Eyedropper tool to select a light red from the Paint window.

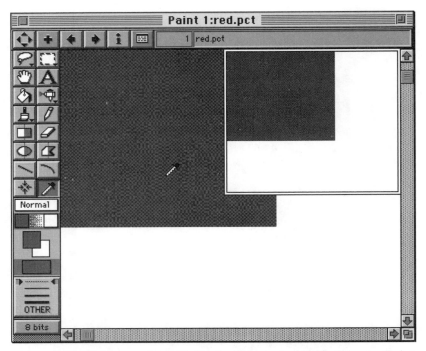

Figure 4-19: *Picking a color with the Eyedropper tool in the Director Paint window.*

Step 8. Double-click on the Selection rectangle tool to select the entire image.

Step 9. From the Effects menu, choose the Fill command to fill the selection with a single color.

Step 10. Resave the movie *red2.dir*. You now have two almost identical movies, with one difference between them: the image in *red1.dir* is dithered, the image in *red2.dir* is undithered.

Step 11. Use Afterburner to create compressed Shockwave movies from both movies.

Look at and compare the file sizes of the Director and the Shockwave movies. The original Director movies will be about 30K in size for *red1.dir* and just over 9K for *red2.dir*. The Shockwave files will be much smaller, of course, about 6K and 3K, respectively.

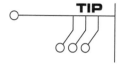

TIP | If the files appear to be larger than this on your hard drive, try copying them to a floppy and viewing the file sizes there, or use a disk utility program to determine the exact size of the files. The Macintosh Finder determines file size by how many hard disk sectors are used by the files, rounded up from the actual amount of data in the file.

Obviously, the movie with the dithered graphic has been compressed by a greater percentage than the one with the flat color image, but the movie with the flat image starts out smaller and ends up smaller. In movies with a number of bitmap images, those small savings add up quickly.

Bitmap Is No Object

Bitmap graphics aren't your only choice when creating graphics for Shockwave movies. Whenever possible, it's a good idea to replace them with object graphics created using the Tools palette. While it's not possible to get all of the texture and smoothness of a bitmap with objects, it is possible to supplement object graphics with strategically placed bitmap images, lending the overall picture more subtlety than simple objects could provide.

The primary reason for using objects is their size. An 8-bit image 448 pixels wide by 300 pixels high is over 130K in size. A similarly sized object graphic is just about 50 bytes—that's more than a 2000:1 size difference. Object graphics need only to store data relating to their shape, color, and size rather than information about every pixel.

Exercise 4-4: 50 Steps to Smaller Movies.

Careful planning can actually help you to create Shockwave movies that are comparable in file size to GIF or JPEG files of the same dimensions. In this exercise, you'll translate the graphic look of a static home page GIF graphic (Figure 4-20), into an animated Shockwave movie that's barely larger than the original GIF.

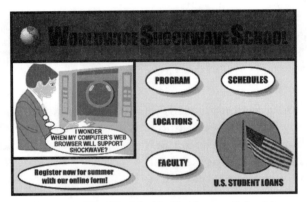

Figure 4-20: *The Worldwide Shockwave School home page GIF.*

Step 1. Open the Director movie *wrldwide.dir* in the EXER0404 directory.

Step 2. An undithered version of the original home page image has been imported into the movie already, as cast member 1. Open the Cast window, double-click on cast member 1, and take a look at this image in the Paint window to decide how we'll Shock this page.

This picture is 448 x 300 pixels wide. (Why not 450 pixels wide? Well, as you'll remember from your Director manual, the width of the movie must be a multiple of 16. 448 divided by 16 is 28.) It has a 4-pixel black border on the outside edge, around the cartoon, and between the two main color areas. The five buttons have drop shadows underneath them to give them some dimensionality, as does the globe in the upper left. The text and graphics are anti-aliased.

What in this image can be turned into an object? The large areas of the backgrounds are the first things that spring to mind. The oval shapes of the buttons, the thought balloon in the cartoon, and the blue circle behind the flag can be created as objects, if we're willing to trade off the anti-aliased edges. The text *could* be done as objects, but the viewer's computer would have to have the appropriate typeface installed to view it correctly, and that's not likely. The flag and globe can't be created with objects. We'll use objects for the shadows, although we won't be able to get soft edges that way.

So here's the breakdown.

Image elements:

- cartoon
- text
- globe
- flag

Object elements:

- backgounds
- buttons
- thought balloons
- circle behind flag
- button shadows
- globe shadow

Here's the outline for this Shockwave movie's script:

- The yellow fill will do a vertical wipe from the bottom to fill the whole screen. With sound effect (whoosh).
- The red banner will do a vertical wipe from the top of the screen. Whoosh.
- An animated (spinning) globe will move across the red banner from right to left, revealing the title as it moves. Whoosh. It remains spinning in its final position.

☯ The cartoon (without thought balloon) will push onto the Stage from the left.

☯ The thought balloon will animate into existence, and a man's voice will speak the words.

☯ The buttons and the flag will pop into position one by one.

☯ In the idle state, the globe will be spinning, the flag will wave, the buttons will have a rollover to indicate that they are active, and the cartoon will have an animated feature which will replay the thought balloon animation when clicked. The word "Shockwave" in the title will flash colors. The buttons will depress when clicked. (You won't do all of this in this exercise, but you need to know what's going to happen in order to decide how to treat the graphics.)

Step 3. Open the Score window and drag cast member 1 from the Cast window into frame 1 of channel 1 in the Score. This will install the *netswin.pal* palette in frame 1.

Step 4. Notice that the black frames weren't mentioned when we were deciding on bitmaps versus objects. That's because the background color of the Stage will provide most of what we need. Bring up the Control Panel and use the pop-up palette to assign black as the background color.

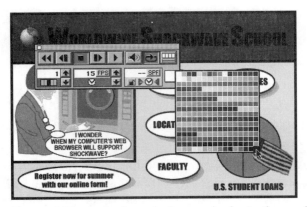

Figure 4-21: *Assigning a background color to the movie.*

Step 5. Bring the Palette window to the front, then use the Eyedropper tool to select the yellow in the graphic so that you can identify the color's exact position in the palette. (It should be 4.) Do the same for the red in the banner (86). We're going to hold off creating the shapes for the background for just a bit, because we don't want to obscure our template image. We'll replace the template in channel 1 with a yellow rectangle later, and reserve channel 2 for a red rectangle.

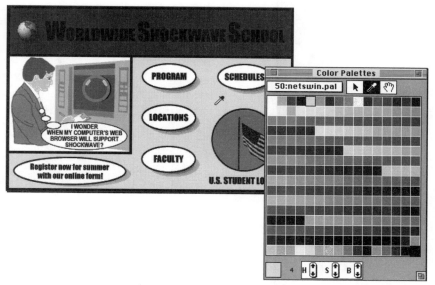

Figure 4-22: *Identifying a color with the Eyedropper tool in the Palette window. The yellow color in position 4 is highlighted and displayed at the lower left.*

Step 6. Scroll to position 49 in the Cast window, select it, and Import the PICT file *type.pct* into the cast. This is a composite of all of the type elements for the image, separated from the other graphics. When the Palette Mismatch dialog box appears, select the top radio button, Remap Colors then OK. This will convert the grayscale image to the *netswin.pal* palette.

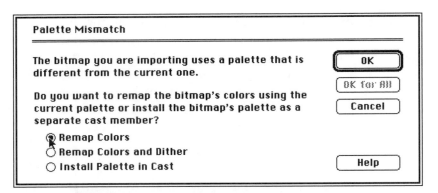

Figure 4-23: *The Palette Mismatch dialog box.*

Step 7. Copy cast member 49, *type.pct*, and paste it into cast positions 3, 4, 5, and 6. We'll use these for the headline in the banner and the text under the flag, erasing the parts we don't want.

Step 8. Double-click on cast member 3 to bring up the Paint window. Erase everything but the word "Worldwide."

Step 9. Repeat step 8 for cast members 4, 5, and 6, leaving the words "Shockwave," "School," and "U.S. Student Loans," respectively, in each.

Step 10. Select cast members 3, 5, and 6, and choose Transform Bitmap from the Cast menu. Set the Color Depth to 2, the Palette to System - Win, and choose Remap to Nearest Colors. This will save valuable memory in the movie.

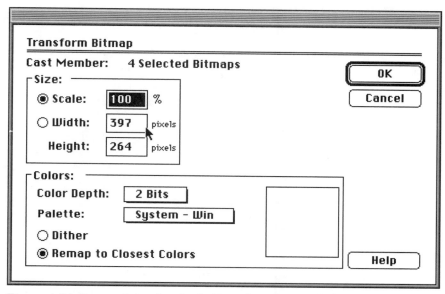

Figure 4-24: *Remapping colors in the Transform Bitmap dialog box.*

Step 11. Select cast member 4 (the word "Shockwave") and choose Transform Bitmap from the Cast menu. Set the Color Depth to 1 and Remap to Closest Colors. This word will change colors as the movie plays, so we need a 1-bit bitmap for the image. Since it'll be changing colors quickly, there's no need to worry about anti-aliasing the edges.

Step 12. Bring the Score window to the fore, and select frame 1 of channel 3 (we're reserving channel 2). Select cast members 3 to 6 in the Cast window, and drag them onto the Stage, positioning them over the template image. Set the Ink effect for these sprites to Darkest, and adjust their position with the arrow keys as necessary.

Step 13. Import the image *tapeman.pic,* into cast position 7. Select channel 9, frame 1, and align the picture with the lower right edge of the picture on the Stage, inside the black border. This leaves two channels between the text elements already placed and the cartoon. Set the Ink effect to Copy.

Step 14. Select channel 7, frame 1 and use the Filled Rectangle tool from the Tools palette to draw a rectangle filled with black on the Stage. Select Sprite Info from the Score menu (Command+K or Ctrl+K). Set Width to 192, Height to 158, and Location to 4 pixels from the left, 83 pixels from the top of the Stage.

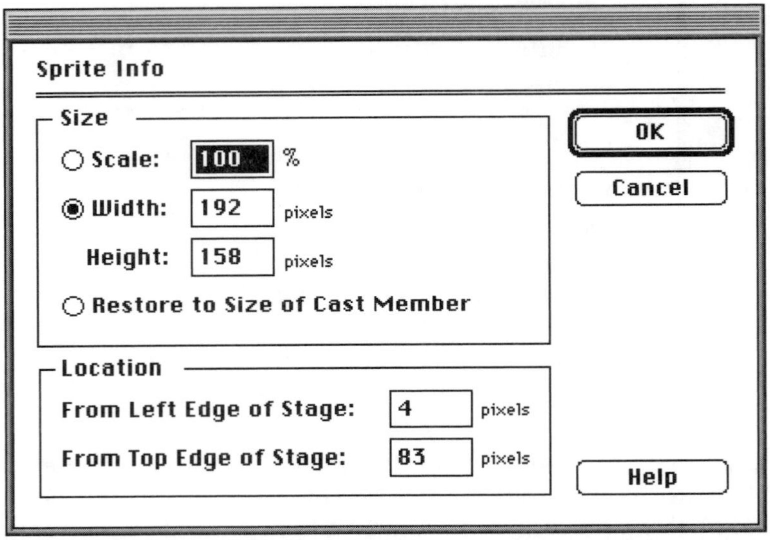

Figure 4-25: *Sizing the rectangle forming the border for the cartoon graphic with the Sprite Info dialog.*

Step 15. Duplicate the sprite in channel 7 by holding down the Option or Alt key, selecting frame 1 of channel 7 and dragging it to channel 8. Set the Width of this sprite to 188 and the Height to 154 with the Sprite Info dialog (leaving the Location settings alone). Set the sprite's foreground color to white with the Tools palette. This rectangle forms a portion of the white background for the cartoon that has been trimmed out of the image. Incidentally, it shows how you can reuse the same cast member with different colors on the Stage at the same time. This shape will be reused for the red and yellow background shapes as well.

Step 16. Duplicate the cartoon image cast member into a new cast position by selecting it in the Cast window and using the menu command Cast | Duplicate (Command+D or Ctrl+D). In the Paint window, erase everything down to the inner ring of the tape in the machine (this will be the other animated element in the cartoon). Double-click the Registration tool to set the registration point to the middle of the image.

Step 17. Duplicate the cropped image of the tape in the Cast window. The two images will be rotated and used for the animation. Open the Paint window, double-click the Selection rectangle tool to select the entire image, and choose Effects | Free Rotate from the menu. Rotate the image counterclockwise until one of the dots is at the bottom of the image.

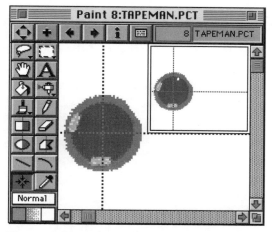

Figure 4-26: *A detail of one of the duplicate tapes from the cartoon image, already rotated and with the registration point indicated by the crosshairs. Notice that the outline has been removed.*

Step 18. Rotate the first copy of the tape clockwise until one of the dots is at the bottom of the image.

Step 19. Use the outline oval tool from the Tools palette to draw a circle (hold down the Shift key to constrain the drawing tool) over the tape's position on the Stage. Set the outline width to 0 pixels with the Tools palette. This clear shape will be a placeholder for a third frame of the spinning tape animation. Use the Sprite Info (Command+K or Ctrl+K) dialog box to set the Location to 119 pixels from the left and 116 pixels from the top.

Step 20. Inside the EXER0404 folder is a directory called GLOBE. Use the Import All button in the File | Import menu item's dialog box to add to the cast all 15 of the PICT files used for the spinning globe.

Step 21. Select all of the images of the globe in the Cast window, hold down the Option or Alt key, and drag them to frame 1 of channel 12 (don't worry about the position on the Stage). This will place the selected cast members in the Score sequentially over a series of frames, similar to using the Cast | Cast to Time menu command. If you open the Score window and drag the playback head across the first 16 frames, you should see the globe spin. In the Score window, double-click on the gray area containing the channel number to select all of the frames of the globe animation, and set the Ink effect to Matte.

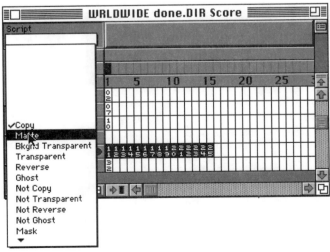

Figure 4-27: *Changing the Ink effect of the globe animation on the Stage.*

Step 22. Select frame 1 of channel 11 in the Score window. Draw a circle on the Stage using the filled circle tool from the Tools palette. Use the Score | Sprite Info dialog to set its size to 32 x 32 pixels, then position it slightly below and to the right of the globe. Choose a purple from the foreground color chip in the Tools palette, and set the Ink effect to Subtract Pin. This Ink is useful for casting shadows that can move across a variety of colors to present a realistic-looking shadow (the darker the object's color, the lighter the shadow).

Step 23. Double-click in the Score on the channel number for channel 11 to select the channel's cells out to the end of the spinning globe animation. Use the menu command Score | In-Between Linear (Command+B or Ctrl+B) to extend the shadow through the entire animation sequence.

Step 24. With the Shift key pressed, double-click again on the number for channel 12, adding the cells containing the globe to the selection. Use the Edit | Cut (Command+X or Ctrl+X) menu command to remove the cells from the Score, and Edit | Paste (Command+V or Ctrl+V) them into the Cast window as a film loop at position 28. Name the loop "Spinning Earth."

Step 25. Select frame 1 of channel 12 in the Score, drag the Spinning Earth film loop from the Cast window to the Stage, and position it over the template. This leaves channel 11 open for now.

Step 26. Select cast position 29. Use the File | Import menu command (Command+J or Ctrl+J) to add PICT files *flag1.pct* and *flag2.pct* to the cast. These are separate stills from the same video clip. Use the menu command Cast | Duplicate (Command+D or Ctrl+D) to make a copy of *flag1.pct*.

Step 27. In the Paint window, set the registration points of the three flag images to the top corner of the flag, using the Registration tool.

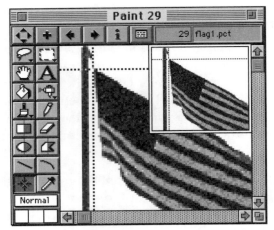

Figure 4-28: *Setting the registration point on one of the flag graphics.*

Step 28. In the duplicate of *flag1.pct* (cast member 31) erase the entire flag, leaving the flagpole. Erase everything but the flag in the other two flag images.

Step 29. Select frame 1 of channel 14 in the Score window. Select the first flag (cast member 29) and the flagpole (cast member 31) in the Cast window (holding down Command or Ctrl while selecting will allow you to select noncontiguous cast members). Drag them onto the Stage into position over the template.

Step 30. Bring the Palette window to the front (Command+8 or Ctrl+8) and use the Eyedropper tool to identify the blue color in the circle behind the flag on the template. Select frame 1 of channel 13 in the Score. With the filled oval tool from the Tools palette, draw a circle over the blue circle on the template. Set its background color with the Tools palette to the blue you identified in the Palette window, make its outline two pixels wide (the second setting from the bottom in the Tools palette), and set the foreground color to black. In the Pattern pop-up palette, choose the solid pattern.

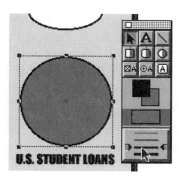

Figure 4-29: *Using the Tools palette to set the width of an outline.*

Step 31. Select frames 1 and 2 in channels 13, 14, and 15, then use the menu command Score | In-Between Linear (Command+B or Ctrl+B) to extend the sprites into channel 2.

Step 32. Select the flag in frame 2 of the Score and the second flag image in the Cast. Use menu command Score | Switch Cast Member (Command+E or Ctrl+E) to swap the second image for the first in the Score.

Step 33. Select the two flag sprite cells in the Score, copy them using Edit | Copy, and make a film loop from them by using Edit | Paste to put them into the Cast window. Call the loop "Waving Flag."

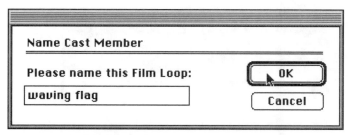

Figure 4-30: *Creating the "Waving Flag" film loop.*

Step 34. Delete the sprites in frame 2 of the Score by selecting them and pressing Delete. Select the flag sprite in frame 1 of the Score and the Waving Flag film loop in the Cast. Use menu command Score | Switch Cast Member (Command+E or Ctrl+E) to replace the image with the film loop in the Score. Reposition the flag on the Stage.

Why wasn't the blue circle included in the film loop? Because in order to give it a rollover effect later on, we want it as a separate sprite for puppeting.

Step 35. It's time to make the buttons. Select frame 1 of channel 21 (reserving 16-20 for the shadows) in the Score window, and drag cast member 32 (the blue circle) from the Cast window to the Score window on top of the button at the lower left. Resize it to match the button, and change its background color to white with the Tools palette color chips. Set the Ink effect to Copy.

Step 36. Copy the sprite in channel 21 to channel 22 by clicking on the cell, holding the Option or Alt key down and dragging it to the cell below.

Step 37. Reposition the sprite in frame 1 of channel 22 over the lowest of the three buttons in a column, and resize it to match the template.

Step 38. Repeat the process in Steps 36 and 37 for the other three buttons. When done, there should be five button sprites in channels 21-25.

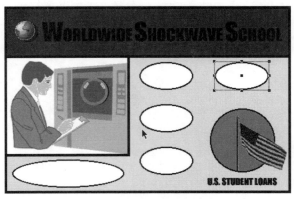

Figure 4-31: *All of the buttons in place, before the addition of text or shadows.*

Step 39. Select the cells in frame 1 of channels 21-25 of the Score. Use the Edit | Copy Cells (Command+C or Ctrl+C) menu command to copy the cells, select frame 1 of channel 16, and Edit | Paste Cells (Command+V or Ctrl+V). This will duplicate the buttons into channels 16-20.

Step 40. Select the cells in frame 1 of channels 16-20. Change the outline width of these shapes to 0 pixels with the Tools palette. Change the background color of the shapes to a shade slightly darker than the yellow of the background. Use the arrow keys to move the selected shapes—now our button shadows—to the right and down about four pixels in each direction.

Figure 4-32: *The buttons, duplicated, offset, and recolorized as shadows.*

Step 41. Almost done with the pieces. Copy cast member 49—the separated text—and Paste it into cast positions 34-38.

Step 42. For cast members 34-38, erase all but the text of one button in the Paint window. One should say "Faculty," one should say "Program," etc.

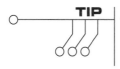

TIP

To check to see if all of the extraneous pixels have been deleted, double-click on the selection rectangle tool to select the entire image—if the selection area is larger then the text you've left, you've got a few pixels on the loose.

Step 43. Select cast members 34-38 in the Cast window. Use the Cast | Transform Bitmap menu command to convert then to 2-bit images using the same settings as in Step 10.

Step 44. Select frame 1 of channel 26. With cast members 34-38 selected in the Cast window, drag them to the Stage into position over the buttons.

Step 45. Now for the thought balloon. Turn channels 7-9 off by pressing the diamond-shaped button next to the channel number in the Score. This hides the cartoon and the two shapes we've used to define its shape and outline, so that we can see the template image.

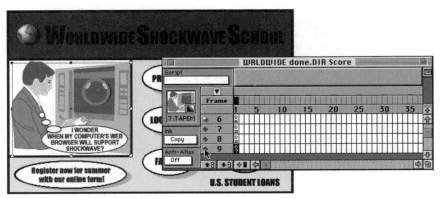

Figure 4-33: *Hiding sprites by turning off their channels.*

Step 46. Select frame 1 in channel 31, and drag cast member 32—the oval shape we used for the buttons—from the Cast window to the Stage, over the bubble containing words. Size it to match the template, make sure the foreground color is black and the background color is white, and set the outline width to 1 pixel with the Tools palette.

Step 47. Copy the sprite in channel 31 into channels 32, 33, and 34. Resize each of these for the other thought bubbles. Make sure they are in order from lower right to upper left.

Step 48. Copy the text from cast member 49 again, and paste it into cast position 39. Erase everything except the text for the thought balloon, and convert it to 2-bit text as above. Turn on channels 7-9. Select frame 1 of channel 35, then drag the balloon text from the Cast window to the Stage and put it into position.

Step 49. Select frame 1 in channel 2, and drag another copy of the rectangle object from cast position 2 to the Stage. Set its color to the red you identified back in Step 3. Use the Score | Spirite Info menu command to set its size to 440 pixels wide x 75 pixels high; 4 pixels from the left and 4 pixels from the top.

Step 50. Delete the template from channel 1, and copy the sprite in channel 2 to channel 1. Use Sprite Info to change its size to 480 pixels by 213 pixels; 4 pixels from the left and 83 pixels from the top. Change its color to the yellow from the template. For housekeeping purposes, delete the template image (cast member 1) and the composed type (cast member 49). Import the sound file *browser.aif*. Use the menu command Save and Compact to eliminate any wasted space in the file, and you have a Shockwave movie with all of the pieces assembled but no animation or scripting yet.

This file will form the basis for later exercises, so be sure to save it. Now that all of the pieces are assembled, we'll add sound, animation, and scripts to this piece in the next chapter, in addition to exploring more Shockwave Lingo.

Moving On

It's important to create your designs for Shockwave movies to fit the capabilities of the technology. In this case, because the original graphic was itself designed with transmission times and graphic file compression in mind, it was likely that a reasonable-sized Shockwave movie could be produced that matched the original almost pixel for pixel. In other situations, that would be difficult or even impossible, leading to enormous files that take minutes to download and simply look pretty. Far better in most cases to sacrifice aesthetics for action.

Through these exercises, you should have a grasp of some techniques that enable you to maximize the visual content of your Shockwave movies while minimizing the size of your files:

- ≋ How to convert images in Photoshop to a standardized (Netscape) palette.

- ≋ How to combine undithered and diffusion dithered indexed-color images.

- ≋ How dithering affects image compression.

- ≋ How creating objects to replace image elements can save incredible amounts of memory in Shockwave movies.

Note that these techniques aren't particular to Shockwave—they'll make *any*Director movie smaller and less of a memory hog. They're not always necessary when you're working in the world of CD-ROM, where there's often plenty of space (at least relatively), but you should always keep them in mind when creating interactive multimedia with Director.

5
Asynchronous Text

Not a particularly thrilling title for this chapter, but the possibilities of what you can do with the commands herein are . . . well . . . not exactly limitless—but pretty darn big. What we've done so far with *GotoNetPage* and *GotoNetMovie* has been relatively simple, directly akin to the Lingo *go* command. The command is executed, and when the file is retrieved, it will be displayed. *GotoNetPage* and *GotoNetMovie* are *synchronous* commands. *Asynchronous* commands—all of the rest of the Shockwave Lingo, in other words—execute while the movie goes on to do other things. Unlike the synchronous commands which dictate that the browser will be displaying some other movie or page when that movie or page is received from the server, the asynchronous commands are generally executed, tested for completion, and only acted upon as the result of another command.

As an example, it's possible to use the asynchronous command *GetNetText* to retrieve a text file from a server, then use the *NetTextResult ()* function to use the retrieved text in a Director movie, without leaving the movie.

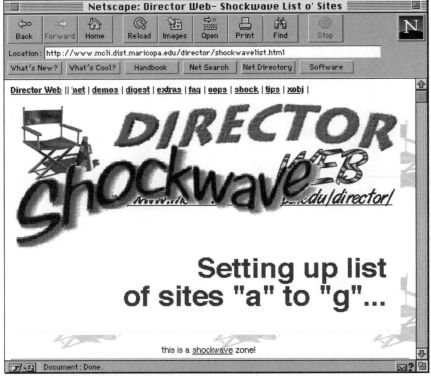

Figure 5-1: *The Shockwave List o' Sites uses* GetNetText *to load updated information into its database.*

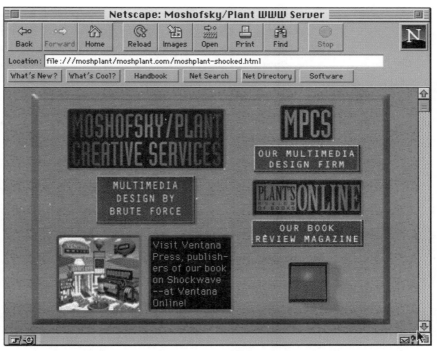

Figure 5-2: *The Shockwave version of the Moshofsky/Plant home page uses* GetNetText *to modify whichever projects are highlighted on a particular day.*

Asynchronous commands, on the other hand, can be used without leaving the current movie. More than one can be executed at a time, transmission failures can be detected, and the commands can be used to load documents that are cached by the browser for faster retrieval when needed. Most of the asynchronous commands are covered in Chapter 6, "Other Asynchonous Operations," but one of the most important ones, *GetNetText,* is the focus of this chapter.

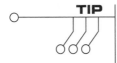

TIP

So far, the commands you've employed have been executed locally, just like opening up a file with any program. The asynchronous commands depend in part on information passed to them by HTTP protocols, and from here on out our examples will need to be resident on a Web server in order to function correctly. If you're unfamiliar with how to upload files to your Web server, contact your server administrator for technical support. Make sure that your server has been set up to support serving Shockwave movies as well.

Getting Text From the Net

The Shockwave Lingo you've encountered so far does one of two things: *GotoNetMovie* can load a new Shockwave movie in the place of an existing movie; *GotoNetPage* replaces the entire contents of the browser window with the contents of any file that can be read by the browser.

GetNetText, however, interacts with the currently playing Shockwave movie itself. The file retrieved with *GetNetText* can become an integral part of the movie, can also be used to modify the movie's behavior, and can even be used to modify information on the server itself.

Before you do all that, though, it's time for a quick demonstration of how to use *GetNetText*.

Exercise 5-1: You can quote me on that.

This exercise lets you create a "Quote of the Day" page with a cool interface. Using a simple text file for the day's quote makes it possible for anyone with the ability to edit a text document to update what's displayed, even if they don't have Director and Afterburner.

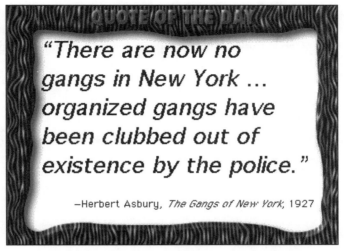

Figure 5-3: *The final version of Quote of the Day.*

Step 1. Open the Director movie *quote.dir* in the directory EXER0601 from the TUTORIAL directory of the Companion CD-ROM.

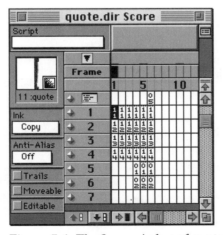

Figure 5-4: *The Score window of* quote.dir.

Step 2. Open the Score window to view this movie. The first three frames show the background for the movie; the last three display the background with the day's quote. Use Command+Shift+U or Ctrl+Shift+U to display the Movie Script.

Listing 5-1.

```
on startMovie
  global state, openQuote, closeQuote, emDash
  put #getQuote into state
  if the machineType = 256 then
    --256 is the code for Windows machines
    put numToChar (147) into openQuote
    put numToChar (148) into closeQuote
    put numToChar (151) into emDash
  else
    --at this point, all other cases
    --are assumed to be MacOS machines
    put numToChar (210) into openQuote
    put numToChar (211) into closeQuote
    put numToChar (209) into emDash
  end if
end
```

This startup script checks for the Lingo property *the machineType* to determine which set of special characters will be used for the quotation marks and em dash preceding the attribution. At this point, the fields are filled with a dummy quotation attributed to Anonymous.

The global variable *state* is used to determine the current action undertaken by the movie. More on that in a moment. The constants will be used later as we put text on the Stage.

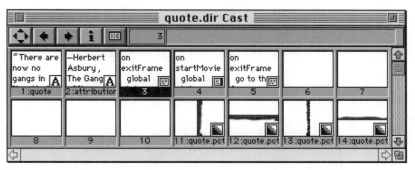

Figure 5-5: *The Cast window of* quote.dir, *showing the graphics which make up the borders of the movie.*

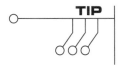

TIP

Notice that the borders of the graphic on the stage have been cut into four separate small images—instead of being left as a single image—to save on file size. Don't neglect byte-thriftiness even when you're just experimenting!

Step 3. Apart from the Movie Script, the only other Lingo in this movie so far is an *on exitFrame* handler in frame 6, which loops the movie back to frame 5. Now, create another Score Script by double-clicking in frame 3 of the Script channel and adding the script in bold below.

Listing 5-2.

```
on exitFrame
  global state
  if state = #getQuote then
    GetNetText "qod.txt"
    put #getting into state
  else
    if (state = #getting) and ¬
      NetDone () then
      handleText
      put #done into state
    end if
```

```
    end if
    if state <> #done then
      go to the frame - 1
    end if
  end
```

As you can see, using *GetNetText* isn't quite as simple as *GotoNetMovie* or *GotoNetPage*. What happens in this script is determined by the current value of the *state* variable. The initial value we set at *startMovie* is the symbol value *#getQuote*. Because that doesn't change between the beginning of the movie and the end of frame 3, the first *if . . . then* statement will be executed, which uses *GetNetText* to retrieve a text file called *qod.txt* from the same directory the movie is in, then changes to *state* variable to reflect that the process has begun. Because all of the conditional statements except for the final *if . . . then* are nested within the first command, they'll be ignored the first time the playback head reaches the end of frame 3. Because the new value of *state* is *#getting,* the *go to the frame - 1* at the end of the handler will kick the playback head to frame 2 before continuing on.

On the second approach to the end of frame 3, with *state* set to *#getting,* the first *else* clause is invoked (because *state* is no longer equal to *#getQuote*), and the conditional statement *if (state = #getting) and NetDone ()* is evaluated. *NetDone ()* is a Shockwave Lingo function which determines whether a particular asynchronous function has finished transferring data from the server, and evaluates to *TRUE* or *FALSE*. If no parameter is used for *NetDone ()*, it returns a value for the most recently called asynchronous command (because only one asynchronous call is used in this example, no parameter is needed).

In a typical Director movie, there would most likely be no need for all this fooling around with states and nested *if . . . then* statements. You'd just write something like this:

```
. . .
GetNetText "qod.txt"
repeat until NetDone ()
  nothing
end repeat
. . .
```

WARNING

The above script is an example of how *not* to write your Shockwave movies! Don't do it!

What you need to know, however, is that Shockwave movies are like sharks: they have to keep swimming or they die. Or, more accurately, Shockwave movies need to have the playback head in relatively constant motion in order to operate correctly. This is because a Shockwave movie, unlike a Director projector, is operating within the browser environment and must ocassionally give up some processor cycles to the browser and whatever else may be running on the computer. This means you must find some way to keep track of what you're currently doing. In this simple example, the global variable *state* does the trick. More complex movies will require that a number of variables be used to keep track of complex situations or that object-oriented programming techniques be used. In Chapter 6, "Other Asynchronous Operations," you'll use Lingo lists to keep track of multiple asynchronous operations.

Once *NetDone ()* has evaluated to *TRUE*, you can be reasonably sure that *GetNetText* has done its job by grabbing the text file called *qod.txt* from the server. Then it's time to do something with the text.

Step 4. The asynchronous function *GetTextResult ()* is the means by which you access text retrieved with the *GetNetText* command. Like *NetDone ()*, when it's used without a parameter (see Chapter 6, "Other Asynchronous Operations" for more on parameters and Shockwave Lingo functions), it gets information about the most recent asynchronous command. Add the handler below to the script in frame 3, below the *on exitFrame* handler (no need to enter in the comments).

Listing 5-3.

```
on handleText
  global openQuote, closeQuote, emDash
  put NetTextResult () into gotText
  --retrieves the text from an
  --asynchronous GetNetText call
  set the itemDelimiter = TAB
  --a tab is used to separate the quote
  --and attribution in the text file
  put item 1 of gotText into theQuote
  put item 2 of gotText into theAttribution
  --puts the raw quote and attribution
  --into temporary variables
  if (theQuote = "") and ¬
    (theAttribution = "") then exit
  --there's no usable data returned from
  --the file
  put openQuote & theQuote & closeQuote ¬
    into theQuote
  --adds curly quote characters
  --to the quote
  if theAttribution = "" then
    put emDash & "Anonymous" into ¬
      theAttribution
  --if there is no attribution then makes
  --quote anonymous and adds em dash
  else
    put emDash & theAttribution into ¬
      theAttribution
    --adds em dash to attribution
  end if
  put theQuote into field "quote"
  --updates the quote text
  put theAttribution into ¬
    field "attribution"
  --updates the attribution text
  put the number of chars of theQuote ¬
    into theSize
  --begins a check which adjusts the text
```

```
    --size if the quote is particularly long
    if theSize > 100 then
      put 18 * 270 / theSize into theSize
      set the textHeight of field "quote" ¬
        to theSize
      set the textSize of field "quote" to ¬
        theSize
    end if
  end
```

This fairly simple handler uses the *NetTextResult ()* function to put the text retrieved from the file *qod.txt* into a variable. The data retrieved is a single text string which cannot exceed 32K in size. In the case of *qod.txt*, the data consists of two items separated by a tab character, but there is no particular format that the text must follow. The *handleText* handler also changes the size of the text in the text blocks to account for larger quotes.

Step 5. Save the Director file *quote.dir*, and use a text editor to open the file *qod.txt*. Enter any phrase you wish to display (no quotes or returns needed), a tab, and an attribution for the phrase. Save the file. (Alternatively, you can use the text file *qod1.txt*, and rename it *qod.txt*.)

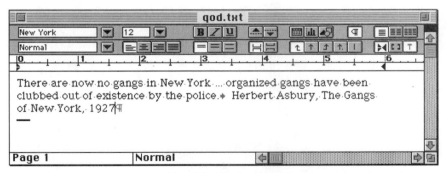

Figure 5-6: *Using Microsoft Word (with the Show Paragraphs option on) to create a quotation for* qod.txt.

Step 6. Use Afterburner to create a *quote.dcr* file from the Director file *quote.dir*.

Step 7. To make use of this Shockwave file, it's necessary to install it and its attendant files on a Web server. The *GetNetText* command is dependent on data sent as part of each transaction between the browser client and the server. Opening the *quote.htm* or *quote.dcr* files will generate an error when the *GetNetText* command is encountered. Copy the *quote.htm*, *quote.dcr*, and *qod.txt* files to a Web server using FTP or whatever method is particular to your situation to put all of the files in the same directory.

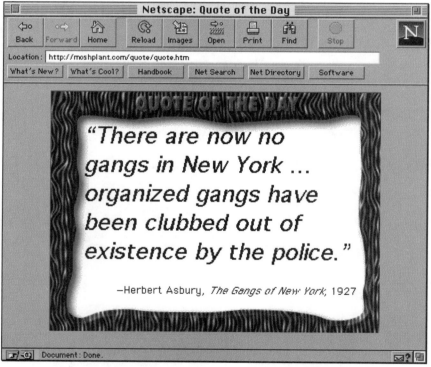

Figure 5-7: *The Shockwave movie* quote.dcr *playing in Netscape Navigator.*

Step 8. Use your Web browser to access the URL *http://www.your-server.domain/your-directory-path/quote.htm*. The Shockwave movie should display your chosen quote in the window. Quit your browser.

Step 9. Edit *qod.txt* once again, changing the information to another quote, another attribution (or rename the *qod2.txt* file to *qod.txt*). Replace the *qod.txt* file on your server with this new version.

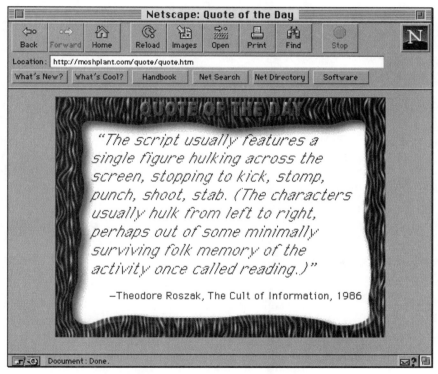

Figure 5-8: *A long quotation in the* quote.dcr *movie.*

Step 10. Once again, load the *quote.htm* file on your server with a browser. The new quote will be displayed on the screen.

Anyone who has the ability to edit a text file and has access to a Web server can modify the quote displayed with this movie. The file *qod.txt* needn't even be located on the same server as the *quote.htm* document, if you use a complete URL for the *GetNetText* command (i.e., *GetNetText "http://www.some-server.domain/directory-path/qod.txt"*). This is just one example of a way to allow quick modification and variability in Shockwave movies.

GetNetText in Charge

Because of Director's flexible nature, text retrieved as the result of a *GetNetText* comand can be used for a variety of situations apart from simply changing displayed text. New data for variables can be read in as text; so can commands to be executed using the Lingo *do* command, and the entire flow of the movie can be changed—without modifying the original Director file—by the use of *GetNetText*.

Exercise 5-2: Modifying movie behavior with *GetNetText*.

If displaying text was the only thing you could do with *GetNetText*, it would quickly grow tiresome. Fortunately, because Director is one extremely flexible program, it's possible to change how a Shockwave movie behaves using essentially the same techniques as in Exercise 5-1.

Step 1. The movie *egrocer.dir* in the EXER0502 directory is a virtual front end for a greengrocer. New fruits and vegetables don't appear magically on the face of the earth every day, so the selection stays relatively stable overall, but depending on the season and availability, the grocer wants to feature some items ahead of others. And she doesn't have to pay some expensive multimedia designer to mess around with the Shockwave movie every day. Go figure.

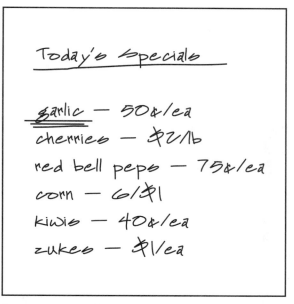

Figure 5-9: *The day's list of items for sale at Egrocer.*

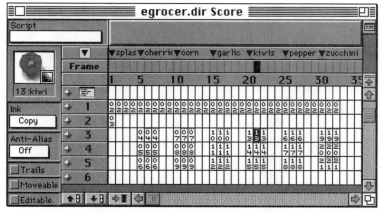

Figure 5-10: egrocer.dir*'s Score window.*

As you can see by examining the various sections of the movie, each marker in the Score displays a different fruit or vegetable, along with a price. Again, our grocer wants to change the order in which these items display, as well as their prices. Not a problem with *GetNetText*.

Figure 5-11: *The Egrocer splash screen.*

Step 2. This version of *egrocer.dir* contains a main splash screen and six sections where the various produce items are displayed. The marker names are fairly descriptive of what's being shown: cherries, corn, garlic, kiwis, peppers-bell-red, and zucchinis. Each section has a heading for and photo of the item, as well as a text field where the day's price can be inserted.

Figure 5-12: *An Egrocer item display screen with default price setting.*

This movie will first display the splash screen, then proceed on to individual sections in an order that will be determined on a daily basis. Once they're all displayed, the process will repeat. The controlling mechanism—a text file—will be kept as simple as possible, both to make its creation easy and to keep the complexity of the parsing engine we use to read it down-to-earth. A comma-delimited file composed of pairs of data items will control the flow of the program and supply the day's prices. The first item of each pair will be the section to be displayed, and the second will be the price.

In a text editor, create a new text file and enter the following line (no spaces):

Listing 5-4.
```
garlic,50¢/ea.,cherries,$2/lb.,peppers-bell-red,75¢/
ea.,corn,6/$1,kiwis,40¢/ea.,garlic,50¢/ea.,zucchinis,
$1/ea.
```

As you can see, the garlic is a hot item today. Save this file as *egrocer.txt*.

Step 3. Back in Director, you need to add in the controls which will change the display of produce items on the screen. To determine what to show, of course, the text file you've just created will need to be read in to the Shockwave movie (*GetNetText*), and the result will need to be extracted (*NetTextResult*) and parsed into individual items.

Since this movie really doesn't get under way until it has a text string to operate on, it makes sense that one of the first things it should do is get that data. Open a Movie Script by pressing Command+Shift+U or Ctrl+Shift+U and create an *on startMovie* handler:

Listing 5-5.

```
on startMovie
  GetNetText "egrocer.txt"
end startMovie
```

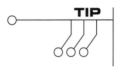

TIP

The URLs you use with *GetNetText* are just like any other text string in Director. Don't forget to put quotes around them—unless you're using a string variable to store the URL.

Step 4. Because you want to keep the playback head moving (maybe it should be called *Shark*wave) you will need to keep track of what's happening during the course of the movie. Once again, you can use a global variable for this purpose. Modify your Movie Script to look like this:

Listing 5-6.

```
on startMovie
  global state
  GetNetText "egrocer.txt"
  put -1 into state
end startMovie
```

Note that in this movie, you're going to be using integer values rather than symbols to keep track of what's happening.

Step 5. In the Script channel of the Score window, double-click on frame 3 to bring up a Score script. In this first section of the movie you need to wait for the GetNetText operation to complete before moving on. Modify the script here to read as follows:

Listing 5-7.

```
on exitFrame
  global state
  if (state = -1) then
    if not NetDone () then
      go to "splash"
    end if
  end if
end exitFrame
```

This determines if the movie has not yet loaded the text (once it's loaded, you'll change *state* to another value), and then checks to see if the *GetNetText* operation has completed. If it has not, the playback head is reset to the marker *splash*.

Step 6. Your next addition will be to handle what happens when *GetNetText* is done.

Listing 5-8.

```
on exitFrame
  global state, control
  if (state = -1) then
    if not NetDone () then
      go to "splash"
    else
      put NetTextResult () into control
      put 0 into state
    end if
  end if
end exitFrame
```

Here, a new global variable is added which will contain the data retrieved by *GetNetText*. Note that the variable has been added to the *global* declaration at the top of the handler.

Step 7. It's time to do something with the text now that it's been read in and extracted. Add the following to the Score Script you've been working on:

Listing 5-9.

```
on exitFrame
  global state, control
  if (state = -1) then
    if not NetDone () then
      go to "splash"
    else
      put NetTextResult () into control
      put 0 into state
      putPrices
    end if
  end if
end exitFrame

on putPrices
  global control
  put the number of items of control / 2 ¬
    into thisCount
  repeat with i = 1 to thisCount
    put item (2 * i) - 1 of control into product
    put item (2 * i) of control into ¬
      field product & "-price"
  end repeat
  put control & ",splash,0" into control
  put 1 into state
end putPrices
```

Figure 5-13: *Egrocer item with price inserted.*

The *putPrices* handler uses every second item value for the price of a product and inserts that into the text cast member named *product & "-price."* Although garlic is listed twice, it really makes no difference; the procedure is just repeated for the field *"garlic-price."*

After the prices have been determined, *control* has two more values added to it. Once the list of products has been cycled through, the movie returns to the splash screen and displays it before looping back through the day's goods.

Setting *state* to 1 readies the movie to continue on.

Step 8. Make another addition to the Score Script for frame 3.

Listing 5-10.

```
on exitFrame
  global state, control
  if (state = -1) then
    if not NetDone () then
      go to "splash"
    else
      put NetTextResult () into control
      put 0 into state
      putPrices
    end if
```

```
        else
          showProduct
        end if
      end exitFrame
```

Then add another handler to the Movie Script:

Listing 5-11.

```
on showProduct
  global state, control
  if state < 1 then put 1 into state
  if state > the number of items of ¬
    control then put 1 into state
  if (state + 1) / 2 <> state / 2 then
    startTimer
    put state + 1 into state
    go to item state - 1 of control
  else
    if the timer < 180 then
      exit
    else
      put state + 1 into state
    end if
  end if
end showProduct
```

This handler will be called at the end of the last frame of each product sequence. The *state* variable will be incremented from 1 to the number of items in the variable *control* (16, once the last pair of items has been added by *putPrices*). The first *if . . . then* statement checks to make sure that *state* is a positive value, the next one resets *state* to 1 if it's greater than the number of *control* items.

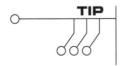

TIP

In an actual-use situation, it is vitally important to do a greater amount of error checking than shown in this example.

This script uses the simple data structure of *control* to advantage by using odd numbers (determined by the script *if (state + 1) / 2 = state / 2*) to reset the timer then increment *state* and go to a new product. While *state* is an even number, the script waits for three seconds (until *the timer* > 180) while it displays the product and price, then it increments *state* to an odd number. On the next call to *showProduct*, the odd value of *state* will reset the timer, and the process begins again.

Step 9. So far, *showProduct* is called only in the Score Script of frame 3. Create a new Score Script for frame 7 (the end of the *cherries* sequence) and add the following syntax to the default *on exitFrame* handler:

Listing 5-12.

```
on exitFrame
  showProduct
  go to the frame - 2
end exitFrame
```

Step 10. Copy the new Score Script you've just created into the last frame of each of the other product sequences, save the movie, and use Afterburner to make a Shockwave movie.

Step 11. Upload *egrocer.dcr*, *egrocer.txt*, and *egrocer.htm* to your Web server in the same directory, and use your browser to access the URL for *egrocer.htm*.

Figure 5-14: *Egrocer in action in Netscape Navigator.*

Step 12. Modify the *egrocer.txt* file to control the prices and sequencing of the movie and upload the new file to your server.

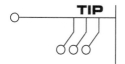

TIP

The caching routines of some browsers may keep you from seeing the updates you make to the controlling text file for this movie unless you quit your browser and restart it between viewings.

CGI Environment Variable Scripting

Interaction through HTTP protocols with programs other than Web servers is accomplished by means of a method called CGI (Common Gateway Interface). The CGI specification enables a program which resides on a server to be executed, operating on data passed to it from the user's browser (or on no data at all, depending on the purpose of the program). The CGI program—which can be written in just about any programming environment from perl on UNIX servers to AppleScript on Mac OS servers—can do something as simple as return an HTML page with the information sent to it, send a URL based on coordinates of a mouse click on an image map, or carry out a financial transaction through a secure database.

HTML form pages are easy to create with editors like Webedit on Windows or PageMill on the Macintosh, but something has to be done with the data. Most ISPs (Internet Service Providers) provide canned CGIs to handle things like image maps, and some provide an e-mail CGI which will send you a message with the information people have filled out your form with. But to automatically do anything with that data—to, say, enter it into an order database and return a page to the viewer with invoice and availability information that has been drawn from the database—something a little more complex is needed.

CGI writing is a subject for a whole other book, but as a Web developer you really won't get the most out of Shockwave until you can send data to a CGI application. True Internet interactivity comes through communication, and without any way to *send* data as well as receive it, your user is just a lone biker on the information superhighway.

There are two methods of data transmission on the Web: GET and POST. POST is the preferred method in most situations, largely because it can support data blocks larger than 1K in size. GET is the method available to Shockwave developers with the first releases.

The GET method sends what is known as an *environment variable* to the server, attached to a URL which specifies the particular CGI application operating on the environment variable. In the case of a simple form which sends information to a database CGI in a server's *cgi-bin* directory, the URL would look something like this for someone who had filled out the First Name field with "Web" and the Last Name field with "Master-3":

Listing 5-13.

```
http://www.server.dom/cgi-bin/
database.cgi?First+Name=Web&Last+Name=Master%2D3
```

The environment variable is delineated from the URL with a question mark, all spaces are replaced with plus signs, and each parameter name/value pair is separated by an ampersand. Additionally, any nonalphanumeric character in the parameter names or values are replaced with a percentage sign and a two-digit hexadecimal code for their ASCII value.

The code below is a set of routines which can be used in Shockwave movies to create valid environment variable data that can be appended to a CGI URL called by *GetNetText* or *GetNetPage*. It's available in the TUTORIAL directory as cast member 1 of *env-var.dir* and should be added to the movie script of any Shockwave movie in which you intend to pass data to CGIs.

Listing 5-14.

```
global cAlpha

on startMovie
  put "0123456789ABCDEFGHIJKLMNOPQRSTUVWXYZ" ¬
    into cAlpha
  --cAlpha is a constant used to test for
  --alphanumeric characters when creating
```

```
      --environment variables for passing to CGI
      --scripts
end startMovie

on clearGet clearThis
   --clears a variable for use as a passed
   --environment variable
   put "" into clearThis
   return clearThis
end clearGet

on addGet getThis, newVar, newVal
   --adds a variable name and value to
   --the environment variable
   put convert (newVar) into getVar
   put convert (newVal) into getVal
   if getThis = "" then
      put "?" & getVar & "=" & getVal into getThis
      --if the variable is empty, adds the question
      --mark separating the CGI URL and the
      --environment variable
   else
      put getThis & "&" & getVar & "=" & getVal ¬
         into getThis
      --adds to an existing environment variable
   end if
   return getThis
end addGet

on convert convThis
   --converts strings into a format suitable for
   -- CGI  environment variables
   put the number of chars in convThis ¬
      into thisLong
   put "" into converted
   repeat with i = 1 to thisLong
      put ¬
         charOrHex (char i of convThis) ¬
          after converted
```

```
    end repeat
      return converted
    end convert


on charOrHex thisChar
   --converts individual characters to environment
   --variable format
   if cAlpha contains thisChar then
     return thisChar
     --the contains operator isn't case sensitive
     --so the cAlpha constant doesn't need
     -- lower-case letters
   else if thisChar = " " then
     return "+"
     --special character for encoding spaces
   else
     return aHex (thisChar)
     --handles other cases where hexadecimal
     --encoding is needed
   end if
end charOrHex


on aHex toHex
   --handles converting non-alphanumeric characters
   --to three-character encoding for CGIs
   put "%" into thisHex
   --non-alphanumeric characters which are in
   --hexadecimal form must be preceded
   --by a percent sign
   put charToNum (toHex) into thisAscii
   if thisAscii = 10 then
     put thisHex & "D0A" into thisHex
     --special case for line feed,
     --note middle character is a zero
   else
     if (thisAscii < 9) or ¬
       ((thisAscii > 11) and ¬
       (thisAscii < 31)) or (thisAscii >255) then
```

```
      return ""
      --characters in these ranges can't
      --be passed to CGIs
    else
      return thisHex & breakHex (thisAscii)
      --all other cases
    end if
  end if
end aHex


on breakHex alphaNot
  --creates two-digit hexadecimal
  --equivalent of alphaNot
  put char (integer (alphaNot / 16) + 1) ¬
    of cAlpha into broken
  --because cAlpha is constructed with the numbers
  --followed by upper-case letters, the first
  --sixteen characters can be used as the
  --hexadecimal digit sequence
  put broken & char ((alphaNot mod 16) + 1) ¬
    of cAlpha into broken
  return broken
end
```

This script has two handlers which you use to create and set variables in your Shockwave movie. *clearGet (whichVariable)* initializes a Lingo variable, and *addGet (whichVariable, parameterName, parameterValue)* adds a parameter name/value pair to the environment variable. The handlers *convert, charOrHex, aHex,* and *breakHex* are all subroutines of *addGet,* and you shouldn't have to call them directly.

Moving On

In this chapter you've learned a powerful way to add easily modified text control structures to Shockwave movies with the *GetNetText* command. You've used the *NetDone ()* and *NetTextResult ()* functions to test whether the command has been completed and to extract the text results from completed commands. If your Web server is running a CGI which allows you to test information sent to it, the environment variable script above will get you started with creating movies that can send information to e-mail, text files, or even databases. In the next chapter, you'll be introduced to the other asynchronous commands, which will allow you to check for transmission errors, determine what types of files have been retrieved, and more!

6

Other Asynchronous Operations

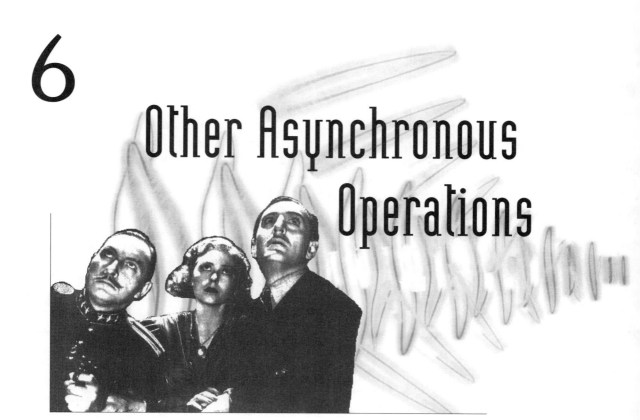

Once you've moved into the world of asynchronous commands and functions, Shockwave moves out of the realm of just putting self-contained Director movies on your Web page and into the world of Internet communications. Just with the toes, but *in*, nonetheless.

Most Web browsers can send out multiple, simultaneous HTTP requests (usually about four at a time). Once an HTML file has been read into the browser, items in the document that refer to other files which should be included when the page is viewed (tags that include a SRC= parameter like IMG and EMBED, and documents in Netscape frames) are placed into a list of items to be requested from the appropriate server. As items at the front of the list are completely received, another item is requested, until all of the items on the list have had retrieval attempts made, or until the viewer has moved on to another page. If the viewer moves on to another page, the browser has to cancel its current operations and retrieve new data. In some cases, when not all of the data is retrieved, the error will cause a lapse in data integrity and either a broken image icon will appear in the page using the image, or a text message stating something like "Transfer Interrupted" will appear in the browser window.

The same procedures need to be followed with Shockwave movies. Improper execution of asynchronous commands can cause infinite loops Shockwave movies that make it impossible to continue without shutting the browser window or quitting the program entirely—not the type of experience that most Web designers want to supply to their viewers.

That means tools are needed to keep track of how things are going in the asynchronous world: ways to determine if operations are complete, if they completed correctly, and what they did. In the previous chapter, three asynchronous operations were used in a specific order:

- **GetNetText**—to start the retrieval of a text item;
- **NetDone ( )**—to test whether the *GetNetText* retrieval is done;
- **GetTextResult ( )**—to extract the text from a *GetNetText* retrieval.

When more than one asynchronous operation is executing, you can't predict which one will get done first—or if they will get done at all. These commands extend the capabilities of Shockwave to managing asynchronous operations—it's up to you to actually *manage* those operations, however. To do that, you'll use the following asynchronous commands and functions:

- **GetLatestNetID ( )**—to identify a particular asynchronous operation.
- **PreloadNetThing**—to store pages, images, and movies in the browser cache for faster retrieval when they're called for.
- **NetError ( )**—to determine the status of a completed asynchronous operation.
- **NetAbort ( )**—to cancel a particular asynchronous operation.

These asynchronous operations round out the Lingo that's been added to Director for Shockwave, and their use will make more complex Shockwave movies and sites possible.

Tracking Asynchronous Operations

One of the most important things you need to know in order to manage a process is how to refer to the individual processes which are occurring. In Chapter 5, only one asynchronous operation was performed at a time. Often, you'll need to retrieve more than one file, because you can't predict where a user will choose to go next, or because several files or graphics will be needed simultaneously. The following exercise demonstrates how Shockwave for Director keeps track of simultaneously occurring asynchronous operations.

Exercise 6-1: Identifying asynchronous operations with GetLatestNetID( ).

In the case of asynchronous operations in Shockwave, each HTTP request is assigned a number, and that number can be retrieved by using the *GetLatestNetID ( )* function. (Note that the parentheses aren't superflouous, although at no time do you use any values between them.)

GetLatestNetID ( ) is a function which returns a positive integer value starting at 1 for the first asynchronous request command issued during a particular session of the Shockwave plug-in. When the plug-in is reloaded (i.e., when a new HTML page is opened) the *GetLatestNetID ( )* counter is reset.

In this exercise, you'll use *GetLatestNetID ( )* along with *GetNetText* and *Net Done( )*, to retrieve four text documents of varying sizes, then display them *in the order in which they finish transferring,* not necessarily in the order they're requested.

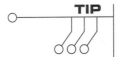

TIP All asynchronous operations are dependent on information provided by a Web server as part of an HTTP header. This exercise requires that the files are resident on a Web server and that access to them is through the server, not by opening them locally.

Figure 6-1: *The original version of* getid.dir.

Step 1. With Director, open the movie *getid.dir* in the EXER0601 directory.

Step 2. Open a Movie Script by pressing Command/Ctrl+Shift+U or selecting the menu item Windows|Script. Add in the following handlers:

Listing 6-1.

```
on startMovie
  clearTracks
end startMovie
```

```
on clearTracks
  global startList, finishList
  put [] into startList
  put [] into finishList
end clearTrack
```

These scripts initialize the list variables used to keep track of the asynchronous operations in the movie. Press Enter to close the Script window.

Step 3. Open the Score window (Command/Ctrl+4) and select frame 3 in the Script channel. Double-click the selected cell or press in the Script Entry area of the Score window to add the following Score Script:

Listing 6-2.

```
on exitFrame
  global startList, finishList

  clearTracksGetNetText "text1.txt"
  add startList, GetLatestNetID ()
  GetNetText "text2.txt"
  add startList, GetLatestNetID ()
  GetNetText "text3.txt"
  add startList, GetLatestNetID ()
  GetNetText "text4.txt"
  add startList, GetLatestNetID ()
end exitFrame
```

These commands begin execution of the process to retrieve the text documents, and use the linear list *startList* to retrieve the number the Shockwave plug-in used to keep track of the process. This exercise will use the same number to determine which retrievals finish first, and to keep track of the cast numbers where the results will be stored. The numbers are added to the list in the order they're issued, so the *startList* will contain items in numerical order. Press Enter to close the Script window.

The text files used in this exercise consist of two short files about 200 characters in length (*text1.txt* and *text3.txt*), one of just over 800 characters (*text4.txt*), and one just under 3,000 characters (*text2.txt*). As you'll probably see in the results of this exercise, even though the shortest file is the first one to be requested by the movie from the server, it won't always be the first one finished. Which is why you use *GetLatestNedID ( )* to keep track of which operation is which.

It is a measure of the depth of desire for change in this country that we've seen not just the ghost of Harry Truman pop up but also, lurking in the corners of the political discussion, the specter of Huey P. Long.

Figure 6-2: *Contents of* text1.txt.

Step 4. In the Score window, at frame 5, add the script that will determine when processes are done, and let the movie know in what order they finish. Double-click on frame 5 of the Script channel to open up a Score Script for the frame, and add the following script:

Listing 6-3.

```
on exitFrame
  global startList, finishList
  if startList = [] then
    --when the startList is empty,
    --all items have been retrieved
    go to "alldone"
  else
    put count (startList) into thoseLeft
    --number of values in the list
    repeat with i = thoseLeft down to 1
      put getAt (startList, i) into j
```

```
        --j now equals the ith value
        --of the list
        if NetDone (j) then
          add finishList, j
          --adds the value of j to the end
          --of finishlist
          deleteAt startList, i
          --removes the value from startlist
          put NetTextResult (j) into field ¬
            count (finishList)
          --puts the text into the next
          --available display field
        end if
      end repeat
      go to "undone"
      --loops if there are still unfinished
      --GetNetText operations
    end if
  end exitFrame
```

This script first determines if there are any items left in *startList*, and, if they've all been removed (which is done as they finish transferring), jumps to the "alldone" marker in the Score.

The *repeat with* loop uses a variable set to the number of items left in *startList* to check the *NetDone ( )* status of each of the remaining data transfers, doing nothing if they're not finished. If they are done, they're added to the end of the unsorted linear list *finishList* and deleted from *startList;* the retrieved text is put into one of the first four cast members.

The movie then loops back to the *undone* marker. Close the Script window by pressing the Enter button.

While reading Huey Long it's easy to understand how the brash
young farmer's boy from poor Winn parish, where 'young bloods of
Huey's age thought it was the height of urban elegance to
saunter into one of the eateries and order 'a chili,'" might
have offended the sensibilities of the established order. Quite
apart from his politics, his campaigning style, with its innovative use of mailed circulars, automobile stumping, radio
speeches, sound trucks, and cruel personal invective was designed precisely to appeal to that part of the populace that
wasn't sitting in the halls and offices of power. Long knew what
appealed to them in part because he was one of them, and though
blessed with a phenomenal memory, razor-sharp wit, and a person-
ality that drove him to work twenty hours a day, he was nonetheless the product of his upbringing in Winnfield, a town where
some of the stores and shops were located in tents, where there
were no sidewalks, no paved streets, and farm stock roamed the
town.

Little of Long's early life is well-documented, perhaps
because no one thought he'd amount to much. Long himself gave a
variety of answers about some episodes in his life, depending on
the audience and time of day. Almost necessarily, the portrait
of Long that Williams paints, drawing on over a decade of
research and interviews with hundreds of Long family members,
friends, associates, and enemies, contains a plethora of contra-
dictory stories. When given the option between positive and
negative views of his subject, Williams predominantly chooses
the former. His decisions are naturally backed up with volumes
of supporting evidence—not the least of which are the actual
accomplishments of Long's tenure as governor and senator.

Long did more than just talk about the things he campaigned
for. When he won the gubernatorial election on second try in
1928, he embarked upon a series of changes that went beyond
reform to outright rebellion against the ruling class. He raised
severance taxes on natural resource industries to pay for
schoolbooks for every child, regardless of whether they went to
public or private school. During his term as governor, the state
built over 2,300 miles of paved roads, 111 bridges, and in 1931
employed ten percent of the men involved in road-building
nationally. He moved to abolish the practices of strait-jacket-

ing and chaining and to introduce dental care at mental institutions (at one, he claimed, dentists extracted seventeen hundred
diseased teeth from inmates). Long's appointee as head of
Angola, still considered one of the toughest prisons in the
country, instituted the state's first prisoner-rehabilitation
program. Long implemented an adult literacy program in Louisiana
that largely served African-Americans, despite the racism of the
overwhelming white majority. The list is extensive and surprisingly progressive for the time, the place, and most particularly
the man he has been portrayed as. Many of his progressive
policies were unthinkable to large sectors of his electorate,
but the breadth of his programs drew in people who supported him
in some areas and not others.

 Williams details the political career of Huey Long exhaus-
tively. Many of the chapters chronicle a blinding array of
events condensed into a period of time that seems far too short
to contain them. What is more incredible is that chapter after
chapter covers a parallel set of events occurring within the
same time frame.

Figure 6-3: *The contents of* text2.txt *file.*

Step 5. In frame 8, add a Score script which will loop the playback head.
Double-click the cell in frame 8 of the Score window, or select the
cell and click in the Script Entry area of the Score window. Put in a
simple loop script:

```
on exitFrame
  go to "alldone"
end exitFrame
```

This will be the display loop which will enable you to take a
look at the results of the text retrievals. Press Enter to close the
Script window.

Used most often merely as a touchstone of rabble-rousing, anti-intellectual, brute force demagoguery, at times Long is shaken aloft as an example of the Bolshevist, fascist, populist end we could all come to should the great unwashed be allowed to have their way with us.

Figure 6-4: *The contents of the* text3.txt *file.*

Step 6. Save the movie with your changes.

Step 7. Use Afterburner on *getid.dir* to create the file *getid.dcr*.

Step 8. Copy the files *getid.dcr*, *text1.txt*, *text2.txt*, *text3.txt*, *text4.txt*, and *getid.htm* to your Web server.

Many know of the Railroad Commissioner, Governor, and Senator from Louisiana only through the fictional mirror of Robert Penn Warren's Pulitzer Prize–winning All the King's Men. Or the stage play. Or the Academy Award–winning movie. Warren's Willie Stark is a tireless self-promoter, a man driven to accumulate power and fortune at the expense of all those around him, whose one contribution to the common good, a hospital, literally backfires when its director shoots him.

The Huey Long of T. Harry William's (again) Pulitzer Prize-winning biography shares all of Stark's qualities and more. The more being specifically the accomplishments and advances that Long brought to a state that, in his time as now, languished near the bottom of the nation not only geographically but in average income (thirty-ninth of forty-eight), farm property value (forty-third), and literacy (forty-seventh). In an era when Wisconsin had four millionaires, Louisiana had one, and if the general poverty of the state wasn't enough,

Figure 6-5: *Contents of the* text4.txt *file.*

Step 9. Use your Web browser to access *getid.htm*. As in the previous chapter's examples, you'll need to use the complete URL (including the http:// header, server name, and directory path) for the *GetNetText* command to work correctly.

After the Shockwave plug-in loads in and the movie begins to play, you'll see each of the four text fields fill in as the complete texts of the various text files are read in. Without opening the text files in a text editor, though, there's no way to tell which is which. Let's remedy that.

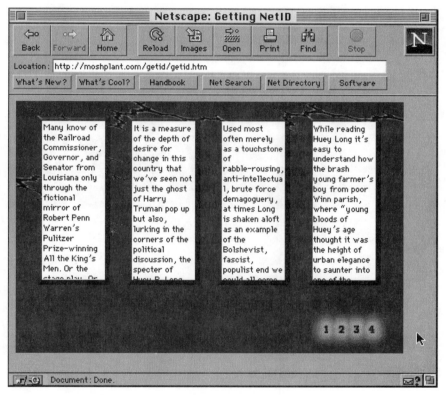

Figure 6-6: *The first playback of* getid.dcr *in the browser.*

Step 10. Open the copy of *getid.dir* you saved with Director. Be sure that the playback head is over frame 1 in the Score window.

Step 11. Open the Cast window and select position 12 in the cast.

Step 12. Bring up the Tools palette (Command/Ctrl+7 or menu item Window | Tools).

Step 13. Use the Text tool to create a text cast member under the first display field on the left. The new cast member should be in position 11.

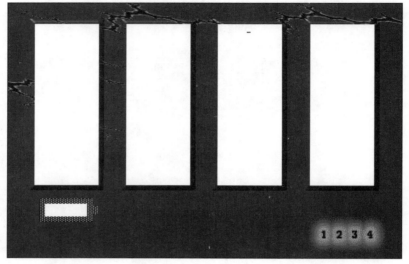

Figure 6-7: *Drawing the identification fields on the Stage with the Text tool.*

Step 14. From the Text I Size menu, select a size of about 24 points.

Step 15. Type in "**0**" (zero).

Step 16. Select cast member 11 in the Cast window.

Step 17. Use the Cast I Duplicate Cast Member menu command (Command / Ctrl+D) to make three copies of cast member 11 in cast positions 12, 13, and 14.

Step 18. Drag each of the duplicate text cast members from the Cast window to the Stage, and place them under the remaining display fields from left to right.

Figure 6-8: *All of the identification fields in place with dummy values inserted.*

Step 19. Double-click in the channel identification area of the first channel holding one of the new text fields. This selects all of the cells in the channel out to the last frame of the movie.

Step 20. Holding down the Shift key, double-click in the last of the channels holding one of the new text fields. You should now have four channels selected, between frames 1 and 8.

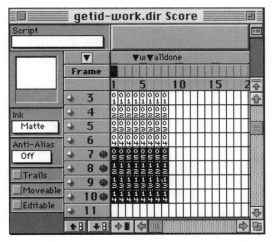

Figure 6-9: *Adding to the selection of all of the cells in a channel.*

Step 21. Select the Score I In-Between Linear menu item to duplicate the four text cast members in frame 1 through frame 8.

Step 22. Open the Score Script for frame 5 and make the modification shown in bold type:

Listing 6-4.

```
on exitFrame
   ...
        if NetDone (j) then
          add finishList, j
          --adds the value of j to the end
          --of finishlist
          deleteAt startList, i
          --removes the value from startlist
          put NetTextResult (j) into field ¬
            count (finishList)
          --puts the text into the next
          --available display field
          put j into field ¬
            count (finishlist) + 10
          --puts value of GetLatestNetID ()
          --into the next identifier field
        end if
   ...
end exitFrame
```

By putting the identification number of the operation into a text field, it will be easier to identify which text file has been placed into a specific display field. Press Enter to close the Script window.

Step 23. Save your modified movie.

Step 24. Once again, use Afterburner to make an updated version of *getid.dcr*.

Step 25. Copy the modified *getid.dcr* to your Web server.

Step 26. Use your Web browser to access the file *getid.htm*. The identification number of the *GetNetText* operation is shown under each of the display fields.

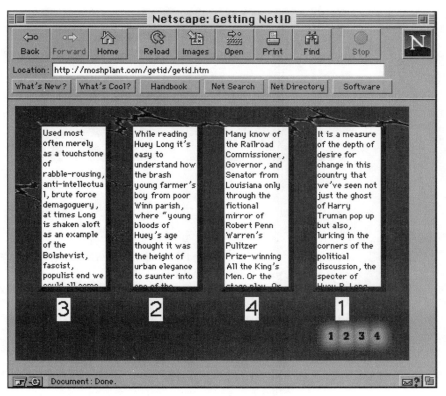

Figure 6-10: getid.dcr *completed with NetID values shown.*

You're going to make a couple of other modifications to the movie before moving on to the rest of the asynchronous operations.

Step 27. Open *getid.dir* again in Director. Be sure that the playback head is over frame 1 in the Score window.

Step 28. Bring up the Tools palette.

Step 29. Use the filled oval tool to draw a small circle on the Stage (use the Shift key to constrain the drawing tool to a 45° angle) at the lower right, about two inches from the right edge of the Stage and just above the lower edge of the Stage.

Figure 6-11: *Drawing the first activity indicator on the Stage.*

Step 30. With the circle still selected on the Stage, use the Tools palette's color selection pop-up palette to set the color to black.

Step 31. Bring the Score window to the front (Command/Ctrl+4). The circle you've added should be selected in the Score.

Step 32. Copy the cell containing the circle from the Score using the menu item Edit | Copy Cells command (Command/Ctrl+C).

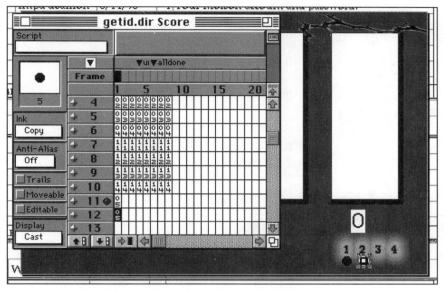

Figure 6-12: *Duplicating the circle in the Score.*

Step 33. Make three duplicates of the circle in frame 1 of the Score by pasting the copied circle into place with the Edit | Paste Cells menu command (or Command/Ctrl+V). As you paste each new circle in place on the Stage, move it to the right, so that it's not overlapping any of the other circles. Note the lowest channel number containing the circle. In the Score, select frames 1 through 8 of the channels containing the circles, and use Command/Ctrl+B or the Score | In-Between Linear menu command to duplicate the lights throughout the movie.

Step 34. Open the Movie Script (Command/Ctrl+Shift+U), and add the Lingo shown below in bold:

Listing 6-5.

```
on startMovie
  clearTracks
  initPuppets
end startMovie
```

```
on stopMovie
  global activeLight
  clearTracks
  put 0 into activeLight
  releasePuppets
end stopMovie

on clearTrack
  global startList, finishList
  put [] into startList
  put [] into finishList
end clearTrack

on initPuppets
  global activeLight
  put XX into activeLight
  --the first channel containing a circle
  repeat with i = activeLight to ¬
    activeLight + 3
    puppetSprite i, TRUE
  end repeat
end initPuppets

on releasePuppets
  global activeLight
  repeat with i = activeLight to ¬
    activeLight + 3
    puppetSprite i, FALSE
  end repeat
end releasePuppets
```

Replace the "XX" in the line *put XX into activeLight* of the *initPuppets* handler with the channel number of the first circle, as you noted in the last step. The *stopMovie* handler clears global variables assigned in the movie and unpuppets the sprites used for the activity lights. Press Enter to close the Script window.

Step 35. In the Score Script for frame 5, make the modifications shown in bold:

Listing 6-6.

```
on exitFrame
  global startList, finishList, activeLight
  if startList = [] then
    --when the startList is empty,
    --all items have been retrieved
    go to "alldone"
  else
    put count (startList) into thoseLeft
    --number of values in the list
    repeat with i = 1 to thoseLeft
      put getAt (startList, i) into j
      --j now equals the ith value
      --of the list
      if NetDone (j) then
        add finishList, j
        --adds the value of j to the end
        --of finishList
        deleteAt startList, i
        --removes the value from startList
        put NetTextResult (j) into field ¬
          count (finishList)
        --puts the text into the next
        --available display field
        put j into field ¬
          count (finishList) + 10
        --puts value of GetLatestNetID ()
        --into the next identifier field
        put activeLight + j - 1 into k
        --determines the appropriate sprite
        --for process j
        set the foreColor of ¬
            sprite k to 255
      else
        --happens if NetDone () is FALSE
        put activeLight + j - 1 into k
```

```
            --determines the appropriate sprite
            --for process j
            if the foreColor of ¬
              sprite k = 255 then
              set the foreColor of ¬
                sprite k to 6
              --color 6 is a red from the
              --Windows palette which is
              --preserved in the combined
              --netswin palette, and is used
              --here to indicate activity for
              --the appropriate GetNetText
              --operation
            else
              set the foreColor of ¬
                sprite k to 255
              --resets the color to black
            end if
            updateStage
          end if
        end repeat
        go to "undone"
        --loops if there are still unfinished
        --GetNetText operations
      end if
    end exitFrame
```

If a *GetNetText* process is still active (NetDone (j) = FALSE), the *else* clause toggles the color of the appropriate circle between black and red. That additional statement in the *then* clause sets the circle to black when NetDone (j) = TRUE. Press Enter to close the Script window.

Step 36. Bring up the Score window.

Step 37. Select an open cell in frame 6.

Step 38. Open the Tools pallete.

Step 39. Choose the Button tool.

Step 40. Draw a button on the Stage, and label it "Get Again." This button will be used to reload the text items.

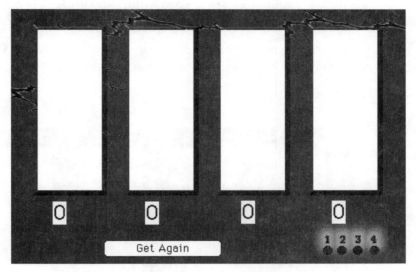

Figure 6-13: *The "Get Again" button in place on the Stage.*

Step 41. Press the Ctrl and Option buttons simultaneously, and click on the button on the Stage to open the Cast Script window for the button. Add the script in bold:

Listing 6-7.

```
on mouseDown
  --mouseDown is used here because
  --mouseUp is unreliable in Shockwave
  clearTrack
  repeat with i = 11 to 14
    put "" into field i
    --empties the identification fields
  end repeat
  go to "startget"
end mouseDown
```

When the button is pressed, the lists will be cleared and the playback head will loop back to the frame containing the *GetNetText* calls. Press Enter to close the window.

Step 42. Open the Score window.

Step 43. Select frames 6 to 8 of the channel containing the button sprite by clicking on the first frame containing the button, holding down the Shift key, and clicking on frame 8 of the same channel.

Step 44. Use the menu command Score | In-Between Linear or Command / Ctrl+B to add the button to all three frames.

Step 45. Save the movie once again.

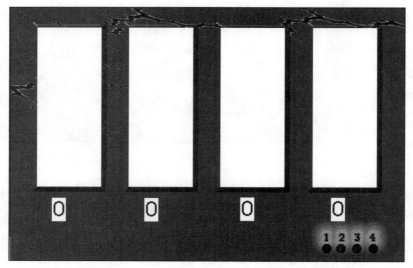

Figure 6-14: *The Stage of* getid.dir *in Director with all elements in place.*

Step 46. Use Afterburner to create a new version of *getid.dcr*.

Step 47. Replace the old *getid.dcr* on your Web server with the new file.

Step 48. Use your Web browser to access *getid.htm* through your Web server.

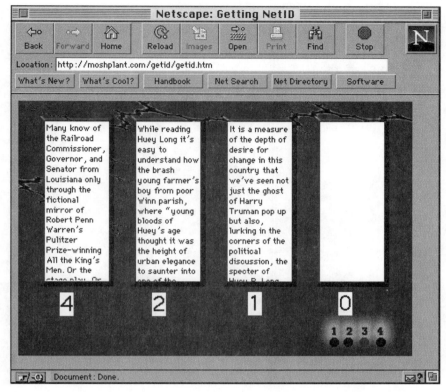

Figure 6-15: *The final version of* getid.dcr *in action, with activity lights indicating currently loading text items.*

Step 49. After the first set of text items has been retrieved, you will see the "Get Again" button created in steps 36-44. Press Get Again to reload the files.

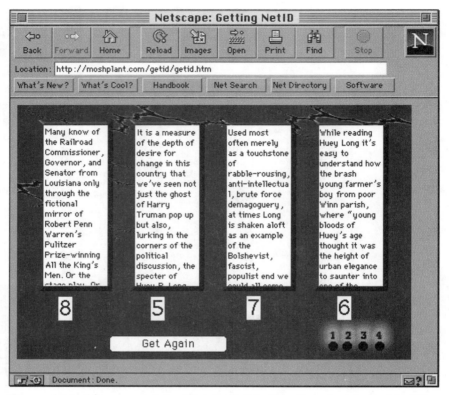

Figure 6-16: *After pressing the "Get Again" button, the values in the identification fields will increase.*

Depending on the speed of your connection, and the conditions between your computer and the file server, you should see some variance between the order in which the files are called and the order in which they are completely received. This will vary according to their size and the individual routes the data takes. Try varying the text in each file (keep in mind that the maximum size for a Director text cast member is 32K), and see how the results differ between individual load cycles. Also notice that the numbers in the identification fields increase with each loop of the entire movie, until the movie is entirely reloaded with a browser reload command or another page has been opened with the browser.

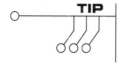

TIP

In most instances, your browser will only load the file from the server once per browser session, using a cached version from your hard drive for subsequent reloads.

Lists are just one way to keep track of a number of asynchronous operations. It's possible to use global variables, objects, more complex list structures, or any other method you prefer to handle them.

Using *GetLatestNetID ( )* is the key to managing asynchronous operations with Shockwave. This exercise has been just an introduction to its possible uses.

PreloadNetThing

Exercise 6-2: Preloading for speed & profit.

If you've ever worked on a large Director project, you're familiar with the concept of *preloading*, or reading a file into memory before it's actually going to be used. In many projects, the Lingo *preLoad* and *preLoadCast* commands can be used to asynchronously load cast members to RAM before they are used by the movie, preventing delays as portions of the cast and linked media are read from CD-ROM or disk.

PreloadNetThing is the Shockwave Lingo equivalent of the existing Lingo commands. In the relatively slow world of the Web, whatever you can do to make things faster and more seamless for the user is worth considering. In this exercise, you'll load in new HTML pages and graphics while the user is viewing a home page so that the pages will come up quickly from the browser's cache of files on the user's hard disk.

Just like *GetNetText*, *GetNetMovie*, and *GetNetPage*, *PreloadNetThing* can work in the background while a movie is playing. Unlike the latter two, it doesn't automatically display the file retrieved in the browser window. Instead, the data is stored in the browser's cache, and when one of the other retrieval commands is executed, the cached data will be read from disk instead of across the Web, greatly reducing access time from the user's viewpoint.

PreloadNetThing can be followed by any valid text object containing a complete or relative HTTP URL.

As its name might suggest, *PreloadNetThing* is a sort of all-purpose command which can be used to load a wide variety of items. Essentially any data which can be retrieved with an HTTP request can be loaded into the cache: HTML pages, GIF and JPEG images, text files, the results of CGI scripts, and Shockwave movies. In situations where the original movie may be playing for a period of time before moving on and there's time to preload a number of other items, *PreloadNetThing* can be used to great effect.

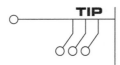

TIP

For this exercise, you're going to use the movie created in Exercise 4-4, "50 Steps to Smaller Movies." If you don't have a copy saved, or haven't done that exercise, use the *wrldwide.dir* file in the EXER0602 directory of the TUTORIAL.

The Worldwide Shockwave School home page will be an animated movie with a spinning globe, a waving flag, and rollover buttons that when pressed will take the viewer to pages with information about the school. Rather than waiting for the user to press a particular button, however, the movie will begin loading the pages that the viewer might want to see into the cache of their browser by means of the *PreloadNetThing* command. This will speed up the viewer's progress through the pages.

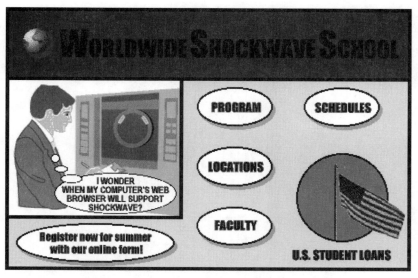

Figure 6-17: *The Worldwide Shockwave School home page movie.*

Step 1. Welcome back to the Worldwide Shockwave School! Open the *wrldwide.dir* movie in Director. The first part of the exercise sets up the basic animation sequence for the movie.

Step 2. Open the Score window (Command/Ctrl+4 or Window | Score from the menu bar).

Step 3. The Score has cells filled only in the first frame so far. All of the elements are in the position they'll occupy for the main loop of the movie. Bring up the Control Panel (Command/Ctrl+2 or Window | Control Panel from the menu bar).

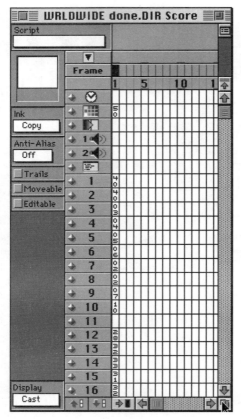

Figure 6-18: *The Score as it was left in Exercise 4-4.*

Step 4. Press the Play button on the Control Panel (or press Command /
Ctrl+P or Enter). The globe in the upper left should revolve and
the flag should wave at the lower right. These are film loops that
you created in Exercise 4-4. (Be sure the Loop button is set.)

Figure 6-19: *The Control Panel with Loop button depressed.*

Step 5. Stop the movie (press the Stop button on the Control Panel or Command/Ctrl+. [period]).

Step 6. Bring the Score window to the front (Command/Ctrl+4 or Window I Score from the menu bar).

Step 7. Select frame 1 or channel 1 in the Score.

Step 8. Scroll to frame 50 in the Score, press the Shift key, and select frame 50, channel 35. You should have a selection block 50 cells wide and 35 cells high.

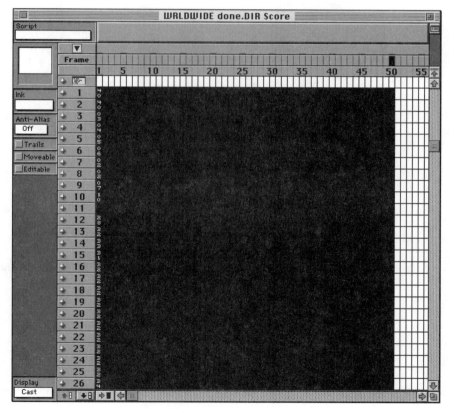

Figure 6-20: *Selecting large blocks of the Score.*

Step 9. Press Command/Ctrl+B or choose Score I In-Between Linear to fill the selection with the contents of frame 1.

Step 10. Drag a marker from the marker well of the Score to frame 50 and name it "Main."

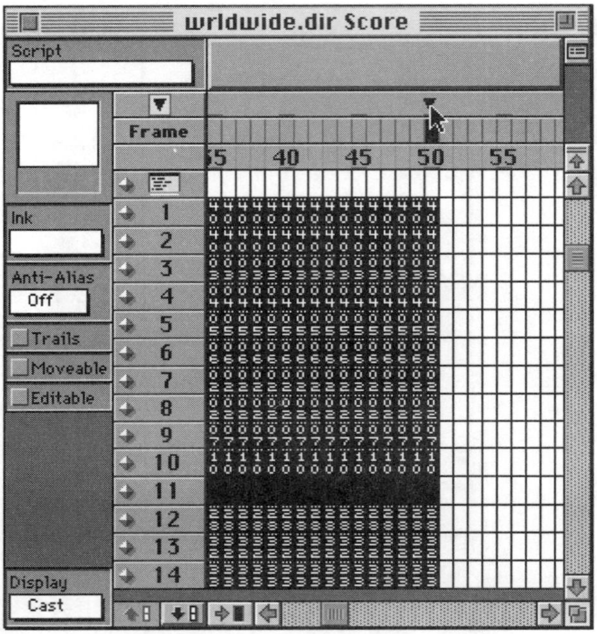

Figure 6-21: *Setting the "Main" marker.*

Step 11. Scroll back to frame 1 and select frame 1, channel 2.

Step 12. Press the Shift key and select frame 5, channel 35 to create a selection 4 frames by 34 channels in size.

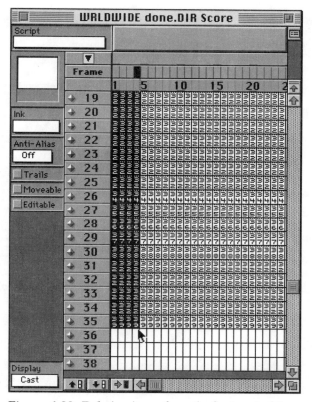

Figure 6-22: *Deleting items from the first part of the movie Score.*

Step 13. Delete all of the cells in the selection by pressing the Del key or using the Edit | Clear Cells menu selection.

Step 14. Select the cell in frame 1 of channel 1 and press the Del key or choose the Edit | Clear Cells menu selection.

Step 15. Select the cell in frame 2, channel 1.

Step 16. Press the Shift key and select the cell in frame 5, channel 1.

Step 17. Choose the Score | Sprite Info from the menu bar or press Command / Ctrl+K to open the Sprite Info dialog box.

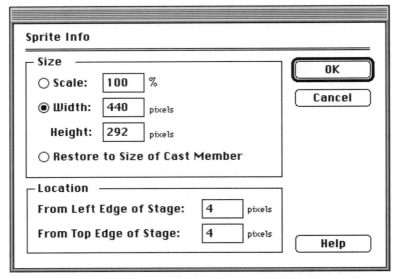

Figure 6-23: *Setting the size of the background object in frames 2 to 5.*

Step 18. Set the width and height of the sprites in frames 2 to 5 to 440 by 292, and the offset to 4 pixels from the left and 4 pixels from the top. This leaves a border of 4 pixels all around the edge.

Step 19. Select frame 1 of the Tempo channel. Double-click in the cell or choose Score | Set Tempo from the menu bar.

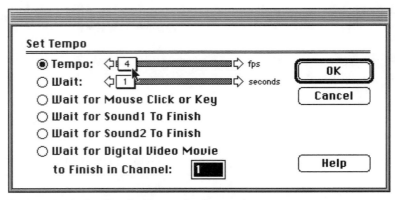

Figure 6-24: *Setting the Tempo for the movie.*

Step 20. Set the Tempo to 4 frames per second and press OK.

Step 21. Select frame 2 of the Transition channel, and either double-click in the cell or choose Score | Set Transition from the menu bar.

Step 22. Set the transition to Wipe Up and the Duration to 1 second. Then press OK.

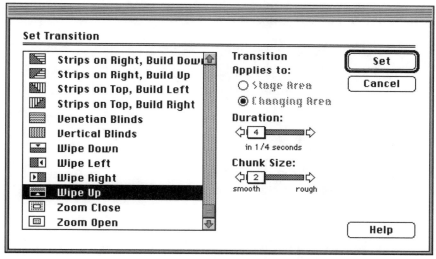

Figure 6-25: *Setting the first transition for the movie.*

Step 23. Select the cells in frame 6, from channel 3 to channel 35 of the Score.

Step 24. Delete the selected cells by pressing Del or choosing Edit | Clear Cells from the menu bar.

Step 25. Select frame 6 of the Transition channel, and either double-click in the cell or choose Score | Set Transition from the menu bar.

Step 26. Set the transition to Wipe Down and the Duration to 1 second. Press OK.

Step 27. Select the cells in frame 7, from channel 6 to channel 35 of the Score.

Step 28. Delete the selected cells by pressing Del or choosing Edit | Clear Cells from the menu bar.

Step 29. Select frame 7 of the Transition channel, and either double-click in the cell or choose Score | Set Transition from the menu bar.

Step 30. Set the transition to Push Left and the Duration to 1 second. Then press OK.

Step 31. Select the cell in frame 8, channel 6 in the Score.

Step 32. Press the Shift key, then select the cell in frame 29, channel 10.

Step 33. Delete the selected cells by pressing Del or choosing Edit | Clear Cells from the menu bar.

Step 34. Select the cell in frame 8, channel 13 in the Score.

Step 35. Press the Shift key, then select the cell in frame 29, channel 35.

Step 36. Delete the selected cells by pressing Del or choosing Edit | Clear Cells from the menu bar.

Step 37. Select the cell in frame 9, channel 12 in the Score.

Step 38. Press the Shift key, then select the cell in frame 28, channel 12.

Step 39. Delete the selected cells by pressing Del or choosing Edit | Clear Cells from the menu bar.

Step 40. Select the globe sprite in frame 8, channel 12.

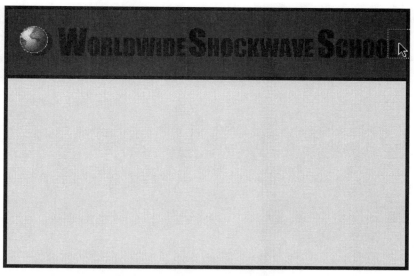

Figure 6-26: *Positioning the globe film loop sprite at the edge of the Stage.*

Step 41. Press the Shift key and drag the sprite to the right edge of the stage.

Step 42. In the Score window, press the Shift key and select the cell in frame 29 of channel 12.

Step 43. Press Command/Ctrl+B or choose Score | In-Between Linear in between the globe animation from its position at the right edge of the Stage (frame 8) to its final position to the left of the text (frame 29).

Figure 6-27: *The in-betweened globe in motion from the right edge of the Stage to its final position at the left.*

Step 44. Select frames 30 to 39 of channel 6.

Step 45. Delete the selected cells by pressing Del or choosing Edit | Clear Cells from the menu bar.

Step 46. Select frames 30 to 39 of channels 13 to 35.

Step 47. Delete the selected cells by pressing Del or choosing Edit | Clear Cells from the menu bar.

Step 48. Select frames 31 to 38 of channels 7 to 10.

Step 49. Delete the selected cells by pressing Del or choosing Edit | Clear Cells from the menu bar.

Step 50. Select frame 30, channels 7 to 10.

Step 51. Use the Ink pop-up menu of the Score to change the Ink effect for the selected cells to Blend.

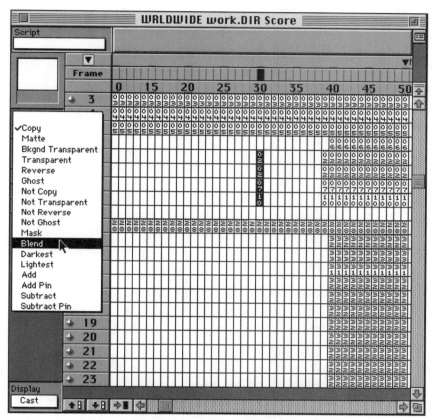

Figure 6-28: *Setting the Ink effect of the cartoon and associated sprites.*

Step 52. Choose Score I Set Sprite Blend from the menu bar and set the Sprite Blend to 0 Percent.

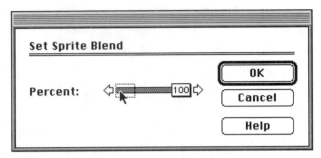

Figure 6-29: *Setting the Sprite Blend value.*

Step 53. Select frame 39 of channels 7 to 10.

Step 54. Use the Ink pop-up menu of the Score to change the Ink effect for the selected cells to Blend. Leave the Sprite Blend of these cells set to 100 Percent.

Step 55. Select frames 30 to 39 of channels 7 to 10. This should include all of the sprites set to a Blend ink effect in frames 30 and 39, as well as the intervening empty cells.

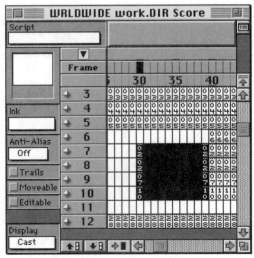

Figure 6-30: *Selecting the cells to In-Between for the Blend effect.*

Step 56. Choose Score | In-Between Special from the menu bar and deselect all of the In-Between options except for Blend. Press OK.

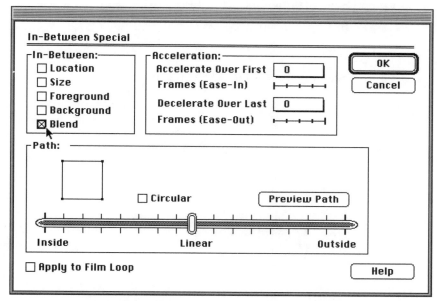

Figure 6-31: *The In-Between Special dialog box.*

Step 57. Select frames 40 to 43 in channel 6.

Step 58. Delete the selected cells by pressing Del or choosing Edit | Clear Cells from the menu bar.

Step 59. Select frames 40 to 43 in channels 13 to 30.

Step 60. Delete the selected cells by pressing Del or choosing Edit | Clear Cells from the menu bar.

Step 61. Select frames 40 to 42 in channel 31.

Step 62. Delete the selected cells by pressing Del or choosing Edit | Clear Cells from the menu bar.

Step 63. Select frames 40 to 41 in channel 32.

Step 64. Delete the selected cells by pressing Del or choosing Edit | Clear Cells from the menu bar.

Step 65. Select frame 40 in channel 33.

Step 66. Delete the selected cell by pressing Del or choosing Edit | Clear Cells from the menu bar.

Step 67. Select frames 40 to 42 in channel 35.

Step 68. Delete the selected cells by pressing Del or choosing Edit | Clear Cells from the menu bar.

Step 69. Select any cell in frame 43.

Step 70. Choose menu item Score | Insert Frame or press Command / Ctrl+] (right bracket) to add a duplicate of frame 43 to the Score.

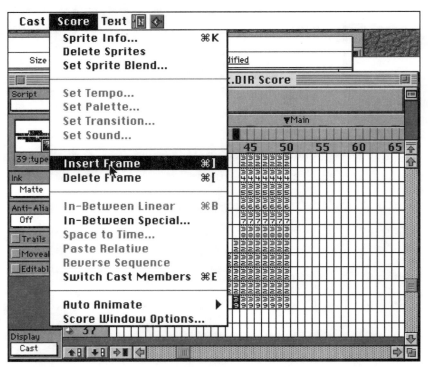

Figure 6-32: *Inserting a frame into the Score at frame 43.*

Step 71. Scroll to Sound channel 1 in the Score and select frames 43 and 44.

Step 72. Choose Score | Set Sound from the menu bar, and set the sound to *browser.aif* (cast member 1).

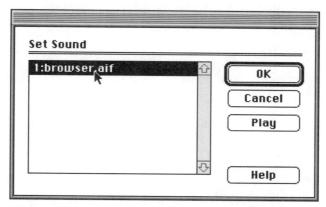

Figure 6-33: *Setting the Sound for frames 43 and 44.*

Step 73. Select frame 44 of the Script channel, and double-click on the cell or click on the Script Entry area in the Score window. Enter the following script in bold:

Listing 6-8.

```
on exitFrame
   if soundbusy (1) then
      go to the frame - 1
   end if
end
```

This script will hold the playback head frames 43 and 44 until the sound i*browser.aif* has completed playing. Press Enter to close the Script window.

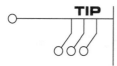

TIP

Use scripts in Shockwave for pauses instead of Tempo settings! You need to keep the playback head moving in Shockwave movies, and the Tempo Wait settings stop the playback head's movement, causing potential conflicts with the browser and other programs.

Step 74. Select frames 45 to 49 of channel 6 in the Score.

Step 75. Delete the selected cells by pressing Del or choosing Edit | Clear Cells from the menu bar.

Step 76. Select frames 45 to 49 of channels 13 to 15 in the Score.

Step 77. Delete the selected cells by pressing Del or choosing Edit | Clear Cells from the menu bar.

Step 78. Select frames 45 and 46 of channels 16 to 18 in the Score.

Step 79. Delete the selected cells by pressing Del or choosing Edit | Clear Cells from the menu bar.

Step 80. Select frames 47 and 48 of channel 16 in the Score.

Step 81. Delete the selected cells by pressing Del or choosing Edit | Clear Cells from the menu bar.

Step 82. Select frame 47 of channel 17 in the Score.

Step 83. Delete the selected cell by pressing Del or choosing Edit | Clear Cells from the menu bar.

Step 84. Select frame 45 of channel 20 in the Score.

Step 85. Delete the selected cell by pressing Del or choosing Edit | Clear Cells from the menu bar.

Step 86. Select frames 45 to 48 of channel 21 in the Score.

Step 87. Delete the selected cells by pressing Del or choosing Edit | Clear Cells from the menu bar.

Step 88. Select frames 45 to 47 of channel 22 in the Score.

Step 89. Delete the selected cells by pressing Del or choosing Edit | Clear Cells from the menu bar.

Step 90. Select frames 45 and 46 of channel 23 in the Score.

Step 91. Delete the selected cells by pressing Del or choosing Edit | Clear Cells from the menu bar.

Step 92. Select frame 45 of channel 25 in the Score.

Step 93. Delete the selected cell by pressing Del or choosing Edit | Clear Cells from the menu bar.

Step 94. Select frames 45 to 48 of channel 26 in the Score.

Step 95. Delete the selected cells by pressing Del or choosing Edit | Clear Cells from the menu bar.

Step 96. Select frames 45 to 47 of channel 27 in the Score.

Step 97. Delete the selected cells by pressing Del or choosing Edit | Clear Cells from the menu bar.

Step 98. Select frames 45 and 46 of channel 28 in the Score.

Step 99. Delete the selected cells by pressing Del or choosing Edit | Clear Cells from the menu bar.

Step 100. Select frame 45 of channel 30 in the Score.

Step 101. Delete the selected cell by pressing Del or choosing Edit | Clear Cells from the menu bar.

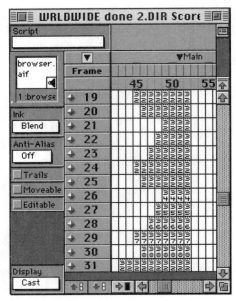

Figure 6-34: *A portion of the Score from near the end of the movie.*

Step 102. Scroll to the Transition channel of the Score. Select frames 45 to 50 of the Transition channel.

Step 103. Choose menu selection Score | Set Transition. Set the transition to Random Rows and the Duration to 2 quarters of a second. Press OK. This will set the transition effect for all of the frames between 45 and 50.

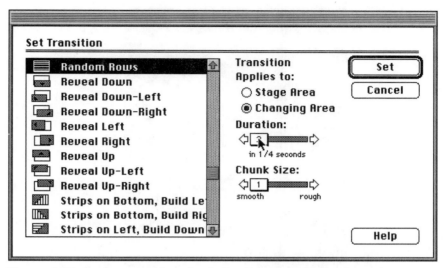

Figure 6-35: *Setting transitions for the buttons appearing on the screen.*

Step 104. Make a selection anywhere in frame 51 (which should be the last frame of the movie since the duplication of a frame in Step 70).

Step 105. Choose menu item Score | Insert Frame or press Command/Ctrl+] (right bracket) to duplicate frame 51 in the Score.

Step 106. Drag the marker labeled "Main" from frame 52 to frame 51.

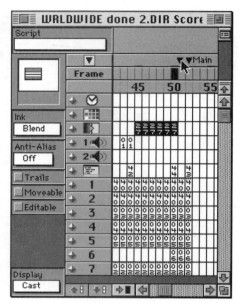

Figure 6-36: *Moving the marker "Main."*

Step 107. In the Script channel of the Score, double-click on frame 52 to bring up a Score Script. Enter the script in bold below.

```
on exitFrame
  go to "Main"
end
```

This sets up the loop for the menu after the animation is done. Press Enter to close the Script window.

Step 108. Press Command/Ctrl+R to rewind the movie.

Step 109. Press Command/Ctrl+Shift+P or Command/Ctrl+Shift+Enter to close the various windows that might be open and to play the movie. You should see the color blocks wipe onto the screen, the text push in from the right side of the Stage, followed by the spinning globe which takes up its position just to the left of the type. The cartoon fades in, and the thought balloon appears, with a voice speaking the lines. The buttons and the flag appear, and in the main loop the globe continues spinning and the flag waves. There are still a couple of animation touches to add to this piece.

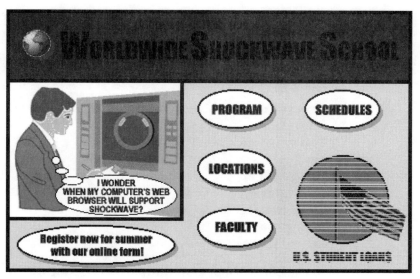

Figure 6-37: *The movie in action so far.*

Step 110. Create a Score Script for frame 50 by selecting the cell in frame 50 of the Script channel and double-clicking. Enter the following script:

Listing 6-9.

```
on exitFrame
  puppetSprite 4, TRUE
  puppetSprite 10, TRUE
  puppetSprite 13, TRUE
  repeat with i = 21 to 25
    puppetSprite i, TRUE
  end repeat
end
```

Sprite 4 is the word "Shockwave" in the banner, sprite 10 is the dummy sprite over the tape reel on the computer, sprite 13 is the shield behind the flag, and sprites 21 to 25 are the buttons. Press Enter to close the Script window.

Step 111. Open the script for the last frame of the movie, frame 52, by double-clicking on frame 52 of the Script channel. Modify the script with the following commands:

Listing 6-10.

```
on exitFrame
  spinTape
  go to "Main"
end

on spinTape
  set the castNum of sprite 10 to ¬
    random (3) + 7
end spinTape
```

At the end of each loop through the "Main" section, the handler *spinTape* will put an image selected randomly from cast members 8 to 10 in place of sprite 10.

Figure 6-38: *The tape reel with an incorrect offset, and Copy ink setting.*

If you play the movie back at this point you'll see some problems with this animation. First, the corners of the tape reel images are showing. More important, the images are offset from where they should be appearing. This is a result of different coordinate systems being used for the bitmap cast members (where the registration point is currently set for the middle of the cast member) and the object cast member we use as a placeholder (whose coordinates are set by the upper left corner of the object). These will be the next items to fix.

Step 112. Double-click in the channel identifier area of the Score window for channel 10, to select the entire channel to the end of the movie.

Step 113. Use the Ink effects menu of the Score window, and set the Ink to Background Transparent.

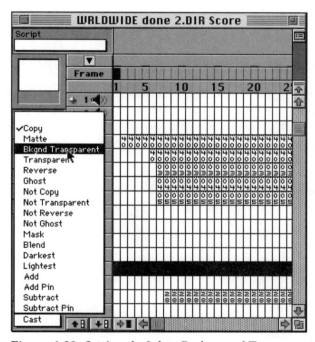

Figure 6-39: *Setting the Ink to Background Transparent for the tape reels.*

Step 114. With the entire channel still selected, choose the Score I Sprite Info menu item. Set the width and height of the placeholder sprite to 38 pixels square, and add about 20 pixels to the offset in both directions. Press OK. When you play this animation back, you may need to make some minor adjustment to the position of the sprite, but it should cover the background image just fine.

Figure 6-40: *The reel sprites stretched just a few pixels larger than they ought.*

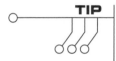

TIP

Because the puppeted sprite maintains its dimensions no matter which cast member is being currently used, disparities in size between the placeholder object and the bitmap sprites can cause odd pixelization effects.

Step 115. The next effect to add will be flashing text for the word "SHOCKWAVE" in the banner. Open the script for the last frame of the movie, by double-clicking on frame 52 of the Script channel. Make the following additions:

Listing 6-11.

```
on exitFrame
  spinTape
  flashShock
  go to "Main"
end

on flashShock
  set the foreColor of sprite 4 to ¬
    random (256) - 1
end flashShock

on spinTape
  set the castNum of sprite 10 to random (3) + 7
end spinTape
```

The word "SHOCKWAVE" will be set to a randomly selected color on each pass of the main loop. Press Enter to close the Script window.

Step 116. Double-click on the identifier for channel 4 to select the entire channel to the end of the movie. Select Copy from the Ink effect menu, then choose Background Transparent from the menu. The previous setting, Darken, prevents the the colorization of the sprite from being visible.

Step 117. Now it's time to work out the rollover effects for the buttons, to indicate active areas. This includes the flag shield as well. Open the script for the last frame of the movie, by double-clicking on frame 52 of the Script channel. Make the additions shown in bold:

Listing 6-12.

```
on exitFrame
  checkButtons
  spinTape
  flashShock
  go to "Main"
end

on checkButtons
  if rollover (13) then
    set the backColor of sprite 13 to 2
  else
    set the backColor of sprite 13 to 137
  end if
  repeat with i = 21 to 25
    if rollover (i) then
      set the backColor of sprite i to 2
    else
      set the backColor of sprite i to 0
    end if
  end repeat
end checkButtons

. . .
```

The *checkButtons* handler determines whether the mouse is over a sprite; it sets the color to a highlight color if it is, or to white (or blue for the circle behind the flag) if it isn't.

Each button has a color set on every loop of the program. Holding the playback head in a repeat loop until the cursor moved off of a button could cause conflicts with the browser over CPU cycles (remember, the Shockwave movie isn't the only potential target of a mouse click when it's a part of an HTML page).

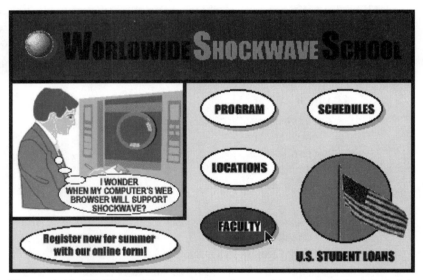

Figure 6-41: *Highlighted buttons before the text bitmaps have had their ink effects corrected.*

If you run the movie now, you'll see that the type over each button may show a white background when the button is highlighted. These next steps eliminate that.

Step 118. Double-click the identifier for channel 26 in the Score window.

Step 119. Press the Shift key and double-click the identifier for channel 30.

Step 120. Select Darkest from the Ink menu of the Score window.

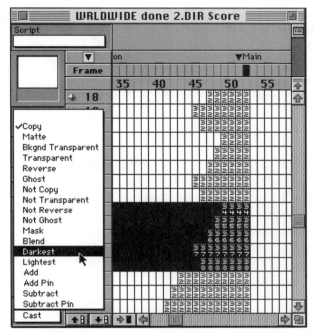

Figure 6-42: *Changing the Ink setting for the button text items.*

Step 121. Your last bit of button legerdemain will be to indicate that the button has been selected with a mouse click and support the standard roll-off/roll-on behavior of a good interface element, all the while keeping the playback head moving so that you have a good little Shockwave movie.

To do this, you need to revamp the script for frame 52 of the Script channel. Double-click the cell to open the Script window and make the changes indicated in bold:

Listing 6-13.

```
on exitFrame
  checkButtons
  spinTape
  flashShock
  go to "Main"
end
```

```
on checkButtons
  doaButton 13
  repeat with i = 21 to 25
    doaButton i
  end repeat
end checkButtons


on doaButton thisButton
  global buttonStatus
  put thisbutton - 20 into statusIndex
  if thisButton = 13 then put 6 ¬
    into statusIndex
  --statusIndex is the position in
  --buttonStatus of the current state
  --of the button
  put getAt (buttonStatus, statusIndex) ¬
    into thisStatus
  --retrieves the button status from
  --the list
  if thisStatus = #up then
    --current button has not been pressed
    if not rollover (thisButton) then
      --button is up and mouse is not over
      press thisButton, FALSE
      light thisButton, FALSE
    else
      --button is up and mouse is over
      if noDown () then
        --no other buttons are down
        if the mouseDown then
          --button is up, mouse is over
          --and mouse is down
          put #down into thisStatus
          press thisButton, TRUE
          light thisButton, TRUE
          moveText thisButton, 1
        else
          --button is up, mouse is over,
          --but mouse is not down
```

```
          press thisButton, FALSE
          light thisButton, TRUE
        end if
      end if
    end if
else
  --this button is already down
  if not rollover (thisButton) then
    --mouse is not over this button
    if not the mouseDown then
      --button is down, mouse has been
      --released not over the button
      put #up into thisStatus
      press thisButton, FALSE
      light thisButton, FALSE
      moveText thisButton, -1
    else
      --button is down, mouse is still
      --down but is not over button
      press thisButton, TRUE
      light thisButton, FALSE
    end if
  else
    --mouse is over this button
    if not the mouseDown then
      --button is down, mouse has been
      --released while over button
      put #perform into thisStatus
      press thisButton, FALSE
      light thisButton, FALSE
    else
      --button is down, mouse is down,
      --mouse is over button
      press thisButton, TRUE
      light thisButton, TRUE
    end if
  end if
end if
if thisStatus = #perform then
```

```
      setAt (buttonStatus, statusIndex, #up)
      perform thisButton
    else
      setAt (buttonStatus, statusIndex, ¬
        thisStatus)
    end if
end doaButton

on noDown
  --returns TRUE if any of the buttons
  --are down
  put true into theDown
  repeat with i = 1 to 5
    if getAt (buttonStatus, i) = #down ¬
      then put FALSE into theDown
  end repeat
  return theDown
end noDown

on press aButton, thisWay
  --handles depressing buttons
  if aButton = 13 then exit
    --flag button doesn't depress
  put the locV of sprite (aButton - 5) ¬
    into vert
  put the locH of sprite (aButton - 5) ¬
    into horz
  --calculates position based on shadow
  --of button
  set the locV of sprite aButton to ¬
    vert + ((thisWay - 1) * 4)
  set the locH of sprite aButton to ¬
    horz + ((thisWay - 1) * 3)
end press

on light aButton, thisWay
  --sets hilight color for buttons
  --or resets if thisWay is FALSE
  if aButton = 13 then
```

```
      put 137 into col
    else
      put 0 into col
    end if
    if thisWay then put 2 into col
    set the backColor of sprite aButton ¬
      to col
end light

on moveText aButton, theWay
  --depresses text along with button
  if aButton = 13 then exit
  --flag button text doesn't move
  set thisText to aButton + 5
  set horz to the locH of sprite thisText
  set vert to the locV of sprite thisText
  set the locH of sprite thisText to ¬
    horz + (3 * theWay)
  set the locV of sprite thisText to ¬
    vert + (4 * theWay)
end moveText

on perform aButton
  --perform will handle button procedures,
  --for now it IDs the button pressed by
  --putting a sprite number in the message
  --window
  put aButton
end

on flashShock
  set the foreColor of sprite 4 to random ¬
    (256) - 1
end flashShock

on spinTape
  set the castNum of sprite 10 to random ¬
    (3) + 7
end spinTape
```

The long *doaButton* handler checks each button for a state stored in the linear list *buttonStatus*, compares it to a couple of other conditions (including whether any of the other buttons are currently depressed, in which case nothing happens, whether the cursor is currently over the sprite, and whether the mouse is down), then decides what happens to the current button.

The other handlers here do the actual work once *doaButton* has decided what will happen (including making the button depress [which automatically hides the shadow], highlighting the button, and moving the text of the buttons where necessary). The perform handler will determine what happens when the button has been activated. Before you can play this section, there are a couple of other changes to make elsewhere.

Step 122. Open the Score script for frame 50 and make the changes indicated in bold:

Listing 6-14.

```
on exitFrame
  global buttonStatus
  puppetSprite 4, TRUE
  puppetSprite 10, TRUE
  puppetSprite 13, TRUE
  repeat with i = 21 to 30
    puppetSprite i, TRUE
  end repeat
  put [#up, #up, #up, #up, #up, #up] ¬
    into buttonStatus
end
```

This script initializes the *buttonStatus* list and adds the button text bitmaps to the puppeted sprites. Press Enter to close the Script window. Close all of the windows except for the Message window. Rewind the movie (Command/Ctrl+R) and play it by pressing Enter or Command/Ctrl+P. As you move the cursor across the Stage, the buttons will be highlighted, and if you click on them, they'll shift slightly, taking their text with them. Click on a button, drag the cursor off of it without releasing the mouse, and drag across other buttons—the original button should remain depressed but not highlighted, and the other buttons should not light up. Release the mouse off of the original button and nothing should happen; release on the button, and a number corresponding to the button sprite should appear in the Message window.

Step 123. Now that your buttons look right, it's time to give them something to do. Open the Score script for frame 52 again and make the modifications in bold to the *perform* handler:

Listing 6-15.

. . .

```
on perform aButton
  repeat with i = 1 to 48
    puppetSprite i, FALSE
  end repeat
  if aButton = 13 then
    GoToNetPage "studloan.htm"
  else
    put ["../register.htm", ¬
      "../faculty.htm", ¬
      "../location.htm", ¬
      "../program.htm", ¬
      "../schedule.htm"] into links
    GoToNetPage getAt (links, aButton - 20)
  end if
end
```

. . .

Press Enter to close the window.

Step 124. Use the menu item File | Save As to save this movie with the name *wrldwid2.dir*.

Step 125. Create a directory on your hard drive called *wrldwide*.

Step 126. Create two subdirectories in *wrldwide* called *images* and *movies*. A common practice on Web servers is to have most or all of the HTML files at root directory level, and images contained in a single directory. This example puts the Shockwave movies in a separate directory as well.

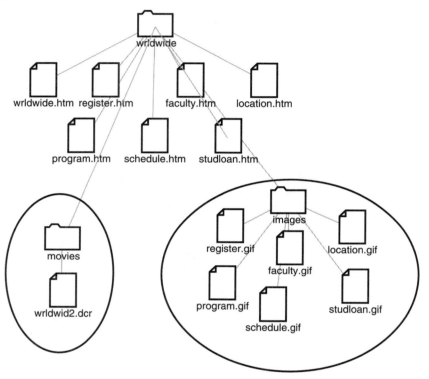

Figure 6-43: *Directory structure diagram of* wrldwide, *showing final file placement.*

Step 127. Copy all of the files with the extension *.htm* from the EXER0602 directory on the Companion CD-ROM into the *wrldwide* directory.

Step 128. Copy the files with the extension *.gif* from the EXER0602 directory to the *images* directory.

Step 129. Use Afterburner to create a Shockwave movie from *wrldwid2.dir*. Name the file *wrldwid2.dcr* and save it in the *movies* directory.

Step 130. Copy the *wrldwide* directory to your Web server.

Step 131. With your Web browser, access the URL to the file *http://www.your-server.domain/your-directory-path/wrldwide/index.htm*.

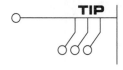

As an example, if user *trotsky* had a directory on the *www.moshplant.com* server which was usually accessed with a URL beginning *http://www.moshplant.com/~trotsky*, the path would be: *http://www.moshplant.com/~trotsky/wrldwide/index.htm*.

The movie will load and should play almost exactly as it did in Director. If you press the buttons, they will load in the appropriate pages and graphics. Take some time to see what kind of speed you get from each page.

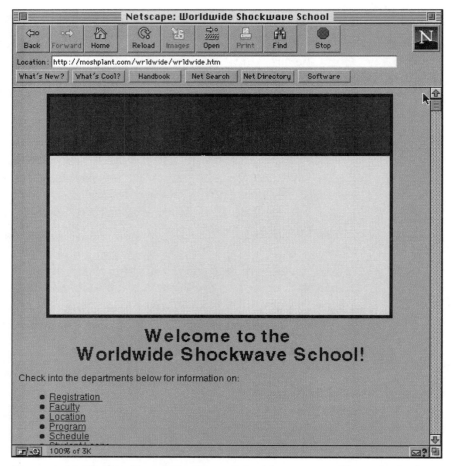

Figure 6-44: *The Worldwide Shockwave School home page with movie playing.*

Next, clear your browser's cache. You'll need to do this in order to truly compare the effects of preloading.

Step 132. Open *wrldwid2.dir* in Director.

Step 133. Open a Movie Script by pressing Command/Ctrl+Shift+U.

Step 134. Enter the following handler:

Listing 6-16.

```
on startMovie
  global loadItems
  put [] into loadItems
  add loadItems, "../images/register.gif"
  add loadItems, "../images/faculty.gif"
  add loadItems, "../images/location.gif"
  add loadItems, "../images/program.gif"
  add loadItems, "../images/schedule.gif"
  add loadItems, "../images/studloan.gif"
  add loadItems, "../register.htm"
  add loadItems, "../faculty.htm"
  add loadItems, "../location.htm"
  add loadItems, "../program.htm"
  add loadItems, "../schedule.htm"
  add loadItems, "../studloan.htm"
  repeat with i = 1 to count (loadItems)
    PreloadNetThing getAt (loadItems, i)
  end repeat
end startMovie
```

If you remember back to Chapter 1, "How the Web Works," the relative URLs added to the *loadItems* list above refer to a parent directory ("../") and a different subdirectory in the parent directory ("../images/"). When you use relative URLs in Shockwave movies, they need to be relative to the movie file, not the HTML page from which it's called.

Press Enter to close the window.

Step 135. Save the Director movie.

Step 136. Use Afterburner to make a new version of the Shockwave movie *wrldwid2.dcr*.

Step 137. Copy the new version of *wrldwid2.dcr* to the *movies* subdirectory on your server.

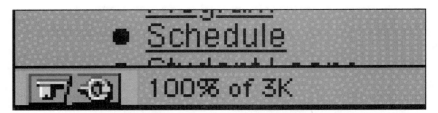

Figure 6-45: *Detail of the browser window, showing preloading while the Shockwave movie plays above.*

Step 138. Access the same URL you used in Step 129. Immediately after the Shockwave movie loads in on the screen and begins playing, you should notice that other files are being read from the server to the cache. Once the animation has finished, try pressing the buttons again to see the difference caused by preloading the other pages. If you examine the items in the *loadItems* list, you should notice that the GIF images—which are generally larger than HTML files— were set to preload first.

Preloading is best used when the movie executing the preload is long enough to hold the viewer's interest while the files are being loaded into the cache. If the user makes a choice which leaves the movie, the preloading items may delay or slow down loading in the items the browser requests next.

NetError () & NetAbort

There are two other Shockwave Lingo commands available to you for the management of asynchronous operations.

NetError ( ) is a function which can take a valid asynchronous ID (from *GetLatestNetID ( )*) value as an argument. Without an argument, *NetError ( )* returns information about the most recently executed asynchronous operation. *NetError ( )* returns an empty text string until the operation is finished, then returns "OK" or a string describing an error.

NetAbort is a command which cancels either the last asynchronous operation, or, when used with a valid asynchronous ID number as an argument, cancels a particular asynchronous command identified by the argument.

Using *NetError ( )* and *NetAbort* can make your Shockwave movies less prone to errors. By testing with *NetError ( )* to see if a particular item has been successfully loaded by *GetNetText* or *PreloadNetThing*, for instance, you run less of a chance that your movie will be loading garbage as data or that your browser will crash when it accesses a broken file. By closing down operations in progress with *NetAbort* when leaving a movie, the browser will work more efficiently and the user experience will be more pleasant.

Below are some modifications to the *wrldwid2.dir* movie which incorporate some of the functionality of *NetError ( )* and *NetAbort*. This first is a modification of the Movie Script.

Listing 6-17.

```
on startMovie
  global loadItems
  put [] into loadItems
  --in this version, loadItems becomes a
  --linear list composed of short property
  --lists, each property list has a text
  --property, thing,containing the relative
  --URL of a preload item
  add loadItems, (addProp loadThis, ¬
    thing, "../images/register.gif")
  add loadItems, (addProp loadThis, ¬
    thing, "../images/faculty.gif")
  add loadItems, (addProp loadThis, ¬
    thing, "../images/location.gif")
  add loadItems, (addProp loadThis, ¬
    thing, "../images/program.gif")
  add loadItems, (addProp loadThis, ¬
    thing, "../images/schedule.gif")
  add loadItems, (addProp loadThis, ¬
    thing, "../images/studloan.gif")
  add loadItems, (addProp loadThis, ¬
    thing, "../register.htm")
  add loadItems, (addProp loadThis, ¬
    thing, "../faculty.htm")
```

```
        add loadItems, (addProp loadThis, ¬
          thing, "../location.htm")
        add loadItems, (addProp loadThis, ¬
          thing, "../program.htm")
        add loadItems, (addProp loadThis, ¬
          thing, "../schedule.htm")
        add loadItems, (addProp loadThis, ¬
          thing, "../studloan.htm")
        repeat with i = 1 to count (loadItems)
          PreloadNetThing getProp ¬
            ((loadItems, i), thing)
          put getAt (loadItems, i) into tempList
          addProp tempList, order, ¬
            GetLatestNetID ()
          --puts the NetID into a
          --new property, order
          setAt loadItems, tempList, i
        end repeat
      end startMovie
```

In the Score script for frame 52 (the main loop of the movie) add a command to the *exitFrame* handler, insert the *checkOps* handler in the script, and make a modification to the *perform* handler.

Listing 6-18.

```
on exitFrame
  checkButtons
  spinTape
  flashShock
  checkOps
  go to "Main"
end

...

on checkOps
  global loadItems
  repeat with i = count (loadItems) ¬
    down to 1
```

```
          --count from the back, because you'll
          --be popping items off of the list and
          --starting at the front will change the
          --index number of a particular item
          put getAt (loadItems, i) into tempList
          put getProp (tempList, order) into ops
          --ops now equals a particular item's
          --NetID value
          if NetDone(ops) and ¬
            (NetError (ops) = "OK") then
            deleteAt loadItems, i
            --the item has finished retrieving
            --and nothing went wrong
          else
            if NetError (ops) <> "" then
              PreloadNetThing getProp ¬
                (tempList, thing)
              --NetError only returns a value
              --when NetDone is TRUE, if NetError
              --is OK, it's been taken care of in
              --above, if it's empty, the
              --operation is still in progress,
              --if anything else, there's been an
              --error and the PreloadNetThing
              --command is reissued
              setProp tempList, order, ¬
                GetLatestNetID ()
              --puts the new NetID into
              --the order property
              setAt loadItems, tempList, i
              --updates loadItems
            end if
          end if
      end repeat
    end checkOps


    . . .


    on perform aButton
```

```
repeat with i = 1 to 48
  puppetSprite i, FALSE
end repeat
repeat with i = count (loadItems) ¬
  down to 1
  put getAt (loadItems, i) into tempList
  put getProp (tempList, order) into ops
  NetAbort ops
end repeat
put [] into loadItems
if aButton = 13 then
  GoToNetPage "studloan.htm"
else
  put ["../register.htm", ¬
    "../faculty.htm", ¬
    "../location.htm", ¬
    "../program.htm", ¬
    "../schedule.htm"] into links
  GoToNetPage getAt (links, aButton - 20)
end if
end
```

. . .

Using a similar strategy in your own Shockwave movies, in addition to strenuous error-checking of text retrieved with *NetTextResult* will go a long way toward preventing lockups and crashes of the Shockwave plug-in and Web browser.

netMIME () & netLastModDate ()

These two functions are included in the specifications for Shockwave Lingo but were not implemented in the first full release of the plug-in. See Appendix C, "The Shocked Lingo Dictionary," for more information.

Moving On

This chapter covered the last of the asynchronous Shockwave Lingo commands and functions, most notably *GetLatestNetID ( )*, *PreloadNetThing*, *NetError ( )*, and *NetAbort*. These commands give you the ability to control the flow of data between a server and the Shockwave movie, to test for failures, and to speed operations.

Now that you are familiar with the Shockwave Lingo, in the next chapter we'll look at some techniques for giving your Shockwave movies impact with one of the most important aspects of Director: sound.

7

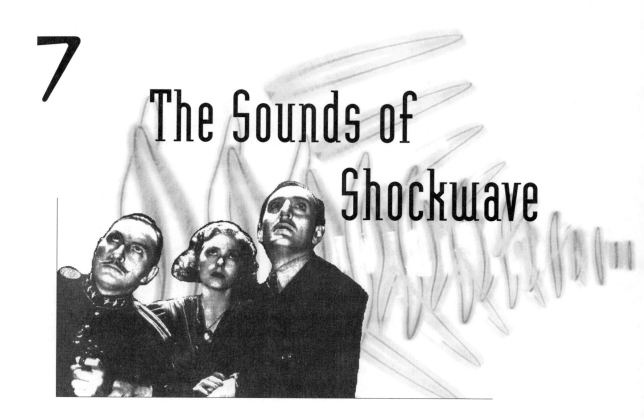

The Sounds of Shockwave

In the race to cram in as many graphics as possible, one of the most neglected areas of multimedia productions is sound. And Shockwave movies are no exception. Digitized sounds are voracious bandwidth-eaters, and consequently they're often not included.

Another strike against sounds in Shockwave is that sound doesn't compress as efficiently as graphics (our tests with Afterburner averaged 20 to 40 percent compression on sounds).

The third strike is that while many design firms and artists have experience in dealing with graphics—and even video—they place professional-quality sound editors and music composers at the bottom of their aquisition priority lists. Creating just the right sound or tune can be as exacting as designing a logo—when Apple introduced their PowerPC line of computers, they hired guitarist Stanley Jordan to create the distinctive chord used for the start-up sound.

In fact, sound is probably one of the most important components of Shockwave movies, if only because so much of the Web is like walking in a graveyard—auralwise. Sound can be used to supplement visual cues, create a mood, and serve as an attention-getter.

When properly prepared and judiciously applied, sound can take a good presentation, move it to the next level of multimedia, and make it something special. You don't need to be a composer to include sounds in your movies (and with Shockwave you won't be using any particularly long soundtracks), but a little bit of sound goes a long way toward making a Shockwave movie a truly complete multimedia production.

Sound is useful in Shockwave movies as short repeating loops used as background music to set the mood, for drawing attention to a particular part of a movie (setting off a sound as the mouse rolls over a particular item, for instance), for giving added feedback when buttons are pushed, etc. All of the same reasons, in fact, that sound is useful in any Director production. In Shockwave you just have to be a little more canny about when, where, and what sounds to use.

Sources

If you've got an electronic music studio with MIDI sequencers and digital mixing software, then you probably won't need to find sounds and music for your Shockwave movies. But if your gig is graphics and/or programming, and your composing skill is limited to two-finger variations on "Chopsticks," then you'll most likely want to pick up some of the numerous clip music collections available.

Figure 7-1: *AMUG's Music Madness Vol. 2 CD-ROM.*

Macromedia includes sound in their ClipMedia CD-ROM series; the Arizona Macintosh Users Group has several discs of sounds and music tracks on their Music Madness series; and many other discs exist as well, ranging from thirty to several hundred dollars in price. Some include all sounds and music at several sampling rates, ranging up to audio CD-quality, and most are both Windows- and Mac OS-readable and allow you to use the sounds royalty-free as long as they are not included in a product for sale.

Make the most of your audio buck by looking for collections that include both special effects and music tracks. Tracks—particularly ones which include short loopable sections—can be used for background or connective music; effects will be useful for button sounds, rollovers, and other event-related sounds.

Slimming Down Sound for Shockwave

Sounds come in a variety of formats, as well as quality levels. Apart from the issue of stereo vs. mono sounds, there is sampling rate and sample depth to consider. Needless to say, in the world of Shockwave movie design you usually give up anything that costs you file size (i.e., bandwidth).

It's important to work with high-quality formats while you're editing sound. In the case of sampled sounds (or, for that matter, digitized images), every time you make a modification to a file you are potentially discarding data. Using a sound filter on a 44 kHz sound sample and converting it to 11 kHz will usually give you a different result than converting first and then using the same filter. It just might make the difference between whether the sound is audible or not. Perform most of your editing work on the best quality sound files you have available to you—then convert them to something you can include in a Shockwave movie.

There are a number of sound file formats on the Mac OS, but the standard for most sounds imported into Director is the AIFF format. Director for Windows can import AIFF (.AIF) files as well as WAV formats. Sound-only QuickTime movies can be used by Director but can't be used in Shockwave movies.

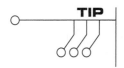

TIP

As with graphics for Shockwave movies, the Link to File button needs to be deselected in the Import dialog box when bringing sounds into the cast.

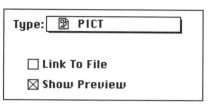

Figure 7-2: *The Link to File button—deselected.*

Digital sound formats like AIFF and WAV represent analog sound waves by testing the sound level at specific intervals and assigning a number to the sound level in a process called *sampling*.

Shown below in Figure 7-3 is a portion of a sound wave in its analog form. Natural sounds usually create continuous waveforms, both in time (horizontal axis) and modulation (vertical axis). The peaks of each major waveform indicate a single soundwave; the number of soundwaves that occur in a second determine its frequency (expressed as cycles per second, *Hertz* or *Hz*), and the higher the frequency, the more high-pitched the sound is. The average human range of hearing is from about 20Hz to 20,000 Hz (20 kilohertz, or kHz).

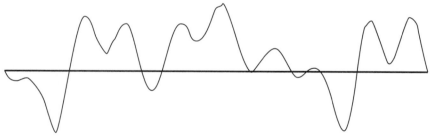

Figure 7-3: *An analog sound wave.*

Imagine the sound digitization process as a grid overlaid on the sound wave. At each point where a vertical line of the grid crosses the wave, the nearest point where a horizontal line of the grid crosses the vertical line is marked. This process approximates the curve of the sound wave with digital information that can be stored on the computer.

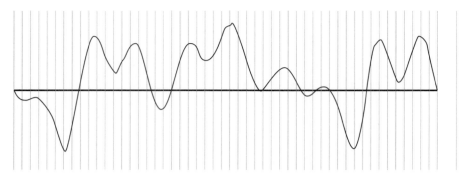

Figure 7-4: *Sound wave overlaid with vertical lines showing sampling points.*

The number of vertical lines used to approximate the sound wave represents the *sampling rate* of the digital sound file. Audio CDs sample sound 44,100 times per second (44.1 kHz or kiloHertz). Due to CD-ROM space considerations and data transfer rates, as well as RAM overhead, many multimedia productions use one-half or one-quarter of that value (22.05 kHz and 11.025 kHz, respectively), as their sampling rate. A sound file with a sampling rate of 11.025 will be only a quarter of the size of the same sound sampled at 44.1 kHz.

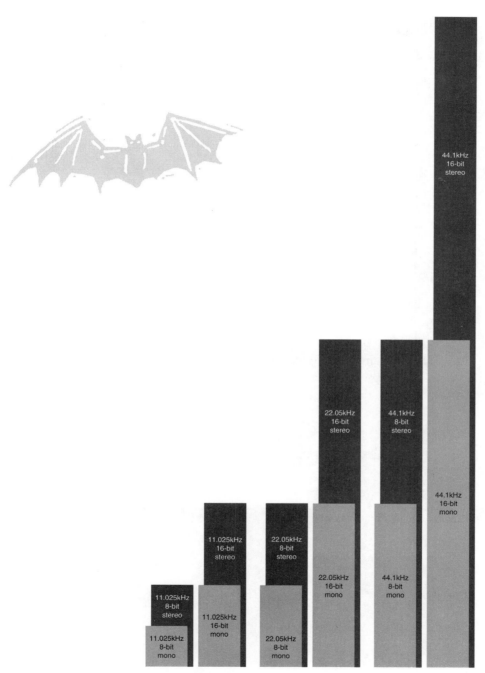

Figure 7-5: *Chart of relative sound file sizes.*

Sounds which have been recorded in stereo require equal amounts of data for each channel; therefore, stereo sounds are twice the size of monaural sounds.

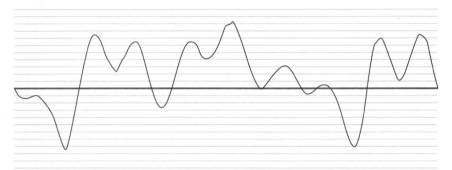

Figure 7-6: *Sound wave overlaid with horizontal lines representing sampling depth values.*

Sample depth, the horizontal lines on our imaginary grid, represents the accuracy of the individual sample. Because individual samples can only be represented by the points where the grid lines cross, the more horizontal lines, the closer the approximation will be to the actual curve.

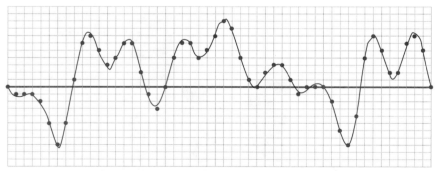

Figure 7-7: *Sound wave with grid showing points approximating the wave.*

The more samples, and the greater the sample depth, the closer the approximation to the original sound. If the sample rate is too low, the harmonic variations in the waveform which give the sound much of its color are lost. If the sample depth is too low, subtleties in the soundwave's amplitude are flattened out. And since those changes create sound in the first place, this can be—as you might suspect—a problem.

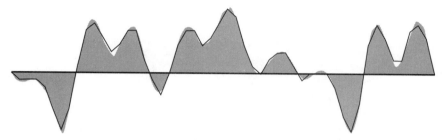

Figure 7-8: *Approximated digital sound wave overlaid on the original analog sound wave.*

Sound quality comes at the expense of file size and bandwidth. Audio CD sound has a sample depth of 16 bits, using two bytes of information at every sample point to provide 65,536 potential levels of amplitude in a soundwave. Most Mac OS and Windows sound-editing programs can create (and Director can import) files with 8 bits of sample depth, which use only 256 amplitude levels but take up only half the space. Many of the same programs (including Macromedia's own SoundEdit 16 software) provide sound compression algorithms which make sounds even smaller, often at a severe loss in audibility. Director will not import sounds in those formats, however.

One second of monaural digitized sound at an 11.025 kHz sampling rate and an 8-bit sample depth occupies (not surprisingly) just over 11,000 bytes on your hard drive. Placing that sound into a Director movie without any cast members or scripts adds roughly 8,000 bytes. Depending on what the sound consists of, it may compress to almost nothing with the Afterburner. (A Director movie containing only a sample of one second of absolute silence actually made a smaller Shockwave movie for us than an empty Director movie.) Or the sound may not compress at all (a second of random noise—the least compressible type of data—in a Director movie compressed to just under its full size for us with Afterburner).

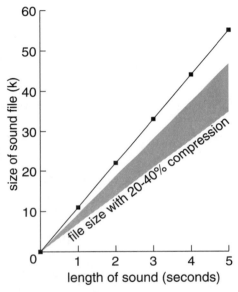

Figure 7-9: *File size estimates for 8-bit, 11.025 kHz monaural sounds, compressed and uncompressed.*

If you figure 1 second of uncompressed 11 kHz sample rate sound at 8-bit sample depth takes up just over 11K and somewhere between 6 and 9K after compression, you can make a pretty accurate estimate of how much sound you want to include in your Shockwave movie. 16-bit, 11K sound will take up twice as much space (12-18 K/sec after compression). 16-bit, 22K sound will double *that* amount (24-36 K/sec after compression). Stereo? Double it again. Remember, these numbers are just rough estimates—compression varies on sound just as it does on images.

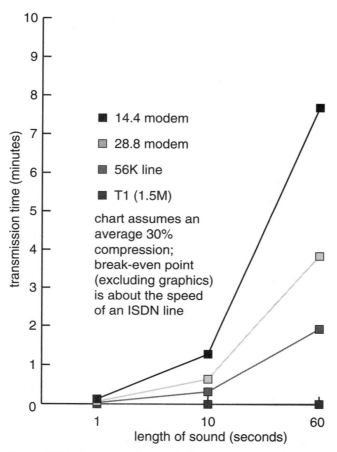

Figure 7-10: *Estimated transmission times for compressed sound portions of Shockwave files.*

All that said, your environment will determine the quality of sound you'll be using in your Shockwave presentations. For general Internet purposes, the smaller the better is the watchword: 11.025 kHz sampling rates with 8-bit sampling depth. (Mac OS computers can handle sampling rates down to 5.564 kHz, but for cross-platform compatibility—this *is* the Internet, where nobody can tell you're a Windows user—11.025 is the least common denominator.) If you're creating something like an in-house reference database where transmission of the files will be across

Ethernet lines, on the other hand, by all means use the highest-quality sound you can get. Audio CD-quality sound (including stereo) can be had for just over 88K/sec uncompressed—that's a megabyte every 11 seconds or so.

Exercise 7-1: What's the Frequency, Kenneth?

This exercise takes you through the steps to take an audio CD-quality sound in Macromedia SoundEdit 16 and convert it to something more manageable for most Shockwave applications. Other sound-editing programs, such as Sonic Foundry's Sound Forge, are capable of similar—if not exactly the same—commands. Here, you'll take the original sampled voice from the Worldwide Shockwave School home page and prepare it for use in a Shockwave movie. This technique isn't necessarily special for Shockwave, but most other Director projects can be a little more forgiving about using higher-quality and stereo sounds. You don't have that luxury in the world of Shockwave.

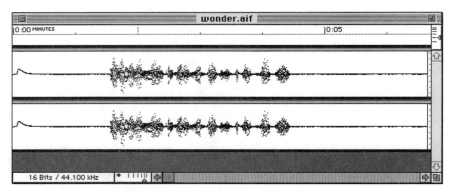

Figure 7-11: *SoundEdit 16 window showing the* wonder.aif *sound.*

Step 1. In SoundEdit 16, open the AIFF sound file *wonder.aif* from the EXER0701 folder in the TUTORIAL folder. Select the Sound | Sound Format menu command. The Rate should be 44.1 and the Bits should be set for 16. Check the Make Default checkbox button and press OK to close the dialog box.

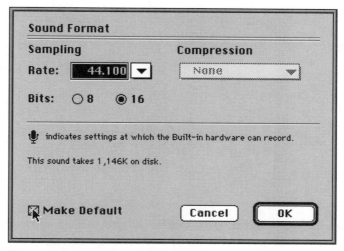

Figure 7-12: *The Sound Format dialog.*

Step 2. From the Sound menu, choose the Mix command to blend the two channels of the stereo sound together, creating a monaural sound.

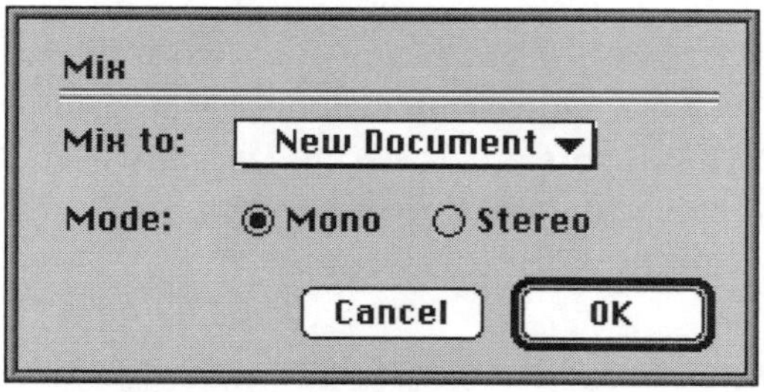

Figure 7-13: *The Mix dialog.*

Step 3. In the dialog box, select New Document from the pop-up menu next to Mix To, and select Mono from the radio buttons below.

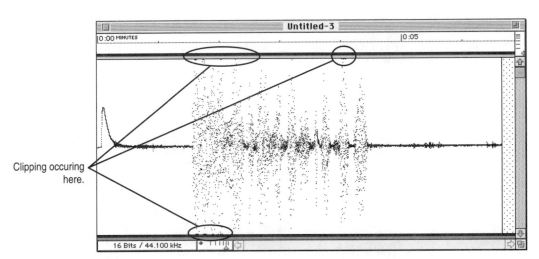

Clipping occuring here.

Figure 7-14: *The mixed sound with clipped area circled.*

Step 4. If you look at the display of the waveform for this sound, you'll notice that the soundwave is cropped off at the top and the bottom of the display. This is known as "clipping," and since it causes degradation of the sound, it's something you should avoid. Play the sound (Command+P or Sound | Play from the menu bar) and listen. When two tracks are mixed together in SoundEdit 16, the values of the waveforms are added; if they are essentially similar, as they are in this case, they become overmodulated and clipped. Close this document without saving it.

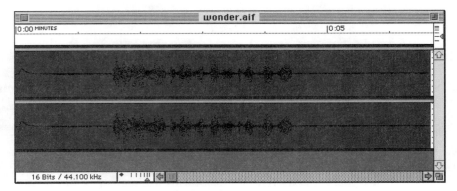

Figure 7-15: *The entire sound selected.*

Step 5. In the original sound file, select the Edit | Select All command from the menu bar, or press Command+A to highlight the entire sound in both channels.

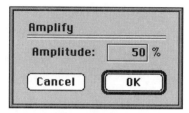

Figure 7-16: *The Amplify dialog.*

Step 6. Because the modulation values of both channels are relatively high, you'll bring them down before mixing them to prevent clipping in the final sound. Choose Effects | Amplify from the menu bar and enter 50 percent for the Amplitude in the Amplify dialog box. This modifies the amplitude—or volume—of the sound. Press Enter to modify the sound.

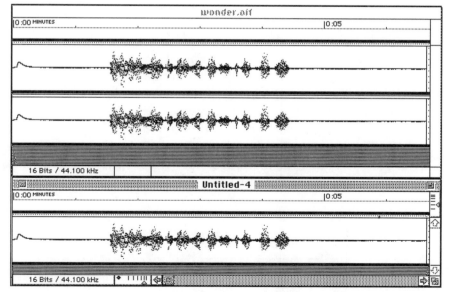

Figure 7-17: *The original sound wave and the mixed sounds with modified amplification.*

Step 7. After the sounds are deamplified, they are ready for mixing. Choose Sound | Mix from the menu bar again, and mix the sounds to a new document with one channel (mono). If you play this new sound, it should be virtually identical to each of the two tracks you mixed together.

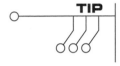

TIP

If you have a sound where the tracks are identical, simply copying one of the tracks and pasting it into a new document will avoid the mixing process altogether. The mixing process is often essential for sounds with multiple voices or instruments.

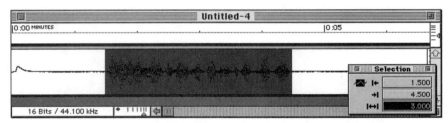

Figure 7-18: *Three seconds of the sound selected via the Selection palette.*

Step 8. The entire sound is originally over 6 seconds long. As you'll notice, long blank spaces appear both before and after the sound. The next task is to get rid of those blank spaces. From the Windows menu, select Show Selection Palette. In the main window, you can see that the voice appears to begin about 1.5 seconds into the sound. Select the first (start) field in the Selection palette and type in **1.5**, then press Tab twice to move to the last (duration) field and type in **3**. Press Tab again, and the 3-second portion of the sound starting 1.5 seconds into the sound will be selected.

Figure 7-19: *The Controls palette with the Option key pressed, showing the Play Loop button.*

Step 9. Press the Play button on the Controls palette, select Sound | Play from the menu bar, or press Command+P to play the selected portion of the sound. If you don't hear the entire phrase spoken, adjust the selection by typing in new numbers for the start and duration fields in the Selection palette and play the sound again. Once you're satisfied that you have the entire phrase selected, copy the selection by using menu command Edit | Copy or pressing Command+C.

Step 10. Create a new document with the File | New menu command or pressing Command+N.

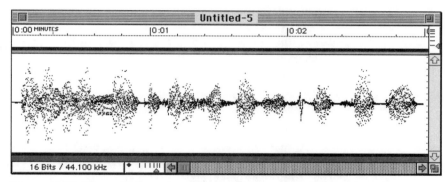

Figure 7-20: *The copied portion of the sound pasted into a new document.*

Step 11. Paste the copied selection of the sound into the new document by pressing Command+V or selecting Edit | Paste from the menu bar. By pasting the selected portion of the sound into a new document, you save yourself the need of selecting each end of the sound and deleting them independently.

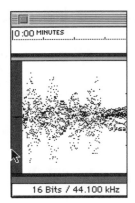

Figure 7-21: *Selecting the first portion of the sound.*

Step 12. Sounds that start suddenly will often "pop" the speakers. In order to prevent this, you'll fade the sound both in and out. Select the very first portion of the sound, from the beginning to just before the first word is spoken. (This should be a selection between 0.050 and 0.075 seconds as shown in the Selection palette.)

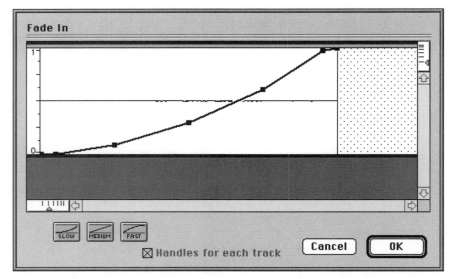

Figure 7-22: *The Fade In dialog, showing the selected portion of the sound after pressing Slow to apply the fade curve.*

Step 13. From the Effects menu, choose the Fade In effect. In the dialog box that appears, press the Slow button then OK to apply the fade.

Figure 7-23: *The last portion of the sound selected.*

Step 14. Select the last portion of the sound and choose the Fade Out effect from the Effects menu. Press the Fast button, then press OK to apply the fade.

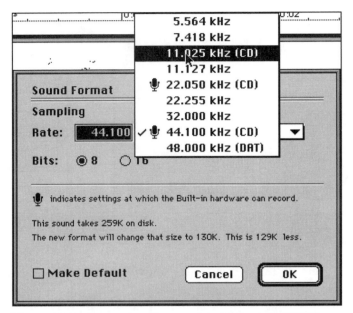

Figure 7-24: *Converting the sound to 8 bits at 11.025kHz.*

Step 15. From the Sound menu, choose Sound Format to bring up the Sound Format dialog box. Set the Rate to 11.025 and Bits to 8. Be sure Compression is set to None, and press OK to close the window and convert the sound.

Step 16. Choose the File I Save menu command and set the File Format to Audio IFF. Save the file as *wonder2.aif.*

This 3-second sound is identical to that used in Exercise 6-2.

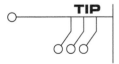

TIP

One of the more useful capabilities of SoundEdit 16 is the Set Loopback menu command. Loopback allows you to create sound files which have a beginning, a looping middle, and an end, unlike setting the Loop property of a sound, which simply starts playing the sound from the beginning on every loop. In a typical Director movie, you can start a sound with a loopback and it will play through the beginning section then loop the middle section until it encounters a Wait for Sound Tempo channel setting. Once it reaches that point, it will continue to the end of the sound instead of looping again. Unfortunately, the same technique doesn't work when looping with the Lingo *soundbusy ( )* function. And since you can't use the Tempo channel's Wait routines in Shockwave, loopback sounds aren't available in Shockwave movies.

Using Sound for a Shockwave Menu

A longer Shockwave movie, interesting as it might be visually, feels a little flat when it's completely silent. Yet putting a long soundtrack can make the movie impossible to download. Making use of short, repeatable sound loops and mixing up the order can help fill in the blank aural spaces.

Exercise 7-2: Loops & Crossfades with Lingo

David Duddleston of Ein Produkt used three sounds played in random order to create a long, nonsequential sound loop for the main menu of his Violet Arcana Shockwave site.

Figure 7-25: *The Violet Arcana main menu.*

Using three different sounds and varying the order helps keep the experience fresh, and—since Shockwave sounds tend to be rather short—avoids the irritating sameness of a single repeat loop. More than three sounds could be used to produce the same effect (using two sounds just doesn't give much randomness), but keep an eye on the size of the files you're creating if you use this technique to use a greater number.

Step 1. Open the Director movie *vashock.dir* from the EXER0702 directory in the TUTORIAL folder.

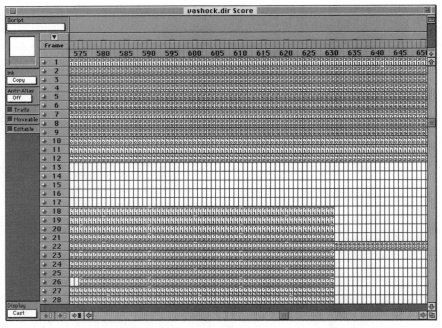

Figure 7-26: *A portion of the Score window for the movie* vashock.dir.

Step 2. This movie is complete except for the sound. If you examine the Score, you'll see about 820 frames of animation, with the first 630 or so being used for an introduction, and the last couple of hundred frames used for the main loop of the menu movie. This movie uses animation hard-wired in the Score combined with *exitFrame* handlers to control sprites and sounds. Open the Movie Script (Command/Ctrl+U) and modify the first handler, *reset*:

```
on reset
  global MouseOn, MouseOnOld, menu
  --these globals are used to maintain information
  --about button states and previous visitation of
  --the movie
  global Smode, fade, onetwo
  --contain information on sound mode,
  --fade state, and current puppeted
  --sound channel
  set MouseOn = 0
  set MouseOnOld = 0
  set Smode = 0
  set fade = 0
  set onetwo = 0
  set the volume of sound 1 = 0
  set the volume of sound 2 = 0
  starttimer
  set the timer = 19*60
  if voidP(menu) then
    --can be used to determine if the menu
    --has been visited in the current session
    set menu = 1
  else
    go to frame 631
  end if
end
```

These additions initialize the sound states you'll need for this movie. Below this handler in the Movie Script is the *checkroll* handler, which highlights the buttons during the main loop of the movie, and a *puppetsprites* handler which is called just before the main loop.

Step 3. Scroll down to the end of the Movie Script and enter the following handler:

```
on sound
  global Smode, fade, onetwo
  if the timer > 20*60 then
    --timer is over 20 seconds
    set oldSmode = Smode
```

```
                    --stores old sound mode
                    set n = 1
                    --n is used as a state variable to
                    --determine if new sound is different
                    --than existing sound
                    repeat while n = 1
                      set Smode = random(3)
                      --picks from three sounds
                      if oldSmode <> Smode then set n = 2
                      --if old sound is not same as new
                      --sound then loop will not repeat
                    set fade = 1
                    --sets fade state to active
                    end repeat
                    if onetwo = 0 then
                      --sound channel two is playing,
                      --begin playing sound in channel one
                      puppetsound 1, Smode+50
                    end if
                    if onetwo = 1 then
                      --sound channel one is playing,
                      --begin playing sound in channel two
                      puppetsound 2, Smode+50
                    end if
                    starttimer
                  end if
                  if fade = 1 then
                    if onetwo = 0 then
                      --fade state is active and new sound
                      --is playing in sound channel one
                      set the volume of sound 1 to ¬
                        the volume of sound 1 + 2
                      --increases volume of new sound
                      set the volume of sound 2 to ¬
                        the volume of sound 2 - 2
                      --decreases volume of old sound
                      if the volume of sound 1 > 254 then
                      --volume of new sound has hit maximum
                        set fade = 0
```

```
          --sets fade state to inactive
          set the volume of sound 2 to 0
          --completely shuts off old sound
          set onetwo = 1
          --makes new sound old sound
        end if
    end if
    if onetwo = 1 then
        --see notes in last section, this
        --code mirrors that above
        set the volume of sound 1 to ¬
          the volume of sound 1 - 2
        set the volume of sound 2 to ¬
          the volume of sound 2 + 2
        if the volume of sound 2 > 254 then
          set fade = 0
          set the volume of sound 1 to 0
          set onetwo = 0
        end if
    end if
  end if
end
```

With this script, each sound loops for 20 seconds. After that period has elapsed, the first *if…then* clause executes, first storing the value of the current sound (global variable *Smode*) in the local variable *oldSmode*. Another local variable, *n*, is used as a check to determine whether a new sound has been chosen. A random number between 1 and 3 is put into *Smode* and compared to *oldSmode*. If the numbers are different, *n* is set to 2, and the repeat loop is exited. The global variable *fade* is set to 1, indicating that it is active. As one repeating loop fades out, the next repeating loop fades in.

The next two *if…then* clauses set a puppet sound to start playing. The channel chosen for play is determined by the global variable *onetwo*, and the sound played is in cast position 51, 52, or 53.

The second major portion of the script executes when the variable *fade* is active. Global variable *onetwo* is checked to see which sound should be faded (when *onetwo* is 0, sound 2 is faded out; when *onetwo* is 1, sound 1 is faded out), increases the volume of the new sound, and decreases the volume of the old sound. When the new sound's volume has reached its maximum (*sound x* > 254), the *fade* variable is set to off, the volume of the old sound is turned off completely, and *onetwo* is set to its opposite value.

Press Enter to close the Script window.

Step 4. Double-click in frame 2 of the Script channel in the Score to bring up a Score Script window. Add the following script to call the *sound* handler at the end of the frame.

```
on exitFrame
   sound
end
```

Press Enter to close the Script window.

Step 5. Select frames 2 to 630 of the Script channel and press Command/Ctrl+B, or use menu comand In-Between Linear to apply the *on exitFrame sound* handler to the first animation sequence.

Step 6. The script in frame 631 of the Script channel sets up the puppet sprites for the buttons, but the frames after that, until frame 821, simply check rollover on the buttons. Add the *sound* handler to the sequence by selecting frame 632 in the Script channel of the Score and clicking in the Script Entry area of the Score window to bring up the existing Score script for editing. Make one small addition:

```
on exitFrame
   checkrollover
   sound
end
```

Press Enter to close the Script window.

You've now added sound to the entire movie. If you play the movie back now, you'll see the letters come drifting out of the lower right, arranging themselves at the top as the buttons come up from the bottom as the movie goes into the main menu loop starting at frame 632. If you stop the movie and play it again, it will seem to start at the main menu loop. By checking to see if a value has been asigned to the *menu* variable in the *reset* handler with the function *voidP(menu)*, the viewer doesn't have to wait through the entire opening sequence again.

Moving On

Sound is an important integral part of any multimedia presentation, including Shockwave movies. As with graphics, however, it's important to use sound as economically as possible. Take your intended audience and transmission medium into consideration when determining the amount and quality of sound to use in your presentation, and use it in ways which vary the experience as well as extend the life of the sound.

In the next chapter, we introduce some techniques to make the most of Shockwave Lingo, to add to your knowledge of graphics and sound.

8

Shockwave Tricks

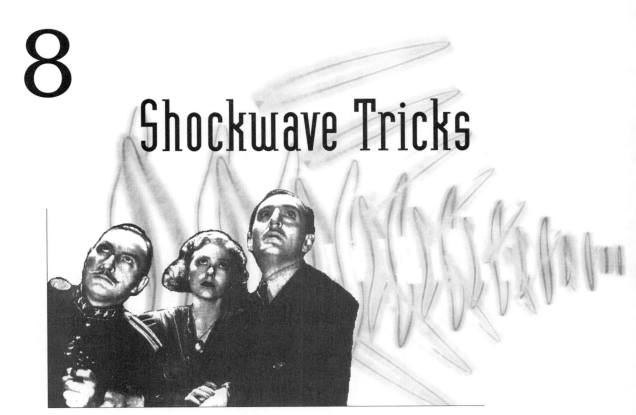

There are many things you can do to make your Shockwave movies work faster, more efficiently, and more transparently for Web surfers. Apart from simply making movies as small as possible, making them do something more than just sit there waiting for the viewer to interact—or worse, *quietly* sit there—should be a primary objective. There are techniques you can use that mostly do the aforementioned—but in ways you may not have thought of.

Take the Measure of Your Browsers

This isn't an exercise but more of a suggestion/command: Nobody's going to see animation that's hanging off the edge of their browser's window. Many multimedia people are used to creating Director movies at 640 x 480 pixels in size. As you've probably seen by now, the movies this book uses are mostly 448 by 300 pixels. That size fits into the unadjusted Mac OS Netscape Navigator window on a 13-inch monitor. The default Windows 95 Netscape Navigator window is about 100 pixels wider and slightly taller. I once spent a lot of somebody's money reworking a Web site that had been designed to look great on an office PC monitor but was far too small on the UNIX workstations with more tightly-packed pixels—the standard equipment for the client's customer base.

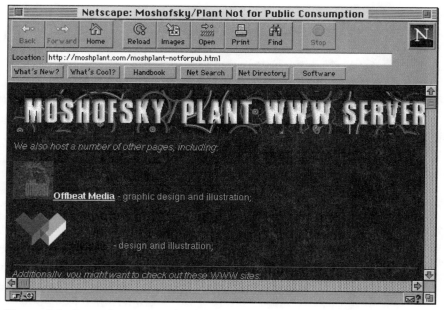

Figure 8-1: *Somewhere out to the right is a really cool animated logo . . . .*

Design your Shockwave movies for your audience. Just because you might have your Web browser window cranked out to the full size of your 21-inch monitor is no reason to expect that everyone viewing the pages you Shock will have the same setup. Look at your movies on a variety of machines. In the world of the Web and multimedia, that's just good sense.

Loader Movies

As much as everyone who uses Director and Shockwave loves their buddies at Macromedia, there's bound to be a few things the company does which irk them. One that cropped up with the Shockwave plug-in was the white window displaying the Macromedia logo that fills the space allocated by the EMBED tag between the time the plug-in loads and the movie begins to play.

Figure 8-2: *The Shockwave version of Purgatory.*

What happens is this: When the browser encounters an EMBED tag, it allocates the requested space within the browser window, which changes the entire space to white. Meanwhile, the Shockwave plug-in begins to load into memory from the hard disk (which may take a few seconds) and the movie itself loads from across the Internet (or your hard drive, if you're opening it locally).

When the plug-in's loaded, it displays the Shockwave logo until it begins playing the movie (which could be a few seconds or several minutes, depending on the size of the movie).

This is all fine and well, but aesthetically it's not the seamless, controlled environment most multimedia producers try to create.

Exercise 8-1: Kicking the whitewalls.

In an attempt to minimize the effect of a blank white box with the Macromedia logo in it, as well as to present something soothing while the real show is about to begin, a number of people use what we'll call a *loader movie*, a very simple movie of minimal size. The loader is usually animated, and its only function is to occupy space on the page, execute a GotoNetMovie, and wait. We use one on the Moshofsky/Plant Web Server Shockwave page. This is how we made it:

Step 1. Open the *moshload.dir* file in Director. You'll find it in the EXER0801 directory of the TUTORIAL folder.

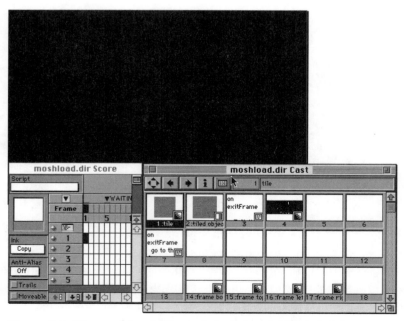

Figure 8-3: *The* moshload.dir *movie in its unadulterated state.*

Step 2. Open the Cast window (Window I Cast from the menu bar or press Command/Ctrl+3). You'll probably only see three items, in positions 1-3, but there are others at positions 14-17, and 26.

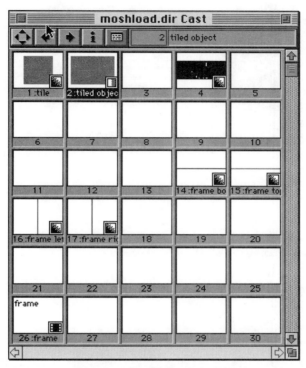

Figure 8-4: *The cast of* moshload.dir.

Step 3. Open the Score window (Window I Score from the menu bar or press Command/Ctrl+4). It should be empty.

Step 4. Drag cast member 2 (labeled "tiled object") from the cast window into the Score at frame 1, channel 1.

Step 5. Select menu item Score I Sprite Info or press Command/Ctrl+K to bring up the Sprite Info dialog box.

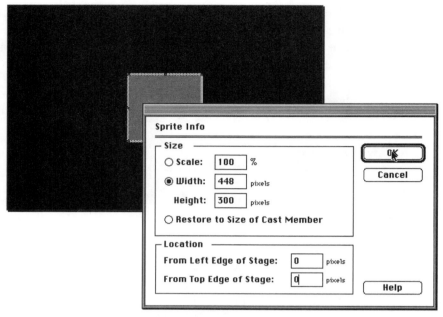

Figure 8-5: *Changing the size of* tiled object.

Step 6. Enter 448 as the sprite's width, and 300 as its height. Set the offset to 0 pixels from both left and top. Press the OK button to close the window.

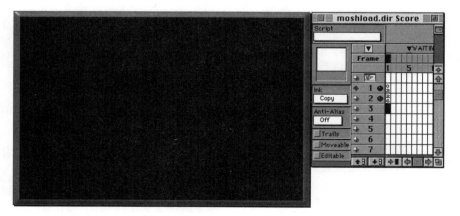

Figure 8-6: *Cast member 26—the frame—on the Stage, with* tiled object *hidden.*

Step 7. Scroll to cast member 26 in the Cast window, and drag it from the Cast window to the Score in frame 1, channel 2. This cast member is a single-frame film loop created from four bitmap cast members that define the edges of the Stage. It should already fit the Stage, and dragging it to the Score centers it on the Stage.

Step 8. Select frames 1 to 5 in channels 1 and 2 of the Score.

Step 9. Use the Score | In-Between Linear menu command or press Command/Ctrl+B to copy the cells in frame 1 to the other selected frames.

Step 10. Drag cast member 3 from the Cast window to the Score in frame 4, channel 3. This is a 1-bit bitmap created from a color graphic used in the *moshplan.dcr* movie.

Figure 8-7: *The logo in place on the Stage.*

Step 11. Open the Tools palette (Window | Tools Palette from the menu bar or press Command/Ctrl+7).

Step 12. With sprite 3 selected in the Score, colorize it with a green selected from the Tools palette foreground paint chip.

Step 13. Use the Ink menu in the Score to set the Ink effect of the sprite to Background Transparent.

Step 14. In the Cast window, select cast member 3, and drag another copy into the Score, to frame 4, channel 4.

Figure 8-8: *Detail of the offset logo cast members.*

Step 15. Move the new copy of the sprite two pixels toward the left and two pixels toward the top of the Stage.

Step 16. Double-click in the Script channel for frame 3 to open the Script window, and enter the following:

```
on exitFrame
  GotoNetMovie "moshplan.dcr"
end
```

This will execute the *GotoNetMovie* command as the playback head leaves frame 3. Press Enter to close the Script window.

Step 17. Double-click in the Script channel for frame 5 to open the Script window, and enter the following:

```
on exitFrame
  go to the frame - 1
end
```

This will keep the movie looping between frame 4 (where the logo sprites are) and frame 5 (where they are not) until the movie called by *GotoNetMovie* is fully loaded and begins playing. Press Enter to close the Script window.

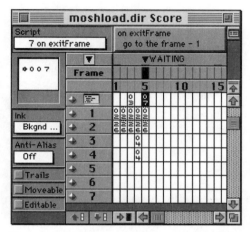

Figure 8-9: *The finalized Score for* moshload.dcr.

Step 18.   Save the movie to your hard drive.

Step 19.   Use Afterburner to convert this movie to a Shockwave movie titled *moshload.dcr*.

Step 20.   Copy *moshload.dcr*, *moshplan.dcr*, and *moshplan.htm* to a directory on your hard drive or Web server.

Step 21.   Use your Web browser to open *moshplan.htm* locally from your hard drive or access the appropriate URL from your Web server. As promised, the page displays in the browser, the plug-in loads, but rather than having to wait for the entire *moshplan.dcr* movie to display, the short loader movie fills the space.

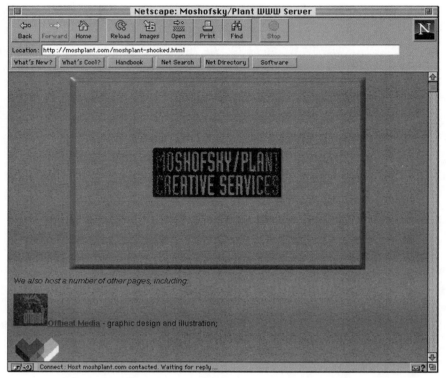

Figure 8-10: *The* moshload.dcr *movie in place on the HTML page, doing its thing.*

This technique saves no time—in fact, it actually adds some seconds to the time before the main movie starts, in most cases. But the time before the blank screen is replaced by a movie doing something—even if that something is minimal—is far shorter.

Exercise 8-2: Electric Mark Twain.

The story about the pseudonym of Samuel Clemens was that he took it from one of the cries of the riverboat men who plied the waters of the Mississippi River. A man standing at the bow of the boat using a rope and a weight would measure the depth of the river, calling out soundings to the pilot. When the water was about twelve feet deep—or two fathoms—the man at the bow would yell "Mark twain!" The books never say if that was good or bad, but the young Clemens must have heard it often enough for the phrase to make an impression.

You can use a loader movie to the same effect as the man in the bow. By measuring the time it takes to download a file of a known size, you can determine what the overall connection speed between server and browser is, and steer users with slower connections to less intensive pages by using the results to determine the next page or movie to be presented. That means creating different versions of material on your site, which can make maintanence frustrating as well as time-consuming but may help you get your message out to a wider range of people.

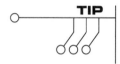

TIP

Connection speed is dependent on many things, including the user's connection, the connection at the server, traffic on both connections, server speed and current connections, and Internet backbone traffic at points between. Assuming that you're measuring the user's speed would be imprudent. Your user might just happen to hit your Web server from a high-speed T1 line at the moment your server is finishing off several other sessions. Give your users the option to try the heavy-duty versions of your pages, even if your initial tests indicate they are unworthy.

Step 1. Open the file *marktwan.dir* from the EXER0802 directory of the TUTORIAL folder.

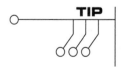

TIP

Because this exercise uses the *GetNetText* command, it needs the HTTP header information sent by Web servers—it won't operate correctly when opened as a local file.

Step 2. Open the Score window (Window | Score from the menu bar or Command/Ctrl+4).

Figure 8-11: *The opening screen of* marktwan.dir.

Step 3. The graph on the stage in frame 1 is a logarithmic scale representing connection speeds ranging from the average slow modem connection (<1 kbps) to the equivalent of a T1 (>1 mbps). There's no way to determine how much data has been read in by a Shockwave command, but by determining the elapsed time while waiting for completion, you know how fast a connection *isn't*. The red gauge on the meter will shrink as the meter runs. It starts at 300 pixels wide.

Make a selection anywhere in frame 1 of the Score and use the Score | Insert Frame command (Command/Ctrl+]) to duplicate the contents of the first frame of the movie.

Step 4. Open a Movie script by pressing Command/Ctrl+Shift+U. Add the following script:

Listing 8-1.
```
on startMovie
  global theTask
  startTimer
  GetNetText "txt10000.txt"
  set theTask = GetLatestNetID ()
  puppetSprite 5, TRUE
end startMovie
```

The file *txt10000.txt* is composed of 10,000 zeros. Press Enter to close the Script window.

Step 5. Double-click in the Tempo channel in frame 1 to bring up the Set Tempo dialog. Set the Tempo to 60 frames per second. Press OK.

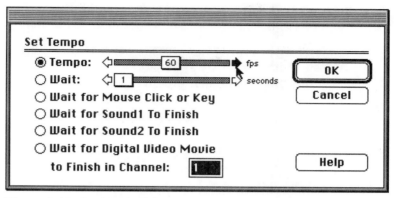

Figure 8-12: *Setting the Tempo.*

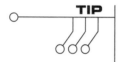

Setting the Tempo as fast as possible will provide the most accurate gauge of the connection speed. Because the timing loop this movie will be using executes at the end of a two-frame loop, it will, at best, be able to provide only 1/30-second accuracy. Setting the Tempo to 10 frames per second would yield less than 1/5-second accuracy. 60 frames isn't recommended for most Shockwave movies.

Step 6. Double-click in frame 3 of the Script channel to add a Score script to the movie.

Listing 8-2.

```
on exitFrame
  global theTask
  if not NetDone (theTask) then

    put the timer into elapsed
    if elapsed > 1200 then ¬
      GotoNetPage "slow.htm"
    --if it's taken 20 seconds to load
    --a 10K file, then the connection
    --is about half the fullspeed
    --of a 14.4 modem connection
```

```
      put elapsed / 60 into ¬
        field "Elapsed Time"
      --displays seconds on the screen
    set width of sprite 5 to ¬
        300 - (integer (log10 ¬
        (elapsed / 0.6) - 1) * 100)
      --changes the width of the progress bar
      --to a value determined by a
      --the elapsed time
      go to the frame - 1
    else
      put the timer into elapsed
      --this section sends the user to
      --various sections based on the
      --amount of time it took to finish
      --the download
      if elapsed < 150 then
        GotoNetPage "full.htm"
      else if elapsed < 300 then
        GotoNetPage "easy.htm"
      else GotoNetPage "slow.htm"
      end if
    end if
  end exitFrame


  on log10 theLog
    return log (theLog) / log (10)
  end log10
```

This script tests the *NetDone ( )* parameter, adjusts the progress bar and loops to the previous frame if the text file hasn't been fully retrieved. If the transfer is finished, the *else* clause determines one of three routes to take, depending on the transfer time.

Step 7. Save the movie.

Step 8. Use the Afterburner to create a Shockwave movie titled *marktwan.dcr*.

Step 9. Copy the files *marktwan.dcr*, *marktwan.htm*, *full.htm*, *easy.htm*, and *slow.htm* to your Web server.

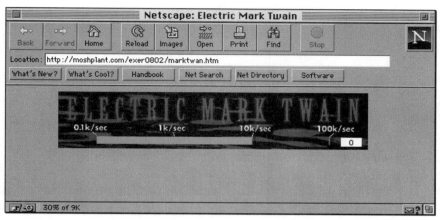

Figure 8-13: *Checking the connection speed using the* marktwan.dcr *movie.*

Step 10. Access the URL for *marktwan.htm,* and the loader movie will determine whether your connection is fast, medium, or slow, and take you to a page displaying its assessment of your connection. The *GetNetPage* commands used in Listing 8-2 can be replaced by other pages or *GetNetMovie* commands (providing that the new movies are the same size as the *marktwan* movie). By adjusting the values in the *else* clause of the *exitFrame* handler, you can determine what *fast* is.

Navigation Bars

One of the more popular uses for graphics in general on the Web is as navigation bars. And as long as there's been Shockwave on the Web, people have wanted to use Shockwave movies as menu bars. The problem has been that no one has come up with a reliable way for the movie to extract information about which page the movie is embedded in. Therefore, using one movie as a button bar on a page will always take the user to the same destination, even if that destination should change from page to page. For a solution, we turned to good old HTML tags and their capacity to target specific points in longer pages. These points are called *anchors*.

Figure 8-14: *A typical static navigation bar.*

An HTML anchor is called by referencing something like *http://aserver.domain/afile.htm#anchor,* where the name of the file is followed by a pound sign or number sign and the name of the anchor (the actual point in the document is indicated by a tag reading *<A NAME="anchor">*).

You can use anchors in HTML documents as part of a *GotoNetPage* command in a Shockwave movie by specifying the URL including the anchor, like this for a full URL:

```
GotoNetPage "http://aserver.domain/afile.htm#anchor"
```

Or just this for a relative URL:

```
GotoNetPage "afile.htm#anchor"
```

Fortunately, when the Shockwave specifications were drawn up, someone had the good sense to make the analogy to markers in Director. The following command will load in the Shockwave movie from the URL and begin playback *at the marker labeled anchor:*

```
GotoNetMovie "http://aserver.domain/amovie.dcr#anchor"
```

Let's give it a whirl.

Exercise 8-3: Markers away.

This exercise will give you some knowledge of how to use *GotToNetMovie* with a URL including an anchor to access specific marker points in a second movie.

Step 1. Open the file *htmltemp.txt* in a text editor and make the changes in bold below:

```
<HTML>
<HEAD>
<TITLE>Markers Away!</TITLE>
</HEAD>
<BODY>
<EMBED SRC="anchorgo.dcr" WIDTH="448" HEIGHT="300">
</BODY>
</HTML>
```

Step 2. Save the text file as *anchor.htm* on your hard drive.

Step 3. Open Director and create a new file.

Step 4. Select File | Preferences from the menu bar to open the Preferences window. Set the Width and Height of the Stage to 448 and 300, respectively. Choose Center for the Stage Location. Press OK to close the window.

Step 5. Open the Tools palette (menu item Window | Tools or Command / Ctrl+7).

Step 6. Select the Button tool and draw four buttons on the Stage labeled "A," "B," "C," and "D."

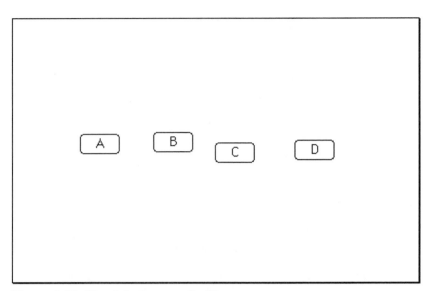

Figure 8-15: *Simple buttons on the Stage.*

Step 7. Select frame 1 through frame 3 in channels 1 to 4 (where the buttons are) and use the menu command Score I In-Between Linear or press Command/Ctrl+B to copy the buttons into frames 2 and 3.

Step 8. Open the Cast window (Window I Cast from the menu bar or press Command/Ctrl+3).

Step 9. Press Ctrl+Option/Alt and click on cast member 1 to bring up the Cast script for the button labeled "A." Enter the changes in bold:

```
on mouseDown
  GotoNetMovie "anchor.dcr#A"
end
```

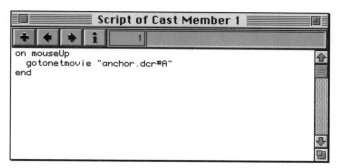

Figure 8-16: *Adding a cast member script.*

Step 10. Select the entire script by pressing Command/Ctrl+A or selecting Edit | Select All from the menu bar.

Step 11. Copy the script with Command/Ctrl+C or menu selection Edit | Copy Text. Press Enter to close the window (don't press Return—it'll wipe out your script!).

Step 12. Press Command/Ctrl+Option/Alt and click on cast member 2 to bring up the Cast script for the button labeled "B."

Step 13. Press Command/Ctrl+A or choose Edit | Select All from the menu bar to select the entire script.

Step 14. Press Command/Ctrl+V or choose Edit | Paste Text to replace the script with the one copied from the button labeled "A."

Step 15. Change the reference to "#A" in the *GotoNetMovie* command to read "#B." Close the window by pressing Enter.

Step 16. Repeat Steps 12-15 for the button cast members labeled "C" and "D."

Step 17. In the Score window, double-click on the Script channel in frame 3 to bring up a Score Script window. Add the script below:

```
on exitFrame
  go to the frame - 1
end
```

Step 18. Save this movie as *anchorgo.dir*.

Step 19. Choose File | New from the menu bar or press Command / Ctrl+N to create a new Director movie.

Step 20. Drag a marker from the marker well to frame 1 and label it "A."

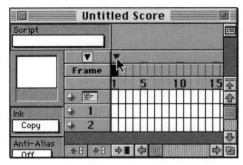

Figure 8-17: *Adding a marker to the movie.*

Step 21. Repeat Step 20 for frames 6, 11, and 16. Label each of the markers "B," "C," and "D," respectively.

Step 22. Select the cell in frame 1 of channel 1.

Step 23. Bring the Tools palette to the front (Window | Tools from the menu bar or press Command / Ctrl+7).

Step 24. Select the Text tool and draw a text box on the Stage. Select a font and size from the Type menu and type in "A."

Step 25. In the Cast window (Window | Cast from the menu bar or press Command / Ctrl+3), select cast member 1. Choose Cast | Duplicate Cast Member from the menu bar or press Command / Ctrl+D to make a copy of the text cast member.

Step 26. Repeat Step 25 two more times. You should have four text cast members, in positions 1 to 4.

Step 27. Double-click on cast member 2 to open the Text window.

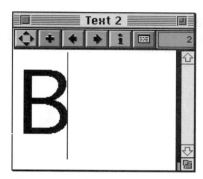

Figure 8-18: *Editing a cast member in the Text window.*

Step 28. Select the text in the Text window and change it to read "B."

Step 29. Press the green forward arrow button in the Text window to edit cast member 3.

Step 30. Select the text in the Text window and change it to read "C."

Step 31. Repeat steps 29 and 30 to change cast member 4 to "D."

Step 32. Drag cast member 2 from the Cast window to the Score in frame 6, channel 1.

Step 33. Repeat Step 32 for cast members 3 and 4, and frames 11 and 16, respectively.

Step 34. Double-click in the Script channel for frame 20 of the Score to bring up a Score Script window. Enter in the usual loop script:

```
on exitFrame
  go to the frame - 1
end
```

Press Enter to close the Script window.

Step 35. With the cell in frame 20 of the Script channel still selected, press Command/Ctrl+C or use the Edit|Copy Cells menu command to copy the cell.

Step 36. Select the cell in frame 15 of the Script channel and press Command/Ctrl+V or use the Edit|Paste Cells menu command to paste the script into frame 16.

Step 37. Repeat step 36 for frames 10 and 5.

Step 38. Select the cell in frame 1, channel 2 of the Score window.

Step 39. Bring the Tools palette to the front (Window | Tools from the menu bar or press Command / Ctrl+7).

Step 40. Select the Button tool.

Step 41. Draw a button on the Stage and label it "Go Back."

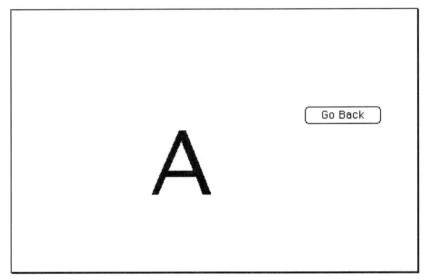

Figure 8-19: *The "Go Back" button on the Stage.*

Step 42. Press Ctrl+Option / Alt and click on cast member 5 in the Cast window to open the cast Script window. Enter the script below:

```
on mouseDown
  GotoNetMovie "anchorgo.dcr"
end
```

This button reloads the movie with the four buttons.

Step 43. Double-click on the channel ID for channel 1 of the Score to select all of the frames of the channel to the end of the movie (frame 20).

Step 44. Press the Shift key and double-click on the channel ID for channel 2 to add all of the frames in channel 2 to the end of the movie to the selection.

Figure 8-20: *Selecting to the end of the movie in channels 1 and 2.*

Step 45. Choose Score | In-Between Linear from the menu bar or press Command / Ctrl+B to fill the selected cells.

Step 46. Save this movie as *anchor.dir*.

Step 47. Use Afterburner to create Shockwave versions of the Director movies *anchorgo.dir* and *anchor.dir*. Save them as *anchorgo.dcr* and *anchor.dcr* in the same folder as *anchor.htm*.

Step 48. Use your Web browser to open the file *anchor.dcr* and press yourself some buttons. Cool, huh?

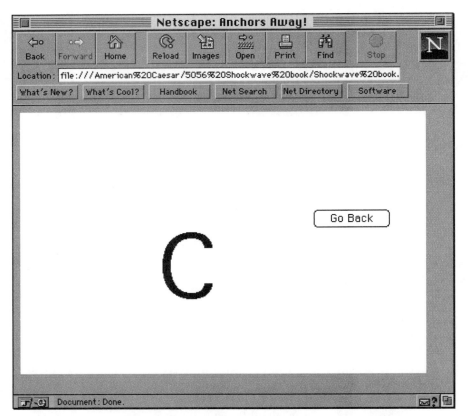

Figure 8-21: *Using URL anchors to target Shockwave movie markers.*

Step 49. Open the file *anchor.htm* with your text editor and make this change:

```
<HTML>
<HEAD>
<TITLE>Markers Away!</TITLE>
</HEAD>
<BODY>
<EMBED SRC="anchor.dcr#C" WIDTH="448" HEIGHT="300">
</BODY>
</HTML>
```

Save the file as *anchorno.htm* in the same directory as *anchor.htm*.

Step 50. Open the file *anchorno.htm* with your Web browser. Obviously, something's wrong.

What's wrong is that while you can use an anchor in a *GotoNetMovie* reference, the same URL just won't work with EMBED.

The goal is to have one movie which can be used as a navigation aid but which won't need to be completely reloaded or rewritten for every single HTML page. To do that, you need to have some way to pass information about the page to the Shockwave movie. If the EMBED command won't do it, you need to figure out some other way.

Exercise 8-4: Behind bars.

This exercise uses anchors, markers, the EMBED command, and the loader movie concept to create a single navigation bar which can be used throughout a site.

Step 1. Copy the directory EXER0804 from the TUTORIAL directory on the Companion CD-ROM to your hard drive. Open the directory and look inside.

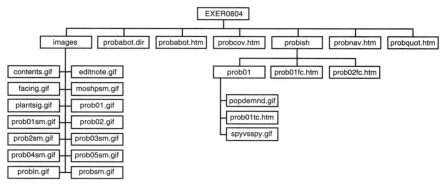

Figure 8-22: *Directory structure for EXER0804.*

This folder has three HTML pages at the main level, a subdirectory with two pages and a subdirectory of its own, with a page inside of that.

Step 2. At the main level of the EXER0804 directory, there are two Director files, *probnav.dir* and *probabot.dir*. Open the *probnav.dir* file with Director.

Step 3. This Director movie is a 448-pixels-wide-by-50-pixels-high navigation bar with buttons for various header sections as well as buttons that will take the user up and down the directory heierarchy. None of the buttons have been scripted to do anything yet. The first order of business is to set up markers for each of the pages we want to be able to navigate to.

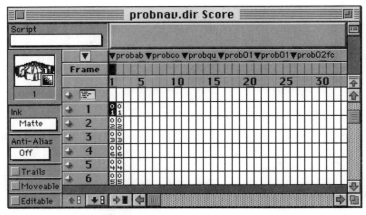

Figure 8-23: *Markers in place for the* probnav.dir *navigation bar movie.*

Drag markers from the marker well to frames 1, 6, 11, 16, 21, and 26. Name them (in sequence) *probabot, probcov, probquot, prob01fc, prob01tc,* and *prob02fc.*

Step 4. Double-click in frame 2 of the Script channel in the Score. Add the usual looping script:

```
on exitFrame
  go to the frame - 1
end
```

Press Enter to close the Script window.

Figure 8-24: *The navigation bar itself.*

Step 5. There are five buttons on the navigation bar. Three represent the HTML files at the main level of the EXER0804 directory. The arrows will be used to move up and down the directory structure. Select frame 1 of the Script channel, press the Shift key, and select frame 2, channel 5. Press Command/Ctrl+C to copy the selected cells.

Step 6. Select frame 6 of the Script channel in the Score.

Step 7. Paste the copied cells using the key command Command/Ctrl+V.

Step 8. Repeat steps 5 and 6 for frames 11, 16, 21, and 26. Each of the markers in the Score should now have a two-frame series of buttons and a looping script.

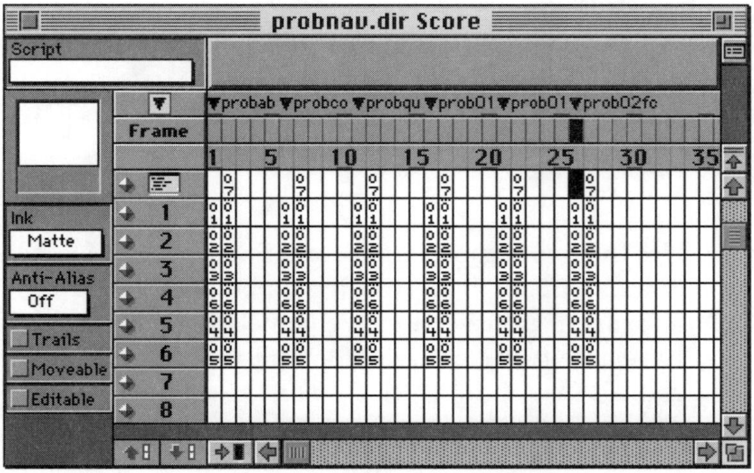

Figure 8-25: *The buttons duplicated throughout the movie.*

Step 9. The three buttons for the files at the main level of the directory will always return the user to the same file. Therefore, a cast member script can be used for those buttons. Press the Ctrl+Option/Alt keys and click on cast member 3 in the Cast window to bring up its cast script. Modify it so that it reads as follows:

```
on mouseDown
   GotoNetPage "probabot.htm"
end
```

Step 10. Repeat step 9 for cast members 4 and 5. Use:

Listing 8-3.
```
on mouseDown
   GotoNetPage "probcov.htm"
end
```

and
```
on mouseDown
   GotoNetPage "probquot.htm"
end
```

respectively.

Step 11. Select cast member 1 in the Cast window.

Step 12. Select frames 1 to 12 of channel 1 in the Score.

Step 13. Use the menu command Score | Switch Cast Members (Command/Ctrl+E) to place cast member 1 in the frames where it appears in the selection in channel 1. The top level pages don't have anywhere higher in the directory to go, and they have two choices for subdirectories, so on these pages you'll use two down arrows.

Step 14. With frames 1 to 12 in channel 1 selected, click on the Script Entry area of the Score window to create a sprite script. This button will load the page *prob01fc.htm* in the subdirectory *probish*. Edit the script to read as follows:

```
on mouseDown
  GotoNetPage "probish/prob01fc.htm"
end
```

Press Enter to close the window. This will assign the Score script to the six filled cells in the selection.

Step 15. Select the range of cells from frame 1 to frame 12 in channel 2. This button will load the page *prob02fc.htm* in the subdirectory *probish*. Edit the script to read as follows:

```
on mouseDown
  GotoNetPage "probish/prob02fc.htm"
end
```

Press Enter to close the window.

Step 16. Select the cells in frames 16 and 17 in channel 1. This configuration of the navigation bar will appear on the *prob01fc.htm* page and this particular button will load a file from higher in the directory structure: the main level. This is where things start to get a little tricky. The Shockwave file navigation bar will reside at the top level of the EXER0804 directory, but the *prob01fc.htm* file will be inside the *probish* folder. A relative URL reference in an HTML page is relative to the position of the HTML page; all graphics, etc., are referenced from that position. Shockwave movies can use relative URLs, but the URL is relative to the Shockwave movie, and if the movie is in a different location than the HTML page, that has to be taken into consideration when writing relative URL references. Press on the Script Entry button and edit the script to read as follows:

```
on mouseDown
  GotoNetPage "probcov.htm"
end
```

The relative URL tells Shockwave to load the *probcov.htm* page from the same directory as the *probnav.dcr* movie. Press Enter to close the window.

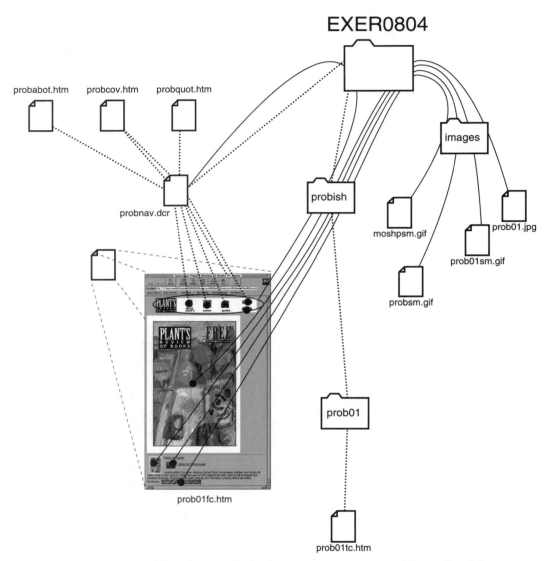

Figure 8-26: *A diagram of the relative calls in the various components of the* **prob01fc.htm** *page.*

Step 17. Select the cells in frames 21 and 22 of channel 1. This section of the *probnav.dcr* movie will be used for the *prob01tc.htm* page, and the button should link to the *prob01fc.htm* page. This is the same link as the cells in frames 1 to 12. Use the Script pull-down menu in the Score window (it should be script 6) to assign the script used in frames 1 to 12 in channel 1 to these frames.

Step 18. Select the cells in frames 26 and 27 of channel 1. This section of the *probnav.dcr* movie will be used for the *prob02fc.htm* page, and the button should link to the *probcov.htm* page at the main level of the EXER0804 directory. This is the same link as the cells in frames 16 and 17. Use the Script pull-down menu in the Score window (it should be script 9) to assign the script used in frames 16 and 17 in channel 1 to these frames.

Step 19. Select the cells in frames 21 to 27 of channel 2 of the Score. These are the down arrow buttons that will appear on the pages *prob02fc.htm* and *prob01tc.htm*. These pages have no subsidiary links in this exercise. Press Del or use menu command Edit | Clear Cells to delete the sprites.

Step 20. Select frames 16 and 17 in channel 2 of the Score. The down arrow for the page this section of the navigation bar will appear on, *prob01fc.htm*, should link to the file *prob01tc.htm*. Click on the Script Entry area of the Score window to create a new Score script and enter the following:

```
on mouseDown
  GotoNetPage "probish/prob01/prob01fc.htm"
end
```

The target page is two directory levels down from the main level where the Shockwave movie *probnav.drc* will be. Press Enter to close the Script window.

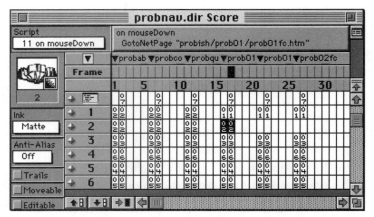

Figure 8-27: *The completed Score of* probnav.dir.

Step 21. Save the *probnav.dir* movie with the menu command File | Save or Command / Ctrl+S, and use Command / Ctrl+O or the File | Open menu item to open the Director movie *probabot.dir*.

Step 22. This movie is empty! It is, however, of the same dimensions as the *probnav.htm* movie, and versions of this movie will be used as loaders for the navigation bar. Open the Score window and double-click on the Script channel in frame 4. Add the loop script as follows:

```
on exitFrame
  go to the frame - 1
end
```

Press Enter to close the Script window.

Step 23. Double-click in frame 2 of the Script channel. Add this script:

```
on exitFrame
  GotoNetMovie "probnav.dcr#probabot"
end
```

Press Enter to close the Script window.

Step 24. Save the movie with the menu command File | Save or Command / Ctrl+S.

Step 25. Double-click in frame 2 of the Script channel. Modify the script like this:

```
on exitFrame
  GotoNetMovie "probnav.dcr#probcov"
end
```

Press Enter to close the Script window.

Step 26. Use the File I Save As menu command to save this movie as *probcov.dir* in the main level of EXER0804 along with *probcov.htm*.

Step 27. Double-click in frame 2 of the Script channel. Modify the script like this:

```
on exitFrame
  GotoNetMovie "probnav.dcr#probquot"
end
```

Press Enter to close the Script window.

Step 28. Use the File I Save As menu command to save this movie as *probquot.dir* in the same directory as *probquot.htm*.

Step 29. Double-click in frame 2 of the Script channel. Modify the script again:

```
on exitFrame
  GotoNetMovie "../probnav.dcr#prob01fc"
end
```

Press Enter to close the Script window.

Step 30. Use the File I Save As menu command to save this movie as *prob01fc.dir* in the *probish* folder along with *prob01fc.htm*.

Step 31. Double-click in frame 2 of the Script channel. Modify the script— you know the drill:

```
on exitFrame
  GotoNetMovie "../probnav.dcr#prob02fc"
end
```

Press Enter to close the Script window.

Step 32. Use the File I Save As menu command to save this movie as *prob02fc.dir* in the *probish* folder along with *prob02fc.htm*.

Step 33. Double-click in frame 2 of the Script channel. Modify the script—this is the last one, I promise:

```
on exitFrame
  GotoNetMovie "../../probnav.dcr#prob02tc"
end
```

Note the extra periods and slash in this URL. Press Enter to close the Script window.

Step 34. Use the File I Save As menu command to save this movie as *prob01tc.dir* in the *prob01* folder along with *prob01tc.htm*.

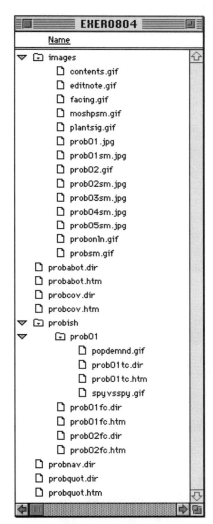

Figure 8-28: *The expanded folder view of EXER0804 on the Mac OS.*

Step 35. Go through each of the 7 Director movies with the Afterburner and create Shockwave movies from them.

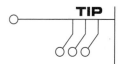

TIP

On the Mac OS Finder in System 7 and later, you can use the View I by Name menu command to see all of the files in the EXER0804 directory, click on the folder triangles to view their contents in the same window (hold down the Option key when clicking on the triangle to open subdirectories as well). Then you can just drag all of the Director files to an alias of the Afterburner icon on the desktop. Each movie being burned will come up with a dialog box asking you where to save the file—just make sure it's being saved into the right place.

Step 36. Use your Web browser to locally open any of the files from any-where in the EXER0804 directory. Clicking on any of the main-level buttons on any page will always take you to one of those three pages; clicking on any arrow will move you one level up or down in the directory structure.

Obviously, this is a fairly simple directory structure, and per-haps it seems like a lot of work to some, but for anyone who's spent any time creating imagemap files, this is a cakewalk.

This is also a bit of a worst-case scenario for navigation bars. This exercise uses relative URLs in order to make it possible to experiment with the files by opening them locally from your hard drive. Using complete (including an *http://* header and full do-main/path info) or absolute (full path info) URLs would eliminate any need to figure out what was relative to what.

Another potential simplifying factor could be the way in which your server is organized. Some administrators prefer to store all HTML files at the main level of the server, with images in one subdirectory and, potentially, movies in another. While not exactly optimal for very large sites (every page has to have a distinct name, and searching for files can be tedious with thousands of individual files in the same folder), again, it cuts down on the likelihood of complex relative URLs.

It probably wouldn't be a good idea to incorporate every single page of your site into one navigation bar (although it would be possible). Adding every single page of a fairly dynamic site could get a little old. But sections of a large site could have their own bars with just a little bit of work for upkeep.

More complex animation, sound effects, better identification of the button destinations, sprucing up the loader movies, and other variables are a cinch to add to navigation bars. Have fun!

Stretching Your Bitmap Dollar

Apart from sound, bitmap images are the most byte-costly elements of Shockwave movies. While the graphics compressors in the Afterburner are very good, there are limits to how far lossless compression schemes such as the ones employed by Shockwave can go.

Exercise 8-5: Tiling objects.

There's nothing like a nice bitmap image to give a graphic some "tooth," a little bit of a rough edge that makes it not so slick-looking. Large bitmaps come at a cost, though, and it's high enough that even CD-ROM developers have to watch out for it. Pity the poor Shockwave designer, stuck with an average user download speed of somewhere between 1 and 3K/sec.

The images below are from two versions of the same movie—one that you've seen part of already in Exercise 8-1: the *moshload.dir* file that was used as a loader for the Moshofsky/Plant Web Server page. The one on the right looks and works identically to the one on the left, but it's one-and-a-half times the size of the other file.

Figure 8-29: *Two versions of the* moshload.dcr *file.*

The trick is to use the Director's ability to tile bitmaps as fills for objects created with the Tools palette.

Numerous tools exist for creating the type of seamless bitmap images that are useful with tiling, including Specular's TextureScape and Xaos Tools's Terrazzo. Others can be purchased as part of CD-ROM image packages like Artbeats's WebTools collection or Jawai Interactive's Screen Caffeine Pro. Whatever you want to use as a tile in Shockwave (or Director, for that matter) needs to be a multiple of 16 pixels in size in each dimension.

Figure 8-30: *KPT Seamless Welder—before and after.*

An invaluable tool for creating tile images is MetaTools's KPT Seamless Welder plug-in for Photoshop and other image editors; it comes as a part of the Kai Power Tools set (available for both Windows and the Mac OS). The same set of plug-ins includes KPT Interform, which allows you to create new textures from the interactions between existing textures.

Once you have an image that you want to use to tile, save it as a PICT file.

Step 1. Start Director and create a new movie.

Step 2. Use the File | Import menu command or Command/Ctrl+J to import the PICT file *tile.pct* from the EXER0805 directory.

Step 3. Double-click on cast member 1, *tile.pct*, to bring up the Paint edit window.

Step 4. Choose Paint | Tiles from the menu bar.

Step 5. Select one of the 8 tile positions underneath the larger windows, choose a tile to replace, then push the button labeled "Created from Cast member #." Use the scroll bars if necessary to select cast member 1.

Step 6. In the Tiles dialog box, you'll see the bitmap on the left as a single pattern and on the right as a tiled pattern. Changing the Width and Height pop-up menus will modify the outline shown around the single tile, either cropping the image (which will most likely make it non-seamless) or leaving large white gaps at the edges (most certainly not elegant). Press OK to close the window.

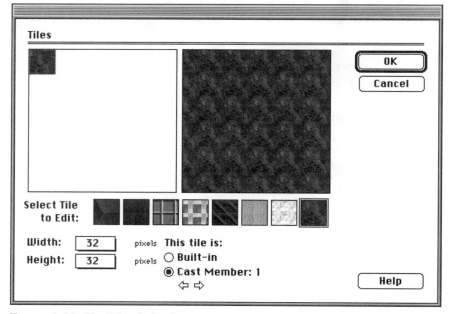

Figure 8-31: *The Tiles dialog box.*

Step 7. Choose the filled circle tool from the Tools palette.

Step 8. Selct the texture you've created in the texture pop-up box of the Tools palette.

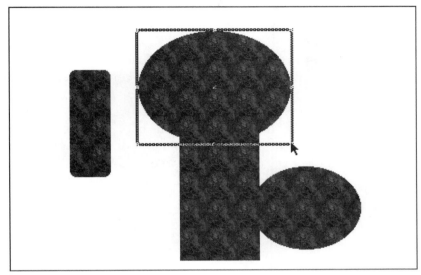

Figure 8-32: *Drawing shapes on the Stage with the tile.*

Step 9. Draw a circle on the Stage with the circle tool. The circle will be filled with the pattern, and the whole thing is very small.

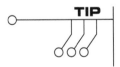

You can draw filled paint shapes using the same tile, but there is no memory saving to be gained, as the tile is immediately converted to a bitmap the size of the new shape.

Moving On

These are just a few of the tips and tricks the early Shockwave designers have come up with. Watch the Ventana Online Companion area for more, along with samples and references to the latest hot sites.

Shockwave is a new and (so far) constantly changing technology, as is the rest of the World Wide Web and—for that matter—multimedia. New techniques are constantly being tried out and developed, and are often shared by members of the community of developers.

During the time I wrote this book, I was constantly connected to some of the best information and day-to-day updates on what people were using Shockwave for and how they were doing it. After you've checked out the appendices in the back of this book, and the Ventana Online Companion, take a look at some of the Web sites below for more of the latest information on what promises to be one of the stars of the World Wide Web: Shockwave for Director.

Macromedia, Inc.

http://www.macromedia.com—The place to go for the latest versions of plug-ins and other Shockwave products.

Direct-L

http://www.tile.net/tile/listserv/directl.html—The home page of the Direct-L e-mail list server, get hundreds of messages a day (mostly about Director)!

Director Web

http://www.mcli.dist.maricopa.edu/director/—The ultimate Web site for Director users, featuring searchable archives of the Direct-L archives, sample movies, and—of course—lots of stuff on Shockwave.

ShockeR

http://www.shocker.com/shocker/info.html—A site dedicated to Shockwave information, known best for the ShockeR e-mail list server, tailored specifically to Shockwave movie creators. Important announcements usually get posted to both ShockeR and Direct-L, but it's been a bit more focused on Web-related subjects.

This book should get you off the ground with Shockwave. By now you're probably already thinking of ways to use interactive button bars with sound and catchy graphics on your (or your client's) site. Remember that none of the techniques in this book are exclusionary; use *everything* at your command to add interactivity to your Web pages—with Shockwave for Director.

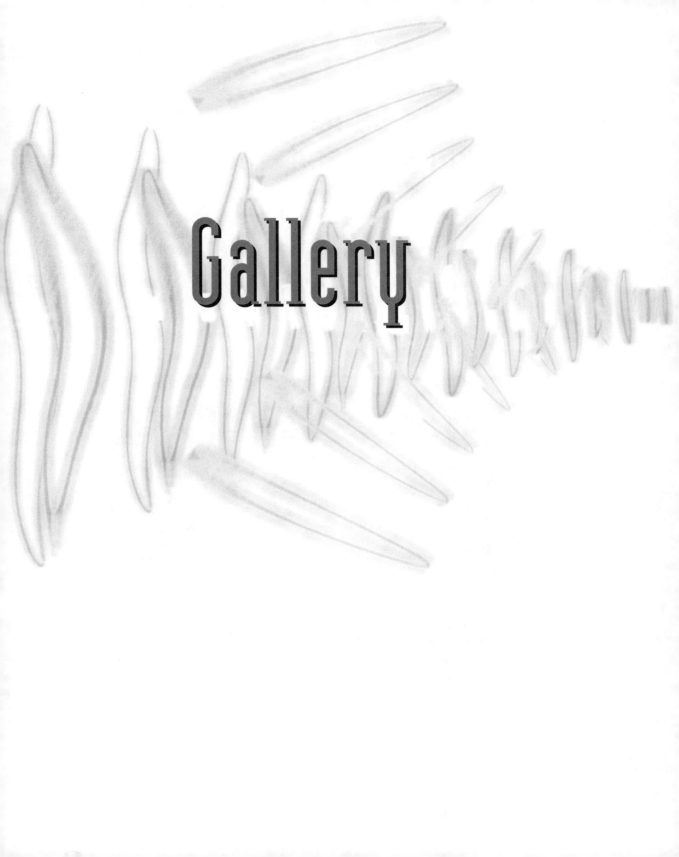

Gallery

CyberKids Shockwave Movie: My Computerized House

Original Story: Wulia Bekoi
Adaptation By: Mountain Lake Software, Inc.

Wulia Bekoi wrote the original story "My Computerized House" in 1994 when she was nine years old. Her story was one of the contest winners in the 1994 CyberKids writing contest. With Wulia's permission, we adapted the original story and art to create a playful set of animations inspired by her work. The purpose of these movies is to demonstrate the potential for using dynamic media for kids on the Web.

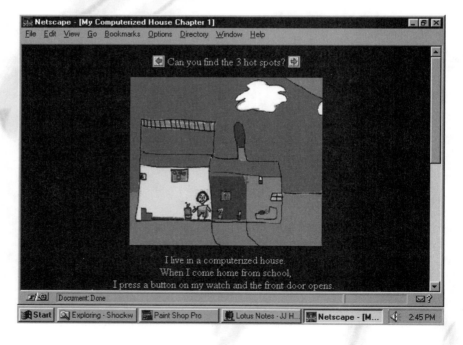

Credits

Dave Berry, dunda@dnai.com, is a consultant who specializes in the design and implementation of Internet, database, Shockwave, and Java applications. Dave is responsible for the implementation of *My Computerized House*, translating the static story into an interactive animation. His wife, Mary Ann Goldstein, assisted with the design and user interface, and their son, Jacob, provided some of the sounds. Dave's home page is http://www.dnai.com/~dunda/dbc.html

Sharon Evans, sevansup@aol.com, a professional digital and traditional artist in San Francisco, assisted with minor adaptations of the original graphics created by Wulia Bekoi. In the past, she has taught art to children and has created paintings adapted from children's original art.

Shara Karasic, shara@mtlake.com, is an online writer and editor for CyberKids and Cyberteens. Shara created the HTML pages for the Shockwave version of "My Computerized House." More recently, she's been reviewing scores of Web sites for a client of Mountain Lake Software.

Julie Richer, julie@mtlake.com, is the president of Mountain Lake Software, Inc., and publisher of CyberKids and Cyberteens Web sites. Julie originated the CyberKids International Writing and Art contest, which was the source of the original story, "My Computerized House," by Wulia Bekoi. Inspired by Wulia's story, Julie provided the vision to animate "My Computerized House" as a set of Shockwave movies.

Mark Richer, mark@mtlake.com, codesigner of CyberKids and Cyberteens Web sites, has been designing software for the past fifteen years. His interests include the Internet, user interface design, and object-oriented software systems. Mark provided project management and user interface expertise in the development of the Shockwave movies and HTML pages. He is currently providing freelance services to several companies and can be reached by e-mail or at (415) 387-4337 in San Francisco, CA.

Mountain Lake Software, Inc. is an educational software publisher in San Francisco, CA, that creates and publishes software products as well as the highly regarded Cyberteens (http://www.mtlake.com/cyberteens) and CyberKids (http://www.cyberkids.com) Web sites.

Mountain Lake Software, Inc.
298 Fourth Ave, #401
San Francisco, CA, 94118

Phone: (415) 752-6515
Fax: 415-752-6506
E-mail: editor@cyberteens.com

How My Computerized House Was Created

When Shockwave was announced and the white paper released in May of 1995, we were very excited about the opportunity to deliver dynamic media for kids on the Web using Macromedia Director. Julie suggested that Dave create an animated version of "My Computerized House," a story by Wulia Bekoi that we published in the CyberKids online magazine.

Although we were excited, the original specification for Shockwave left out many of the technical details we needed to begin the project. A goal from the beginning was to produce something that would get exposure during Macromedia's rollout, so we didn't want to wait to get started. Even though we were not participants in the Shockwave beta program, the Direct-L mailing list and Macromedia's Web site provided enough information for us to realize our goal.

Design

Our approach from the beginning was to focus on the content and not try to stretch the technology, because many Shockwave implementation issues were still unclear. Details on movie borders, new Lingo commands, compression, and HTML extensions were not available at first. All we knew for sure was that we would be able to play a Director movie inside of the Netscape Navigator browser window without a helper application.

Bandwidth is clearly a major consideration and constraint when designing a Shockwave application. Macromedia had suggested 100K for a maximum file size for Shockwave movies, to be delivered over a 14.4 modem connection. Someone on the Direct-L (Macromedia Director) mailing list had pointed out that ten 60K movies would be much more effective than one 600K movie. This, in essence, validated our choice of "My Computerized House" for a set of Shockwave movies because it consisted of ten chapters, each accompanied by a simple picture and a short description. By limiting each movie or chapter to 100K, Dave could keep within Macromedia's guidelines and still include some playful animations, sounds, and user interactions.

Navigation between the movies and the Web pages was an early challenge that we easily resolved by deciding that all of the links to Web pages, including going to the next and previous movie, be specified with HTML and GIF images on the Web page—that is, outside the borders of the Shockwave movies. We also experimented early on with using a matching border color in the Director movie and the HTML page, but discarded that idea in lieu of a simple black background which would hide the border of the movie within the Web browser's window.

In general, we decided not to use any feature that has traditionally been problematic in cross-platform Director development. This includes custom palettes, Movies In A Window (MIAW), menus, digital video such as QuickTime, text, or any other linked media. In our design, all of the data had to live in a self-contained Director movie and be platform-independent.

Implementation

With the major technical design issues behind us, it was now just a matter of delivering ten cross-platform Director movies from pre-existing bitmap files. We made 8-bit graphics using the Macintosh system palette, allowing Director to map the colors. After some experimentation with the images, we settled on a 4" x 3" movie size which fits into the Web browser's window on a 640 x 480-resolution monitor. The images when originally imported had a lot of texture, some of which had to be cleaned up because of the color-mapping differences in the Photoshop document and the Mac system palette. Some of the texture was preserved while other areas were smoothed out. The text was converted to 1-bit bitmaps to avoid font substitution issues.

The majority of the time spent on graphics was in scraping the interesting items on the pages we wanted to animate, and providing suitable replacement for that area in the background bitmap cast member. Once the new cast members we wanted to animate were created, it was just a matter of providing a Lingo framework for the animation. Using Lingo's Parent/Child object-oriented scripting capabilities and single frame animation, we put together a simple set of objects that were created at the beginning of the movie and checked in the score script of the animation. Here's the entire score script for the first movie.

```
global firstPass, gObjects

on exitFrame
  go the frame
end

on enterFrame
  if firstPass = TRUE then
    set firstPass = FALSE
    initClouds
    initBallonText
    initHand
    initDoor
    initCat
```

```
    else
      moveClouds(getAt(gObjects, 1))
    end if
end

on idle
  doHeadCheck(getAt(gObjects,2))
  doHandCheck(getAt(gObjects,3))
  doCatcheck(getAt(gObjects,5))
end
```

Because the Shockwave plug-in was not available during testing, we used a Director helper application that played the movies in a separate application window. By putting the Director movies on an Internet site, we were able to gauge how long it took to download the movies. By overlaying the window of the helper application onto the Netscape browser window, we were able to demo the movies as they would ultimately look using Shockwave.

The sounds were key to the project, and we used a Media Vision sound input device and an Advent microphone to create them. They were input to and edited on a PowerMac 7100/AV with SoundEdit Pro. It was very important to fully exploit sound while not sacrificing file size so that the sounds represented roughly only 20 percent of the overall file size. After some experimentation, we discovered that MACE compression did not work on Windows, so we had to normalize all of the sounds to 8 bits at 11.127 kHz uncompressed.

We finished the final movie right after the pre-Beta Shockwave plug-in for Windows was released to developers. This last movie just lists credits, but it includes an interesting random music sequence derived from a single hum into the microphone. We stepped up the notes to create an 8-note scale and randomized the playback order and interval to simulate a computer playing music as the credits rolled.

Finally, we'd like to share some of our thoughts and experiences as early adopters of Shockwave. We began working on this project shortly after Macromedia announced Shockwave and released a white page in May 1994. First of all, we had to have confidence that Shockwave would be delivered in the coming months and that it would be successful. Second, we had to visualize how it would look and work without having the actual Shockwave software to test. By making conservative but solid design decisions as described above, we were able to design movies that worked well without having the plug-in in our hands.

When a pre-Beta release of Shockwave was announced for developers only on the Direct-L mail list, Macromedia representatives mentioned that they would put links on their Web site to third-party Shockwave pages—if a working URL was submitted within a week. Because we were almost done with our project, we had a significant advantage over others who were waiting for the plug-in before doing serious development. As a result, *My Computerized House* was an early favorite and was included on Macromedia's Shockwave Gallery page. We still think it's cute and fun, but by getting it out early we certainly maximized the impact of our efforts.

Cyberteens Shockwave Movies

Creator: Mountain Lake Software, Inc.

This is a collection of Shockwave movies that were created as a dynamic and abstract expression of the themes in several of the main sections of the Cyberteens Web site (http://www.mtlake.com/cyberteens):

1. Cyberteens *Connection*, a bulletin board
2. *Games*, online games
3. *Launchpad*, a database of URLs for young people
4. *Zeen*, an online magazine

Credits

Jennifer Alexander, jennalex@sirius.com, a freelance digital artist in San Francisco, is actively exploring the visual and expressive aspects of the new technologies. Beginning her career as a scene designer for the theatre, she is now bringing her sense of vision and drama to the digital world. It is her goal to create interesting environments and experiences in cyberspace that break all of the laws of gravity. Some of her work can be found at http://www.imaja.com/Change/Jennifer/J.Alexander.html.

Kirk Keller, kirk_keller@socketis.net, has done freelance multimedia authoring and computer animation since 1988. He programmed and appeared in the popular SPG-Blast Shockwave game, one of the first Shockwave applications on the Internet and the first site to be named by Macromedia as the Cool Shocked Site of the Moment (**note:** he was the cute one in glasses). Samples of Kirk's work can be found at: http://selfpub.www.columbia.mo.us/~kirk_keller. Kirk is planning to create an online magazine in the next year with Matthew Kerner on Macromedia Director authoring.

Matthew Kerner, c642133@showme.missouri.edu, is a student at the University of Missouri, studying Communications. He has been doing freelance graphic design and multimedia development since 1994. Matthew has created several Shockwave applications using object-oriented programming techniques. He also contributed to the development of SPG-Blast (**note:** he was the other cute one in glasses). Matthew is planning to create an online magazine in the next year with Kirk Keller on Macromedia Director authoring. Matthew's home page is http://www.missouri.edu/~c642133. He can be reached by e-mail or at 18502 East 27th Terrace South, Independence, Missouri 64075-1526.

Mark Richer, mark@mtlake.com, codesigner of Cyberteens and CyberKids Web sites, has been designing software for the past fifteen years. His interests include the Internet, user interface design, and object-oriented software systems. Mark represented Mountain Lake Software, Inc. as project manager for the Cyberteens movies. He is currently providing freelance services to several companies and can be reached by e-mail or at (415) 387-4337 in San Francisco, CA.

Mountain Lake Software, Inc. is an educational software publisher in San Francisco, CA, that creates and publishes software products as well as the highly regarded Cyberteens (http://www.mtlake.com/cyberteens) and CyberKids (http://www.cyberkids.com) Web sites.

Mountain Lake Software, Inc.
298 Fourth Ave, #401
San Francisco, CA 94118

Phone: (415) 752-6515
Fax: 415-752-6506
E-mail: editor@cyberteens.com

How the Cyberteens Movies Were Created

Jennifer had been creating graphics for the CyberKids and Cyberteens Web sites for several months when Mark asked her to create original art for a Shockwave movie for Cyberteens. Jennifer came up with a new visual concept for the Cyberteens site. As Jennifer recalls,

> "My intent was to create an animation that could be part of a series, with characters and environments that would repeat through varying situations. The different sections of the site should be reflected in the characters and the action. Working with symbols that teenagers could relate to and would enjoy looking at was also important. It was a vital choice to go with symbolic imagery that dealt with the abstract nature of cyber-space. And so, after stewing on it for a few nights, creating some rough drafts, I presented my ideas to the other Cyberteens folks (Shara Karasic, Julie Richer, and Mark Richer). Next I arrived at the point where I began determining the action sequences and creating the artwork, which was done in Adobe Illustrator and Adobe Photoshop."

We still needed a Director programmer to create the Shockwave movies, so we turned to the Direct-L (Director) mailing list for help. We were pleasantly surprised to get several responses on such short notice during the Christmas holidays. Both Matthew and Kirk replied independently, though they had worked together on previous projects. Using the Internet, we transferred files and e-mail messages back and forth, and completed the project on a short deadline—without Kirk and Matthew in Missouri ever actually meeting with Jennifer and Mark in San Francisco! The most remarkable part of the process was how Jennifer, Matthew, and Kirk communicated their ideas about the animations by electronic communication only. These animations were truly created about, for, and *in* cyberspace.

Jennifer supplied Matthew and Kirk with the animation cels (i.e., different pictures of how the objects looked when in motion) as well as a general description of how the animation should look. The description was open enough to give Matthew and Kirk room for changes to suit programming needs or even add some ideas. They determined how the animation would work and selected the fewest number of cels they could use.

The overall description of the animation was general enough that they could add elements as the animation progressed. In the *Connection* movie, for example, Jennifer's instructions were simply that the eyes would come out of the side of the screen. As Kirk began animating them, he realized that they looked like a couple of fish. So he finished the animation with this in mind and added the water sound.

In general, animations should be created using Lingo as much as possible. However, if the animation is complex or if you're on a tight deadline, using the score is a good idea.

Here's an overview of each of the Cyberteens Shockwave movies.

Overview of the Connection Movie

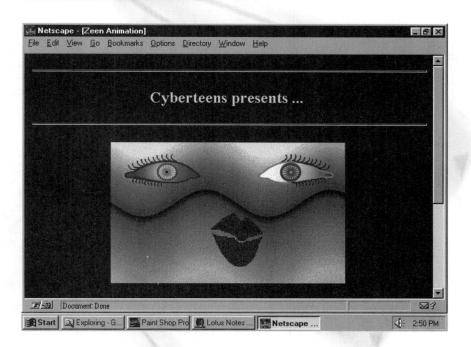

This movie presented a difficult task. The animation in this movie required several elements to be moving up and down and turning. This would require several different cast members and, thus, increase the size of the movie. To reduce this somewhat, Kirk used the scaling features in Director to simulate some movement. When the eyes turned, Kirk would set one keyframe of the eyes at full size (frame 78) and another with them scaled to one pixel width (frame 84). Kirk then animated in between these two keyframes. At the end of this sequence, Kirk then added a keyframe of the eyes going in the opposite direction, scaled to one pixel in width (frame 85). Kirk then set another keyframe of this same cast member scaled to full size (frame 90) and animated in between them.

This technique works great for animations such as flipping tiles or rotating logos. Although the complexity of this animation required that Kirk use frames for this scaling technique in the score, this technique can be even more effective (and faster) if Lingo is used to do the scaling. For an example of this, check out Kirk's home page at: http://selfpub.www.columbia.mo.us/ ~kirk_keller.

Overview of the Games Movie

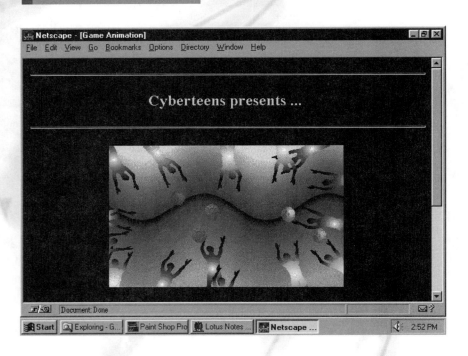

Sometimes you have to be a little creative when working on a tight deadline and with few resources. In this animation, what was needed was the sound of a volleyball being hit by players. The only problem was that we really didn't have time to go out and capture audio of a volleyball being hit. So instead, Matthew captured audio of Kirk hitting a soda can with an ink pen. Matthew then took this sound into Sound Edit 16. There Matthew slowed down the tempo of the sound and added a slight amount of reverb. The result was that kind of metallic sound that a volleyball makes when you hit it.

Overview of the Launchpad Movie

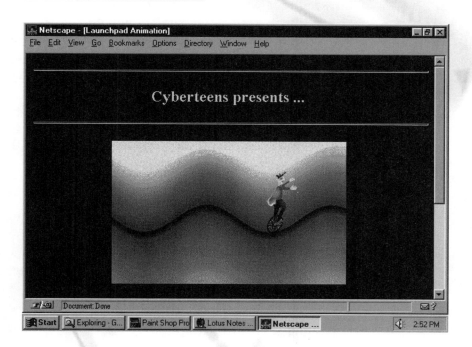

This animation required that one general sound (the squeaking of the unicycle wheel) be synched with the animation to help create the illusion of the unicyclist speeding up or slowing down. To do this, Kirk simply split the sound effect into two parts—a squeak-up and a squeak-down sound. When the unicylist slowed down, the number of frames between the two sounds would be increased.

The complexity of this animation required that the cels of the animation be placed by hand in the score instead of being animated with Lingo. To make the animation more believable, Kirk followed these two rules.

1. This type of animation is not uniform.

If you look at the animation in the frames of this movie, you will see that the movement is not uniform. Some cels of the animation remain for one frame. Some cels remain for two or three frames. This is important in order to convey the instability of riding on a unicycle.

2. Use exaggerated movement to "telegraph" the direction in which your animated character will go.

Jennifer supplied Kirk with several animation cels of the unicyclist. These cels gave Kirk the general idea of how the artist wanted the unicyclist to move. Of these cels, Kirk then picked the ones that best exaggerated the forward and backward movement of the unicyclist. Note that movement exaggeration is a standard technique that has been used for years in traditional animation.

Overview of the Zeen Movie

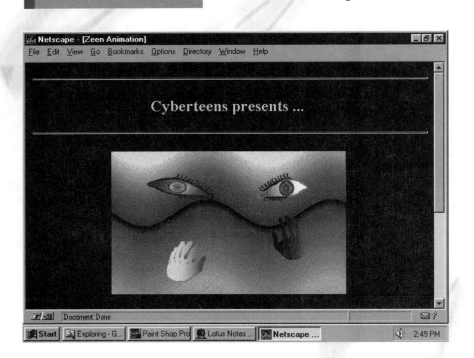

In this movie, Matthew used a layering of the background graphics similar to what was used in the SPG-Blast game. In this case, Matthew took the graphic Jennifer created and split it into two graphics of sky and hills. Matthew then layered the reader (in channel 2) between the sky (channel 1) and the hills (channel 4) so that the end effect was the reader coming up from behind the hill.

In this animation, the movement was fairly simple. We just needed a book with a trail of three books flying through the air. This is a perfect candidate for Lingo-based animation.

Matthew took 46 cels (or cast members) of the book flying. The trailing books would simply be old positions where the lead book had flown. With this in mind, channels 7 to 12 were set as puppet sprites. Lingo was used to set which cel (or cast member) they were to display as well as where they were to be positioned on the stage. This resulted in an animation that only took up two frames in the score. At the end, when the reader pops up, Lingo then hides the members of the book trail one at a time.

Pretty Good Golf

Programmer: Gary Rosenzweig

The original concept for *Pretty Good Golf* was to come up with a simple golf game that would be small enough for people without high-speed internet connections to play. I didn't want this restriction to affect the features of the game. There would have to be full 18-hole courses, a selection of clubs, a score sheet, and a screen design and interaction that would make playing it fun.

The hardest obstacle was to be able to represent a golf course without taking up several hundred K of data. If each hole was represented by a bitmapped image, even at 4-bit color depth, then every hole would be about 100K. This means that an entire course would be about 1.8 meg.

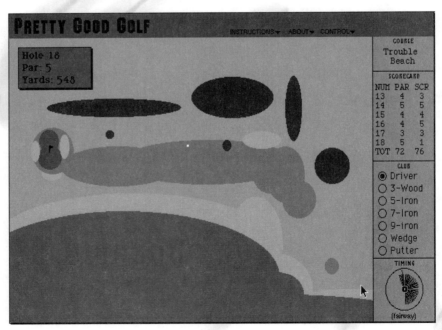

The solution was to use Director's vector graphics. The oval shape seemed to lend itself to golf course design. Groups of trees, lakes, the green, sand traps, and the fairway could all be represented by one or more ovals. I dedicated about 30 sprite channels to ovals. They are all at different positions and have different color assignments.

Now, I just needed a way to load new courses. I could have just created one course for the game and placed it in 18 frames, one for each hole. However, this would have meant having a whole different Shockwave movie for each course.

What I did was use a Director list to describe what a hole should look like. Most sprites were just ovals, with a particular rectangle and color. The only other items were the starting position of the ball and the position of the flag. There were also miscellaneous items like the par for the hole and the position of the hole's sign.

Each hole had its own list with all of these items specified. Then the entire course was a list containing all 18 of these holes. Once it became a list, I could convert it to a string and save it to a text file. It is these files that are loaded over the Internet when a user chooses to play other courses. The "Sample Course" is just stored as text in a cast member inside the Shockwave movie.

This technique kept *Pretty Good Golf* down to about 64K compressed, which includes the "Sample Course." The largest elements inside it are the short sounds, created by my friend Jay Shaffer, who is an expert at producing quality audio with tight file-size restrictions. I can't overemphasize the importance of being able to get more for less when it comes to sound—which is the biggest file-size hog Shockwave developers need to control.

Pretty Good Golf can be found at http://www2.csn.net/ ~rosenz/shock.html. It was featured as Shockwave Site of the Day by Macromedia on February 16, 1996.

WebInvaders

Programmer: Raúl Silva

When we set up AfterShock's home page we wanted to have good examples of Shockwave authoring. We realized that the most demanding use for Shockwave would be to create an arcade game. We wanted a game people were already familiar with, therefore WebInvaders was an obvious choice.

While writing WebInvaders I came upon what is a common problem with Director. Just the invaders alone took up all 48 channels. This would be fine if I did not have to have missiles, bombs, barriers, and so on to worry about. I solved the problem by using composite cast members for the invaders. The invaders really take up only 18 channels. This is done by overlapping two sprites each with 3 invaders on top of each other.

This is a chart I used to figure out the binary combination for each possible combination of invaders.

This complicated things, because I not only had to detect a collision with a sprite but also figure out where on the sprite the collision would take place so that I could remove the appropriate invader. This was solved by a simple if...then routine that calculated where the missile actually hit. For example, if it hit on the top and the top invader was there, then the sprite would change to the cast member with the missing top invader.

This is a slightly modified version of the script. I took out some things that don't relate to the discussion and simplified a few things. It should give you a good idea of how to detect which (if any) invader was hit:

```
on checkInvaderHit me
    --gMissileSprite number is a global that holds the
    --sprite channel for the missile

    --pMySprite is a child property that holds the
    --sprite channel for its group of invaders
    global gMissileSpriteNumber

    --Is there a collision?
    If sprite gMissileSpriteNumber intersects pMySprite then

    --set up a variable with the vertical position
    --of the sprite
    set myVLoc to (the locV of sprite  pMySprite) - 28
    --NOTE: 28 is half the height of a full invader sprite.
    --It cannot be done dynamically because the height will
    --vary if there are less than 3 invaders on it. We
    --subtract it from the vertical position
    --of the sprite to find out the location of the
    --TOP of the sprite.

    --set a variable with the vertical location of the missile
      set VmissileLocation  to the locVof sprite
gMissileSpriteNumber

    --was the top invader hit?
    --we add 13 (which is the height of the top invader)
    --to determine the range. This will check the top
    --13 pixels of the sprite for a collision.
      if VmissileLocation < myVLoc+13 and VmissileLocation >
myVLoc then
```

```
--if not already destroyed then...
    if getAt(pmyList,1) then

--Set the position for this alien to 0
    setat(pmylist,1,0)

--Replace with the proper cast
--(replace cast is a user defined handler. Its shown
--after this script)
    replaceCast

    --We are done here
    exit
  end if
 end if


--was the middle invader hit?
--we use a range between 24 and 35. 35-24=11 The
--height of the second invader! We start at 24 to
--account for the empty space between the top and
--middle invaders,
 If VmissileLocation > myVLoc+24 and VmissileLocation <
myVLoc+35 then
    if getAt(pmyList,2) then
      setAt (pmyList,2,0)
      replaceCast
      exit
    end if
  end if


--was the center invader hit?
  if VmissileLocation > myVLoc+47 and VmissileLocation <
myVLoc+57 then
    if getAt(pmyList,3) then
      setAt (pmyList,3,0)
      replaceCast
      exit
    end if
  end if
 end if
end
```

In order for this to work, I had to keep track of the status of each sprite (to know which invader if any was missing). Each of the 16 sprites has a list that holds this information. The list is structured in a binary system. If all invaders are present, then the list is equal to [1,1,1]. If only the middle invader is missing then the list is equal to [1,0,1]. When the sprite collides with a missile, it first checks where it happened and then looks to see if that position is 0 or 1. If the position is 1, then it converts the binary list to a decimal number. For example, [1,0,1] equals 5 in decimal. Once it knows this, it looks for the number of the cast member named "5" and assigns it to the sprite.

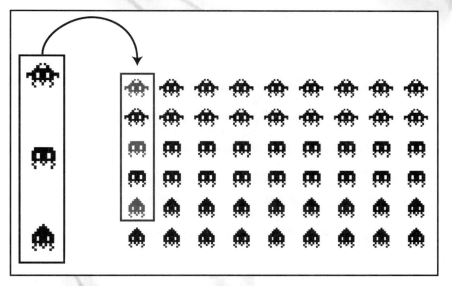

Each column of invaders is made from two overlapping sprites. Instead of 48 sprites, this compositon now uses 18!

Whenever a collision between the missile and an invader is detected, this script is called up to remove the dead invader:

```
on replace cast

-- Define a variable that will hold the cast name of
-- the sprite.
-- It starts out with a numerical value but we will convert
-- it to a string at the end.
    set myCastName to 0

-- *simple binary to decimal converter*

-- Check each of the 3 values on this child's status list and
-- add the corresponding value if necessary

   if getAt(myInvaderlist,1) then set myCastNum ¬
      to myCastName +1
   if getAt(myInvaderlist,2) then set myCastNum ¬
      to myCastName +2
   if getAt(myInvaderlist,3) then set myCastNum ¬
      to myCastName +4

--If myCastname is not zero then set the cast number
--of the sprite to the string equivalent of myCastName.
   if myCastName then
      set the castnum of sprite mySprite to the number ¬
         of cast string(myCastName)
   else

-- If myCastName is equal to zero then set the cast number
-- of the sprite to 0. (Which will make it disappear)
      set the castnum of sprite mySprite to myCastName
   end if
end
```

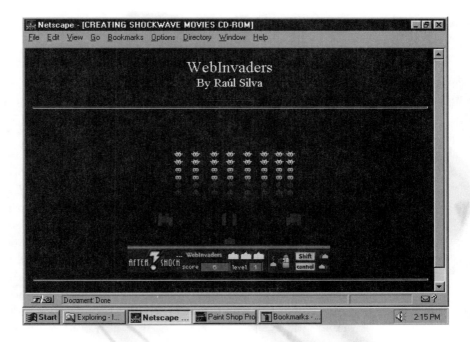

Credits

Raúl Silva has been working with Director since 1989. He is one of the leading Director experts in the nation. Recently he founded AfterShock, a company that develops interactive titles for the Web. AfterShock's page can be reached at http://www.ashock.com. Raúl's home page can be reached at http://www.tezcat.com/~raul.

Bouncing Miaws!

Programmer: David Yang

This movie was created to test the Shockwave technology when it first came out. I wanted to create a simple game without spending too much time and too many resources.

All the sound effects, music, and artwork were created in-house using standard production tools: SoundEdit 16, Adobe Photoshop, and of course Macromedia Director. Voices (with help from my wife) were digitized into SoundEdit 16 and were manipulated and saved as 11.025 kHz (for minimal space and compatibility for cross-platform playback). The initial version did not have a music track; I created the music later on and it was digitized into SoundEdit 16 as well.

To create simple animated effects, each miaw is made up of six casts (three for bouncing and three for recycling). The house and the background were also hand-drawn in Director's paint window. Adobe Photoshop was used for scaling, cropping, and creating the credits screen.

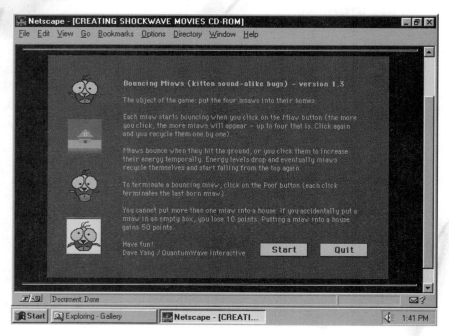

Programming

I programmed the movie using parent/child (object-oriented) methods to simplify keeping track of individual animated casts. Each miaw offspring behaves according to the "rules" set out for them: moving, recycling, and landing. Creating and destroying these miaw objects are handled in the movie script by sending messages to each individual offspring. When a miaw is created, it is placed in the actorList; this list is used to keep track of objects for receiving the stepFrame message. Sprites are also "recycled" as new miaws are created and old ones destroyed. Full source to the movie is included, as well as stand-alone versions for both Macs and PCs.

Obstacles When Creating the Movie

There was one thing that took more time than others during the development of this game: trying to figure out why the Mac version performed much slower than the PC counterpart (both stand-alone versions play at normal speed). This problem is most noticeable when the mouse is moved rapidly when the movie is playing inside Netscape 2.0 (including beta and final versions); Microsoft's Internet Explorer (Version 2.0b3) performs slightly better. As of this writing, the problem with the speed performance on the Mac still exists with the final version of the Shockwave plug-in for Director 4.0 and Netscape Navigator 2.01.

As this has been a rapidly developed game, there is much to be improved. I would like to hear from anyone who has made improvements based on this game and/or anyone interested in creating interactive multimedia on the Internet. Please visit my Web site for the latest updates.

Credits

David specializes in interactive multimedia design, programming, and consulting. His background includes both technical and creative training in computer mathematics, graphic design, and computer graphics.

David formed his company, QuantumWave Interactive, and has been creating a variety of multimedia projects, including corporate presentations, 2D and 3D animations, commercial CD-ROM titles, touch screen kiosks, and interactive multimedia on the Internet. He is also a multimedia consultant and an instructor for the Bell Centre for Creative Communications in Toronto, and has contributed articles for an international computer graphics magazine.

David can be contacted at: qwi@astral.magic.ca or via his Web site: http://www.magic.ca/~qwi.

Nomis & ShockFish

Programmer: Joseph Fish of Multi Digital Media, Inc.

Nomis and ShockFish were created by Joseph Fish of Multi Digital Media, Inc. They were designed to show the usefulness and functionality of Macromedia's new Shockwave plug-in. Multi Digital Media, Inc. is a Cary, North Carolina, company that specializes in multimedia and Internet solutions. Since 1994, MDM has excelled in the creation of multimedia programs and Internet Web site design. This expertise has enabled MDM to be at the forefront of Shockwave development, where packing a lot of information into a small file is the name of the game.

Multi Digital Media, Inc.
659 Cary Towne Blvd. #155
Cary, NC 27511
1-800-45MULTI
(919) 319-9788
http://www.mdmi.com

ShockFish was designed to illustrate adding animation to a Web site utilizing a very small-size file. To start, a small and large fish animation was imported into Director, then animated into a series of frames. The only Lingo code used was to allow the click on the center image to GotoNetPage. This file, after compression with Afterburner, is only 11K.

Nomis is an example of an interactive game with motion, sound, and random multilevel game play.

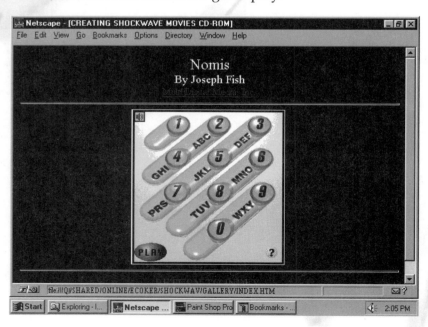

Nomis uses Director's built-in programming language, Lingo, to create the game play. The main functions are explained below.

TonePress is the function called by pressing one of the game buttons. The game buttons pass the variables, Sprite Number (Spr), and Tone (Tne) to the function TonePress.

```
on TonePress Spr, Tne    <-- This is the function
  global SEQUENCE, COUNTER, TEMPO, SISSY, SOUNDER
  if the frame = 17 then
    if SOUNDER = 1 then  <-- See if the sound is on or off.
If on play the sound.
    puppetsound "tone "&Tne
    end if
    set the blend of sprite Spr to 100  <-- Show the button.
    updatestage
    startTimer
    repeat while the stillDown is TRUE < -- Keep showing it
and play the sound while pressed.
      nothing
    end repeat
    set the blend of sprite Spr to 0 <-- Hide the button.
    updatestage
    puppetsound 0 <-- Turn off the sound.
    if value(getaProp(SEQUENCE, COUNTER)) <> Spr ¬
      then  <-- Check to see if selection is correct.
      puppetsound "Wrong"
      repeat while soundbusy(1) is TRUE
       nothing
      end repeat
      set the blend of sprite value(getaProp(SEQUENCE, ¬
      COUNTER)) to 100     <-- Show the correct answer
      if SISSY = 1 then
        put 0 into SISSY
      else
        put 1 into SISSY
      end if
      go to "LOSER"
    else
      if COUNTER=count(SEQUENCE) then <-- Check to see if
this is the last button in the sequence.
```

```
        startTimer
        repeat while the timer < 15
          nothing
        end repeat
        go to "STARTER1"
      else
        set COUNTER=COUNTER+1
      end if
    end if
  end if
end TonePress
```

The exitFrame script below is what controls the game play. It uses random numbers to add to a series of numbers that gets longer and longer. It also keeps track of the level and increases the play speed every six button presses.

```
on exitFrame
  global TEMPO, SEQUENCE, TIMEAROUND, SOUNDER
  set TIMEAROUND=TIMEAROUND+1
  if TIMEAROUND=6 then go to "BOOSTER"  <-- The BOOSTER frame
increases game speed.
  else
    GETRAN <-- Gets a random number using the function below.
    startTimer
    repeat while the timer < 25
      nothing
    end repeat

    repeat with i=1 to count(SEQUENCE) <-- Playback the series
      if SOUNDER = 1 then
        puppetsound the name of cast ¬
        value(getaProp(SEQUENCE, i)-3)  <-- Play the tone.
      end if
      set the blend of sprite getaProp(SEQUENCE, i) ¬
        to 100  <-- Show the button
      updatestage
      startTimer
      repeat while the timer < TEMPO/2  <--Pause where TEMPO
is the game level.
```

```
        nothing
      end repeat
      puppetsound 0  <-- Stop the tone.
      set the blend of sprite getaProp(SEQUENCE, i) ¬
        to 0  <-- Hide the button.
      updatestage
      startTimer
      repeat while the timer < TEMPO/2
        nothing
      end repeat
    end repeat
    go to "RESPONSE"
  end if
end
```

GETRAN is the function that gets the random number and appends the list SEQUENCE with it.

```
on GETRAN
  global SISSY
  if SISSY=1 then <--Checks if the player is in "Sissy Level".
    put RANDOM(6) into RANNUM
    set RANNUM=RANNUM+3
    append SEQUENCE, RANNUM
  else
    put RANDOM(10) into RANNUM
    set RANNUM=RANNUM+3
    append SEQUENCE, RANNUM  <-- Appends the variable RANNUM
to the end of the list SEQUENCE.
  end if
end
```

How could Nomis take more advantage of new Shockwave functions? Use PreloadNetThing to load in different play fields during play, and then use GotoNetMovie to jump to those new play fields. Use GetNetText to import a list of high scores.

These are just some of the ways that Shockwave can be used to create not only straight animation but actual interactive games and other programs to add life to a Web site.

Space Pirate

Programmer: Gary Rosenzweig

The idea for *Space Pirate* came to me about one month after Shockwave had been released for public beta. At that point, most people, including myself, were creating short and simple arcade-style games. These games reminded me of the first games for the Apple II and other computers in the early '80s. It looked like the computer gaming evolution was repeating itself on the Internet.

For instance, in 1993 the Web could only show basic text information, just like the early university mainframes. Then, in 1994 and 1995, static graphics and simple text games started to appear. Shockwave seemed to have the same affect on the Internet that the introduction of the Apple II and Commodore computers had on the computer industry. The restrictions with those were that they were slow and had limited graphics capabilities. The limitation of Shockwave was the slow speed of the Internet.

So I tried to remember what came after the simple arcade games in the early '80s. Several things came to mind, but the one that stuck was the simple trading game. The one I played, and I cannot remember its name, had you as the captain of a trading ship in the far east during the 1800s. You started with little and traded for profit until you were rich.

I then converted this to the flashier idea of space travel and began working on *Space Trader*. Right in the middle of building the movie, I became bored. I needed something more exciting to work on. So *Space Trader* became *Space Pirate*. I added "Attack," "Plunder," and "Steal" to the list of options.

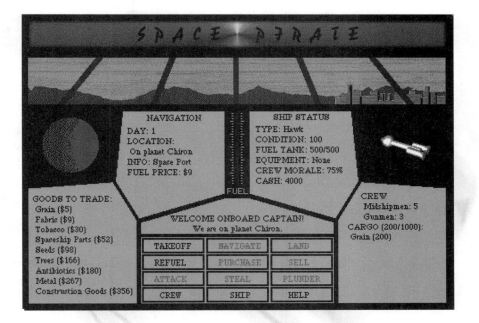

The difficult part of making the game was to present decent graphics without ending up with a 1 meg Shockwave movie. This was complicated by the fact that I wanted players to be able to travel to about 200 planets, each one looking different when seen from the spaceship's window.

I solved this problem by combining several random graphic elements. First, I started with a type of atmosphere—just four different patterns. I threw in "stars" as a fifth pattern, since I already had that image for use during the space travel part of the game. Next, I placed on top of that a matted image of scenery. These are usually mountains, but one option is to have no scenery at all, for a "bland" world. Then, I placed a Director box over the whole image and used a color and a blend setting to tint the entire world.

Once that was done, the man-made objects needed to appear. For instance, for a "Space Port" world, I randomly placed together four different city "modules" to make a somewhat unique city skyline. The three figures show three different variations.

The result is that I had hundreds of thousands of random combinations of scenery. I generated each random planet at the beginning of the game and stored it in a large Lingo list. The user can then revisit worlds during the game and get the same scenery. Space Pirate can be found at http://www2.csn.net/~rosenz/ shock.html. It was featured on the Director Web site as the "coolest shockwave site we have seen yet" for several weeks.

Quatris & 'Stroids

Programmer: Dan Berlyoung

I am in the process of earning my Masters degree in Instructional Technology at Kent State University. My consulting business is a part-time gig that keeps me current on the latest technology and also keeps me visible in the local business community. I started out doing technical support for a local computer retailer and then for a vertical market integrator. Gradually I moved over into the multimedia end of things, working with MPEG, Authorware, laser discs, and CD-ROM writers along the way. I spent all of 1995 working on an educational children's game that was created entirely in Director. Eating, sleeping, and breathing Director for 12 months teaches you a thing or two, and it pays pretty well too. So I decided to go back to college, get my Masters degree and consult on the side.

I've always enjoyed staying on the leading edge of computer technology, so renting myself out as a "technology connoisseur" was a logical thing to do. Director, Shockwave, Java, and the Net in general are the hot things. But five years (maybe fewer) from now they won't be, and something else will be hot. So I ride the wave in front of everybody else and help them get to where I am.

Working with Director and creating multimedia titles was my primary focus until the Web hit and changed everything. Shockwave has opened up an entirely new direction for me. The Internet is not so much a new tool but a new kind of "paper and printing press." I feel like one of the original printers with his brand-new Gutenberg press. The possibilities are (big surprise) endless.

My clientele ranges from radio stations to major shoe corporations. Really, anyone who wants to get a message out to the world. Some want to squeeze it onto a single floppy disc, others want to use a whole CD. And now they have the Web, which along with an incredible list of advantages has an equally large set of limitations.

Saturday!
Dan L. Berlyoung
965 Hunt Street
Akron, Ohio 44306-2410
(330) 785-1326
1dan@mailhost.net
www.mailhost.net/~saturday

Why & How the Movies Were Created

The two games I created, Quatris and 'Stroids, were the result of a good guess and surprisingly few hours. In the middle of 1995, I had heard several rumors that Macromedia was going to bring Director to the Web somehow, and judging from the bandwidth currently available I figured that the movies would have to be as small as possible. So, I decided to see how far and how small I could take Director.

Quatris started out as a game I wrote in BASIC on an Apple][some eight years ago while I was still in college. I figured rewriting it would be a good exercise. It turned out to be a bit more challenging than I had initially thought, but nevertheless I finished it—and was more than a little surprised with its final size and playability.

Heartened by this first success, I then went on to write 'Stroids, a re-creation of the venerable arcade game from yesteryear. This game presented a new set of challenging but not insurmountable problems. My main concern was speed, but with the presence of several comments from users out on the Web asking me to "slow it down," this seems not to be a problem.

Step-by-Step Procedure

Quatris

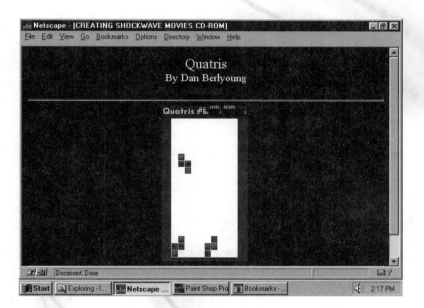

The main hurdle I had to overcome while writing Quatris was the simple fact that the Quatris playing field consisted of a 10 x 20 grid containing 200 individual blocks that had to be completely independent of each other. Simple for a bitmapped screen, but Director, as we are all painfully aware, has only 48 sprite channels. I ended up being able to do it with only 40 tracks, with 8 left over for interface elements.

The inspiration for the solution came from the hi-res graphics screen of the Apple]I . It represented each pixel of the screen with a bit from a byte of memory. That way one byte could handle 7 pixels. (The 8th pixel was for a color-shifting mechanism that is too arcane for me to go into now.) Remembering this, I thought, "Why can't I do this with a sprite channel in Director?" And that's what I did.

To start, I created 32 sprites which contained cast members that represented all the different ways 5 blocks (or pixels) could be turned on and off. For example, the first actor had nothing in it, no blocks turned on. [   ] The second, had the first block turned on [x], the third [x], the fourth [xx] and so on up to the 32nd [xxxxx]. Then all I needed was to code up several binary boolean functions (Lingo could really use these!) so I could turn on and off specified bits inside the number that would represent the cast member I would use. (Namely I needed a binary AND function to turn on and off specified bits.) By using this method, I could handle 10 blocks (one of 20 rows) with only 2 sprite channels. At 2 channels per row and 20 rows, this comes out to 40 channels.

After creating those basic routines, the rest of the game was a simple matter of creating a main event loop that checked the keyboard, updated any falling shapes, and checked for collisions and completed rows.

'Stroids

The big challenge in writing 'Stroids was that I had to be able to manage a variable number of objects all with different locations, appearances, velocities, and life spans. The key word here was "objects," and that meant using the dreaded "Parent/child" object-oriented part of Lingo that we all love and fear.

What I developed was a generalized Lingo parent/child object that I called an "Oid" that represented a visible, moving thing on the screen.

This object when birthed first off searches for an open sprite channel and grabs it. It then sets up some location, velocity, and appearance properties, depending upon values sent to it. I could have had it insert itself into the "actor list," list but I wanted to keep the "rocks" and "bullets" separate, so I maintained two lists that contained references to each object in these two classes.

As with Quatris, the game consisted of a main event loop that looked for key presses and sent update messages to all objects on the screen. The objects themselves took care of movement, collision checking, and lifetime expirations (bullets). The thing that shocked me the most while writing this game was that the bulk of the "Oid" object definition and the main event loop took only four hours to write. The remaining ten hours or so were spent adding all the fluff, such as scoring, number of ships remaining, and figuring out how to split one asteroid into two more moving at slightly different vectors.

Using this same dynamic sprite allocation object definition (Oid), I am working on a "Missile Command" type of game and finding it equally easy to create.

Whack-A-Mole

Creator: mindframe

About mindframe

mindframe is a multimedia firm located in St. Paul, Minnesota. The company was founded in 1994 by John Barton and Steve Etzell with the objective of providing high-quality multimedia production for Twin Cities businesses. mindframe provides programming, design, and consulting services.

mindframe employs five full-time people, a few part-timers, and contractors who are mostly programmers, graphic artists, and musicians. Most of the employees have been with mindframe for over a year and a half. Our work appears on over 1,000,000 CD-ROMs worldwide and we have produced several Web pages. Through our full-time employees and part-time employees, we have talents in C, PERL, Director, digital video, music composition, art and design, HTML, Authorware, and more. We develop programs for all platforms, including Macintosh, DOS, Windows 3.1, Windows 95, and UNIX.

mindframe belongs to several local trade groups including the IICS and the Multimedia Round Table.

If you would like to learn more about mindframe, feel free to visit our Web site: http://www.mindframe.com.

e-mail: info@mindframe.com
Phone: (612) 646-8967 (ask for Troy)
Fax: 612-646-1675

Credits

John M. Barton: mindframe's head graphic artist. John has worked as an illustrator and graphic designer for eight years in the Twin Cities area. He works mainly on the Macintosh but has also mastered 3D Studio, and Director on the PC. John has also mastered Shockwave for Freehand. When he's not working, he enjoys spending time with his wife and daughter as well as working on his classic 1986 Ford Taurus. Prior to mindframe, he was the Art Director for Wayzata Technology, a small CD-ROM publisher located in Minnesota.

Steven J. Etzell: mindframe's head Director programmer. Steve has been programming multimedia in Director for three years. Steve works on Macs, PCs, and UNIX computers. He also programs in C and PERL and encodes digital video on mindframe's Optibase MPEG boards as well as QuickTime on their A/V Macs. In his free time he enjoys water skiing, tennis, golf, hockey, basketball, and many other sports he doesn't get to play anymore while going to school and working. His techie interests lie in intelligent agents, Web agents, and many facets of information systems design. He is also picking up Java for fun and profit. Prior to mindframe, Steve was a multimedia programmer at Wayzata Technology, a small CD-ROM publisher located in Minnesota.

Paul A. Weier: Paul is mindframe's System Administrator. He is responsible for maintaining mindframe's Internet connection on their Sun SparcStation and was the chief architect of Whack-A-Mole. Among his talents, he excels in CGI scripting, PERL, the tools of UNIX System Administration, C programming, and video games. His interests outside of work are video games, movies, books, splatball, volleyball, and home improvement. Prior to mindframe Paul was a UNIX applications programmer for a local investment company.

Troy D. Lanoux: mindframe's sales and marketing expert. Troy has also been trained in the art of HTML programming and he has even created his own Web page. Troy is an active board member of the Midwest Direct Marketing Association and is the leader of a SIG of the IICS. In his free time, Troy enjoys water skiing, raquetball, tennis, and video games.

Nathan C. Steinbauer: mindframe's customer support rep and account executive. Nathan is responsible for much of our usability testing and quality assurance. In Nathan's free time he enjoys listening to music, going to concerts, reading, going to movies, competitive sport fishing (named Mr. Bass 1993 by the Baxter Bass Snatchers), and critiquing fine coffee.

Justin Yahnke: mindframe's apprentice programmer and graphic artist. Justin is currently a student at the Minneapolis College of Art and Design. He is a skilled graphic designer as well as a programmer. Justin did much of the "grunt" work on Whack-A-Mole. Justin is also a talented musician, an expert video game player, a martial arts expert, and a hippie of the '90s. Justin is also the only member of mindframe known to have a tatoo.

Kelly Klein: mindframe's current slave from the University of St. Thomas. She is a student at St. Thomas, studying Quantitative Methods/Computer Science and Mathematics. Kelly performs various duties for mindframe that include HTML programming, PERL scripting, system administration, and being an advisor on program design and creation. She is also becoming an expert in network security, Java programming, and data encryption.

About Whack-A-Mole

Whack-A-Mole was conceived by mindframe's System Administrater, Paul Weier. Everyone in the office was trying to come up with a cool Shockwave app to put on our Web page. Paul came up the the concept and wrote a short specification of how the application should work. When he finished the specification, he handed it to Steve Etzell to begin production.

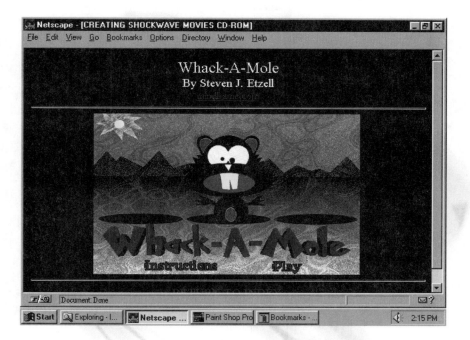

Etzell looked at the spec written by Weier and requested some graphics from John Barton. Barton created the graphics seen in Whack-A-Mole. When the graphics were completed, Etzell selected some music that was composed for a proof-of-concept of a video game that mindframe worked on in 1995. The music was written and produced by Matt Keen who was mindframe's student slave at the time. Matt Keen has since forsaken multimedia programming and doomed himself to the hell of programming databases. Etzell then created the introduction and a shell of the rest of the game. He then passed the work onto Justin Yahnke to be completed.

Justin took the game from the meaningless shell it was and made it into the game it is. Once Yahnke completed the game, it went through a quick beta-testing cycle and was placed on the mindframe Web page. Etzell and Yahnke worked together to fix the existing bugs and they continue to update the game.

How Whack-A-Mole Was Produced

We used several pieces of software on both Macs and PCs to create Whack-A-Mole.

- Infini-D for the Mac
- Adobe Photoshop 3.0.1
- Director 4.0.4 for the Mac
- Director 4.0.4 for the PC
- Afterburner for the Mac
- Served on Sun Sparcstation running solaris 2.4 on the NCSA HTTP server.
- SoundEdit Pro
- DeBabelizer 1.6.5

The game play was designed by Paul Weier and handed to Steve Etzell as an e-mail document. Etzell reviewed the document with Weier to make sure that the requirements were clear. Etzell and Weier worked together to decide how to make the game small enough to download over the Internet as well as big enough to be playable.

They chose the screen size and the number of elements for the screen, and decided on a target size for the movie (250K). Most of the elements outlined in the original specification were implemented in the game.

Etzell then asked Barton for some graphics for the game. Barton created the mole graphics in Infini-D and Photoshop. It took him about 5 hours to come up with the graphics seen in the game. The graphics were in Photoshop PICT format in 24-bit color.

When Barton completed the graphics he gave them to Etzell for review. Etzell took the graphics and ran them through DeBabelizer to create a common 256-color palette and converted all the graphics to that 8-bit palette. Once the graphics were DeBabelized, Etzell imported the PICT files into Director.

Etzell then went to work on the audio selections for the movie. Since space is a big issue in Shockwave movies, Etzell trimmed the background music from its original length, looped the clip, and saved it in an 8-bit 11Khz AIFF file using SoundEdit Pro for the Macintosh. He then selected several sound effects from some clip-audio CDs in the company CD library. He also trimmed and edited the audio clips from the CDs using SoundEdit Pro, ultimatly saving the clips as 8-bit 11Khz AIFF files.

Once the audio editing was complete, he imported the sounds into the Whack-A-Mole Director file. He spent about half a day creating the introduction screen and the rest of the shell for the game. The text elements of the game were created using the text tool in Director and saved as PICT files, since the fonts would not be usable on other machines—especially as a Shockwave file.

After the shell was created, the specification file, the Whack-A-Mole Director file, and all of the raw graphical and audio elements were handed to Yahnke to be completed. Yahnke spent about two days on the logic and programming of the rest of the game. Yahnke requested new graphics for the mallet and for smaller moles. Once Yahnke completed the game, he handed it over to Weier and Etzell for testing.

Etzell took the game, reviewed the code quickly, and then ran it through the beta version of Afterburner for the Macintosh. Etzell gave the file to Weier to place on a test Web page. While the game was being tested by other people in the office, Etzell reviewed the Director file and the code to see if anything could be optimized. Etzell found a few lingering graphic elements and sound files that could be deleted from the cast. He also slightly modified the code for the play of music and for the instructions screen.

After everyone in the office had a chance to review the game and write down their comments, Etzell and Yahnke worked on fixing bugs and adding simple functionality. The Shockwave game was then tested on many different machines on different platforms. The game was tested using an alpha version of the Shockwave plug-in for Netscape 2.0 on a Macintosh 840A/V, a Pentium-based Windows 95 machine, a 486 running Windows 3.1, and several smaller Macs.

Once the fixes were in place and the game made it through the office testing, the game was placed on the mindframe.com Web page. The page evolved through comments by outside users that accessed the game. We also made modifications to the game from user comments.

Some of the problems encountered in the process of producing Whack-A-Mole were as follows:

- Large audio file sizes.

- Large graphics.

- Working with alpha and beta versions of the Afterburner and Shockwave plug-ins.

- The new Lingo commands for Shockwave.

- Speed of download and speed of play of the game on different machines.

- The sound effects were quirky on Windows machines.

There are several things that we wish to do to the game but are having trouble finding the time to make the modifications. These are some of the things we want to add to the game:

- A multiple entry for the game (with or without instructions).

- The introduction would be a separate Shockwave file from the game file.

- A flashy introduction screen complete with instructions.

- Keeping track of the high score.

- Selection of different music, sound level capabilities, and different "splat" sounds.

- Addition of different things to "Whack," and different whacking tools.

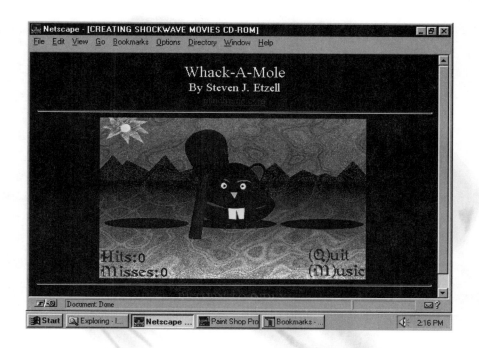

Appendix A

About the Online Companion

Bring your Web pages to life with Shockwave! The *Shockwave Online Companion* is your one stop location for Shockwave resources on the Internet. It serves as an informative tool as well as an annotated software library aiding in your exploration of Shockwave's powerful development environment.

The *Shockwave Online Companion* links you to available Shockwave newsgroups, Web pages, and e-mail discussion groups. So you can just click on the reference name and jump directly to the resource you are interested in.

Perhaps one of the most valuable features of the *Shockwave Online Companion* is its Software Archive. Here, you'll find and be able to download the latest demos, utilities, and other software that is freely available on the Internet. Also with Ventana Online's helpful description of the software you'll know exactly what your getting and why. So you won't download the software just to find you have no use for it.

The *Shockwave Online Companion* also links you to the Ventana Library where you will find useful press and jacket information on a variety of Ventana offerings. Plus, you have access to a wide selction of exciting new releases and coming attractions. In addition, Ventana's Online Library allows you to order the books you want.

The *Shockwave Online Companion* represents Ventana Online's ongoing commitment to offering the most dynamic and exciting products possible. And soon Ventana Online will be adding more services, including more multimedia supplements, searchable indexes, and sections of the book reproduced and hyperlinked to the Internet resources they reference.

To access, connect via the World Wide Web to http://www.vmedia.com/director.html

Appendix B

About the Companion CD-ROM

The CD-ROM included with your copy of *Shockwave!* contains a wealth of valuable software, including the Shockwave plug-in for Windows and Macintosh. Providing the plug-in will save you valuable downloading time and gets you up and running fast. Also included is a step-by-step tutorial that walks you through building a Shockwave movie. The Gallery of movies represented within the book also can be viewed on the CD. And the author's examples and code are conveniently placed on the CD as well.

Installing the CD-ROM is simple. If you are running Windows 95, insert the CD in the CD-ROM drive and double-click the My Computer icon. Double-click on the Shockcd_pc icon. Then double-click the viewer.exe icon. You'll see a welcome screen that introduces the CD.

If you are running Windows 3.11, insert the CD in your CD-ROM drive and with Windows running, select File, Run from the Program Manager. Then type **D:\VIEWER** (where D: is your CD-ROM drive) in the command-line box and press Enter. You'll see a menu screen offering several choices.

If you are using a Macintosh, insert the CD in your CD-ROM drive and double-click on the Viewer icon. The CD will launch and you'll see an introduction screen.

After the initial introduction, a menu screen appears. You can choose CD Contents, Tutorial, Ventana, or Hot Picks. Click on a choice.

If you choose CD Contents a laboratory scene is displayed. Click on Shockwave to install the Shockwave plug-in on your hard drive. The switches at the top of your screen copy Shockwave samples to your hard drive. Click on the Web crawler in the lower right corner to view sample Shockwave movies. Click on the folder to view a listing of the sample code contained within the book.

If you choose Tutorial, a Shockwave tutorial is displayed. You can use this tutorial to step through creating a Shockwave movie.

If you want further information about Ventana, click on the Ventana option.

To view information about other upcoming Ventana titles, click on Hot Picks. A graveyard scene appears on your screen. Each grave represents a Ventana title. Click on the tombstone to see a description of the book. Click on Printer Order Form to receive information on ordering the book. Click on the tombstone to return to the Hot Picks menu.

Appendix C

Shockwave Lingo

There are 11 new Lingo commands for Shocking your Director movies. These commands provide your Shockwave movie access to the network. Most Lingo commands immediately return a result; Shockwave commands and functions are dependent on the Net access time. The network is essentially an asynchronous place. It takes time to get things from the Net; however, the user can continue interacting with a Shockwave movie during an asynchronous operation. Most of the network commands involve starting an operation, then checking to see if it has been completed, and finally getting the results.

These new commands are not recognized by the Director development environment. In order to develop your Shockwave file, you will need to use simulated handlers (see Intercepting Shockwave Commands later in this appendix) to intercept these new commands to avoid script errors. Once you are satisfied with the file's performance off the Net, the file can be tested on the Net from your hard drive, before Afterburning (compressing the Director file), using the open file command in Netscape 2.0.

Intercepting Shockwave Commands

To intercept these commands during development, it is recommended that you place the following movie scripts in your movie. Remember to comment them out before Afterburning or testing on the Net.

```
Movie Scripts
(comment this out before using in your html)

on GetLatestNetID
return 1 -- thisNetID
end
----------
on GetNetText URL
alert "Getting net text from..." & RETURN & url
end
----------
on GotoNetMovie shockwaveURL
alert "Loading" && shockwaveURL

set the itemdelimiter to "/"
  put the last Item of movieURL into targetMovie
  set the itemdelimiter to ","

go to movie targetMovie --in same directory during
development
end
----------
```

```
on GoToNetPage URL
  alert "This would have taken you to web page:" &
RETURN & URL endon NetAbort thisNetID
put "Operation Aborted"
end
----------

on NetDone  thisNetID
--simulate the time lag at the end of a net operation
  cursor 4
  starttimer

repeat while the timer < 90  --1.5 seconds
    nothing
  end repeat

cursor -1
  return TRUE
end
----------
on NetError thisNetID
return "OK"
end
----------

on NetLastModDate thisNetID
return the date
end
----------

on NetMIME thisNetID
return "MIME type"
end
----------

on NetTextResult thisNetID
return "Some Net Text"
end
----------

on PreloadNetThing  URL
alert "This would have preloaded:" & RETURN & URL
end

--end moviescript
```

GetLatestNetID

function

Syntax   GetLatestNetID

Description   This function returns a unique identifier for the last asynchronous operation which was started.

The Shockwave movie counts each URL call after it is loaded. If the first call is **getNetText** "http://whatever.txt" then check for netdone(1) or NetTextResult(1).

Checking for NetDone(1) immediately after the URL call may return true because the last net operation was the movie loading, so allow a little delay before checking. Testing for Net operations within this new asynchronous environment may require programming around the time delays presented by the Net.

Example

```
on exitFrame
    GetNetText  "http://www.yoursite.com/text.txt"
end

on exitFrame
  global currentNetID
  set currentNetID = GetLatestNetID()
end

--skip a frame to allow for moving frame head

on exitFrame
  global currentNetID
  if netDone(currentNetID) then
    put NetTextResult(1) into field "displayTextField"
    updatestage
```

```
        else
          go to the frame - 1
        end if
      end
```

See also   **NetTextResult, NetDone, NetError**

GetNetText

command

Syntax   **GetNetText** *uri*

Description   This command starts the retrieval of an HTTP item.

Lingo can import this item as text using the **NetTextResult**() function. The universal resource identifier (URI) specifies the HTTP item to be retrieved. The current version of the Shockwave plug-in only supports HTTP URLs.

Example
```
on exitFrame
   GetNetText  "http://www.yoursite.com/text.txt"
end
```

Director tests the state of the asynchronous operation and posts the results using the following Lingo script:

```
on exitFrame
   put NetTextResult(1) into field "displayTextField"
   updatestage
end
```

Note: Shockwave cannot simultaneously read and write. Checking netError(1) after the GetNetText call will show an OS error.

See also   **NetTextResult**

GOTONETMOVIE

command

Syntax   `GotoNetMovie` *uri*

Description   This command retrieves and goes to a new Director movie from the network. The new movie occupies the same display area as the calling movie. The universal resource identifier (URI) specifies the HTTP item to be retrieved. The current version of the Shockwave plug-in only supports HTTP URLs.

This command is the Shockwave version of the **go to movie** "whatmovie" commands used in regular Lingo. Like the regular version, global variables will stay resident in the new movie.

If you have more than one movie on a page, only one movie can call for a second movie at a time. If several movies issue a GotoNetMovie command during the same period of activity, only the first GotoNetMovie command is executed.

Note: The current movie will continue playing until the next is loaded, then, without warning, it will terminate and go to the next one.

Example
```
on exitFrame
    GotoNetMovie "http://www.yoursite.com/nextShock.dcr"
end
```

See also   **PreloadNetThing**

OTONETPAGE

command

Syntax   `GotoNetPage` *url*

Description   This command opens a URL, whether it's a Director movie or some other MIME type. Using GotoNetPage opens a new page within the net browser. The universal resource locator (URL) specifies the HTTP item to be retrieved. The current version of the Shockwave plug-in only supports HTTP URLs.

Note: The current movie will continue playing until the page is loaded, then, without warning, it will terminate and go to the new URL.

Example   ```
on exitFrame
    GotoNetPage "http://www.yoursite.com/nextPage.html"
end
```

**See also**   **PreloadNetThing**

# ETABORT

<div align="right">**command**</div>

**Syntax**     `NetAbort` *NetID*

**Description**   This command cancels the network operation referenced by NetID without waiting for a result.
```

Example
```
on mouseUp
  global currentAsynchronousOperation
  NetAbort currentAsynchronousOperation
end
```

See also   **PreloadNetThing, NetDone, NetError**

NETDONE    function

Syntax   **NetDone** *NetID*

Description   This function returns true when the asynchronous network operation referenced by the NetID is finished. Until that point, it returns false. The NetID can be obtained at the start of any asynchronous operation by using the **getLatestNetID** function.

Example
```
on exitFrame
  global nextMovie
  set nextMovie = "http://www.yoursite.com/
nextShock.dcr"
  PreloadNetThing  nextMovie
end

on exitFrame
  if NetDone(1) then
    if NetError(1) = "OK" then goToNetMovie nextMovie
    -- or you can goToNetPage if preloading an HTML
  else
    go to the frame - 1
  end if
end
```

Note: In order to prevent the system from being tied up, it is recommended that you keep the playback head moving between at least two frames while your movie plays.

The movie counts the URL calls after it is loaded, so if the first call is getNetText url, then check for netdone(1) or NetTextResult(1). Checking for NetDone() immediately after the URL call may return true because the last net operation was the movie loading. Testing for Net operations within this new asynchronous environment may require programming around the time delays presented by the Net.

See also   **PreloadNetThing, NetError, goToNetMovie**

ETERROR   **function**

Syntax   **NetError**_NetID_

Description   This function returns an empty string until the asynchronous operation referenced by the NetID is finished. It returns "OK" if the operation was completed successfully or a string describing the error if the operation failed.

Example
```
on exitFrame
  global nextMovie
  set nextMovie = "http://www.yoursite.com/
nextShock.dcr"
  PreloadNetThing  nextMovie
end

on exitFrame
  if NetDone(1) then
    if NetError(1) = "OK" then GoToNetMovie nextMovie
    -- or you can GoToNetPage if preloading an HTML
```

```
      else
        go to the frame - 1
      end if
    end
```

See also   **PreloadNetThing, NetDone, GoToNetMovie**

NETLASTMODDATE   function

Syntax   **NetLastModDate***NetID*

Description This function returns the date last modified string from the HTTP
            header for the item referenced by NetID.

Example   ```
            on exitFrame
              PreloadNetThing "http://www.yoursite.com/text.txt"
            end
            ```

            Director tests the state of the asynchronous operation and posts
            the results using the following Lingo script:

            ```
            on exitFrame
              put NetLastModDate(1) into field "How old am I"
              updatestage
            end
            ```

            Note: This function can be called only from the time NetDone or
            NetError reports that the operation is complete until the next
            operation is started. Once the next operation is started, Director
            discards the results of the previous operation in order to conserve
            memory.

See also   **PreloadNetThing, NetDone, NetError**
            ```

NetMIME

function

Syntax   **NetMIME** *NetID*

Description   This function returns the MIME type of the HTTP item referenced by NetID.

Example
```
on exitFrame
    PreloadNetThing  "http://www.yoursite.com/text.txt"
end
```
Director tests the state of the asynchronous operation and posts the results using the following Lingo script:
```
on exitFrame
    put NetMIME(1) into field "what MIME am I"
    updatestage
end
```

Note: This function can be called only from the time NetDone or NetError reports that the operation is complete until the next operation is started. Once the next operation is started, Director discards the results of the previous operation in order to conserve memory.

See also   **PreloadNetThing, NetDone, NetError**

NETTEXTRESULT

Syntax   `NetTextResult`*NetID*

Description   This function returns the text result of the operation. For a **GetNetText** operation, this is the text of the HTTP item. This function can also be used in conjunction with other NetPage operations that produce a text result like Java Scripts.

Example
```
on exitFrame
    GetNetText  "http://www.yoursite.com/text.txt"
end
```

Director tests the state of the asynchronous operation and posts the results using the following Lingo script:

```
on exitFrame
    put NetTextResult(1) into field "displayTextField"
    updatestage
end
```

Note: This function can be called only from the time NetDone or NetError reports that the operation is complete until the next operation is started. Once the next operation is started, Director discards the results of the previous operation in order to conserve memory.

See also   **GetNetText, NetDone, NetError**

PRELOADNETTHING   **command**

Syntax   `PreloadNetThing` *uri*

Description   This command starts preloading an HTTP item into the local file cache. The universal resource identifier (URI) specifies the HTTP item to be referenced. The universal resource identifier (URI) specifies the HTTP item to be retrieved. The current version of the Shockwave plug-in only supports HTTP URLs. This item can be anything, including other Director movies, an HTML page, a graphic, etc. This command is like a preLoadCast for the Net.

The item is stored in the Netscape disk cache on the end user's hard drive. The preloading occurs asynchronously, allowing the user to interact with the current movie while it is happening. Your movie should check periodically for the **NetDone**() function to determine when it has finished loading. Usually the item can be viewed immediately after preloading; however, if the end user's cache is set too low, the item may be removed from the disk cache before your Shockwave file can use it.

Note: There is a limit of four asynchronous operations at a time. Be sure to check for the completion of each event before attempting to start new ones.

Example
```
on exitFrame
   global nextMovie
   set nextMovie = "http://www.yoursite.com/
nextShock.dcr"
   PreloadNetThing  nextMovie
end

on exitFrame
   if NetDone(1) then
     if NetError(1) = "OK" then goToNetMovie nextMovie
     -- or you can goToNetPage if preloading an HTML
```

```
        else
          go to the frame - 1
        end if
      end
```

See also   **NetDone, NetError, GoToNetMovie**

There are a number of Lingo commands that do not work with the current Shockwave plug-in. Some of these are bugs, others are because of the security restrictions on the Net.

Lingo Commands not available in Shockwave:

Control resource files

```
openResFile
closeResFile
```

Window commands

```
open window
close window
```

File Handling Commands

```
importFileInto
fileName of cast
fileName of window
getNthFileNameInFolder
moviePath
pathName
searchCurrentFolder
searchPaths
saveMovie
```

Printing Commands

```
printFrom
```

System-related Commands

```
open

quit
restart
shutdown
mci
```

Other things to consider:

The Tempo features in the score will not function properly, if at all, in Shockwave. Instead, it is recommended that all tempo operations, including Lingo pauses, be handled by using Lingo in Shocked movies.

Pause

Pauses should be handled as a frame loop between two or more frames.
example:

```
frame 1    marker "start"
on exitFrame
end

frame 2
on exitframe
   go to the frame - 1  -- or go to "start"
end
```

Wait for sound

Waiting for a sound to finish should be checked by using the soundBusy() function.

example:

```
frame 1    marker "start"
on exitFrame
   if not soundBusy(1) then go to "nextThingToHappen"
end

frame 2
on exitframe
   if soundBusy(1) then
      go to the frame - 1 -- or go to "start"
   else
      go to "nextThingToHappen"
   end if
end

frame 3  marker "nextThingToHappen"
on exit frame
   --whatever
end
```

Wait for Mouse Click

In the script channel, type this script:

example:

```
on exitFrame
   go the frame
end

on mouseUp
   go the frame + 1
end
```

Wait For N Seconds

In the script channel, type the following script.
example:

```
on exitFrame
   set N =   -- set N to the number of seconds you want
to wait

if the timer > (N * 60) then
     startTimer
   else if the timer < (N * 60) then
     go the frame
   end if
end
```

KeyUp

KeyUp lingo commands will not work. Use KeyDown instead.

System lockout

If you leave the system in a repeat loop, the user will not be able to access anything. This even locks out access to the Netscape browser. Loop between frames instead.

Using XObjects

Xobjects can be used with Shockwave movies; however, you must allow the user to download the Xobject you want to use before you start the movie.

The XObject needs to be placed in the same folder or directory as the Shockwave plug-in.

It's important for the XObject to be in the folder or directory where the Shockwave plug-in is located because that's the only folder or directory where an openXlib statement that's in a shocked Director movie looks for XObjects. The openXlib statement ignores any path you give it.

On Windows 3.1 computers, XObjects need to be in the directory named NP16DSW. The default location for the NP16DSW directory is C:\NETSCAPE\PLUGINS.

On Windows 95 computers, XObjects need to be in the NP32DSW folder. The default path for the NP32DSW folder is C:\Program Files\Netscape\Navigator\Program\Plugins.

On Macintosh computers, XObjects need to be in the Plug-ins folder. The default location of the Plug-ins folder is in the Netscape Navigator folder.

If you create a movie that calls an XObject and the XObject isn't in the same folder or directory as the Shockwave plug-In, users will get an error message that says Script error: Xlib file not found. To avoid the error message, it's a good idea to display an alert message at the beginning of the movie asking users to make sure the XObject is in the correct folder. To open an XObject, include code such as this in the startMovie handler:

```
on startMovie
    global myXObject
    -- The following line makes sure the XObject doesn't
already exist.
    if objectP(myXObject) then myXObject(mDispose)
    openXlib "LibraryName"
    set myXObject = LibraryName(mNew)
end startMovie
```

It's good practice to close any XObject you've opened when done.

```
on stopMovie
    global myXObject
    if objectP(myXObject) then myXObject(mDispose)
    closeXlib "LibraryName"
end stopMovie
```

Appendix D

What You Can't Do With Shockwave

A number of standard Director functions are unavailable when using Shockwave. Operations that require access to local files or system-level commands are disabled for security purposes. Some Tempo channel commands are also disabled, as they would interfere with browser operation.

Local File Access

Reading and writing to local files is disabled in Shockwave for Director for security purposes.

- The functions of the FileIO XObject are not implemented in the plug-in.
- OpenXLib command is disabled.
- OpenResFile command is disabled.
- CloseXLib command is disabled.

- CloseResFile command is disabled.
- importFileInto command is disabled.
- saveMovie command is disabled.
- searchCurrentFolder function is disabled.
- getNthFileNameInFolder is disabled.
- searchPaths function is disabled.

Linked Media

Linked media files on either the Web server or Web browser machines are not implemented in the initial releases of Shockwave, as they are a subset of local file access operations.

- All QuickTime movies are imported as linked media in Director 4, therefore all QuickTime functions are unavailable in Shockwave.
- Graphics or sounds imported into a Director movie with Link to File checked in the Import dialog will not be available to a Shockwave movie made from the Director file.
- Movie in a window (MIAW) commands are unavailable to Shockwave movies.
- open window command is disabled.
- close window command is disabled.
- fileName of cast function is disabled.
- moviepath function is disabled.

Tempo Settings

Tempo settings that stop the motion of the Playback head in the Score are disabled in Shockwave to prevent CPU cycle competition. This is essentially all Tempo channel settings except the settings for frames per second.

- Wait x seconds is disabled.
- Wait for Mouse Click or Key is disabled.
- Wait for Sound1 to Finish is disabled.
- Wait for Sound2 to Finish is disabled.
- Wait for Digital Video Movie to Finish in Channel x is disabled.

System-Level Commands

For security reasons, system-level commands and XObjects that allow control over the user's machine or connected devices are disabled in Shockwave.

- printFrom command is disabled.
- open command is disabled.
- quit command is disabled.
- restart command is disabled.
- shutdown command is disabled.
- mci command is disabled.

Appendix E

File Size Estimates

Most users sign on to the Internet at transmission speeds of 14400 kbs or less. So, it is best to keep the movie size as small as possible—even before compressing it with Afterburner. Long load times will probably send your user to another site. Games are forgivable to a point, but animated banners, bullets, or sound clips are unforgivable if they are too large. If you are going to include a large movie in your Web page (over 200K), consider loading a smaller movie first and then using GotoNetMovie to download the main movie. Or consider breaking the larger movie into a series of smaller chunks and preloading the next segment as the current segment begins playing.

Content	Size	14.4 kbs	28.8 kbs	64 kbs	1.5 mbps
small movie or movie segment	30K	30 secs	10 secs	6 secs	1 sec
small complete movie	100-200K	180-300 secs	90-180 secs	20-40 secs	1 sec
large complete movie	200-500K	6-12 mins	2-4 mins	90 secs	3 secs
very large movie	1 Meg	You're joking	Still joking	3 mins	6 secs

Table E-1: *Download Times at Common Modem Speeds.*

Appendix F

Configuring Your Web Server for Shockwave

To configure your Web server for delivery of Macromedia Shockwave for Director files, you will need to change the configuration of the server to recognize the .dcr files created by Shockwave as a distinct MIME type.

The configuration should be altered to serve file names ending in .dcr with a MIME type of "application/x-director". This will tell the server to send the proper information ahead of your Shockwave files so that browsers will know to use the Shockwave plug-in to view the file.

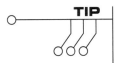

TIP

You can serve uncompressed Director .dir and protected .dxr movies as well as Shockwave .dcr movies by adding lines to your configration file for each of those extensions as well, keeping all information the same except for the extension.

For UNIX Servers

Contact your system administrator to add the following information:

◈ MIME type: application

◈ Sub Type: x-director

◈ Extension: .dcr

For MacOS Servers

MacHTTP

Add the following line to the .config file:

```
BINARY .DCR TEXT * application/x-director
```

WebSTAR

Run the WebSTAR Admin program and choose Suffix Mapping from the Configure menu. Make the entries showing in the figure below and press the Add button.

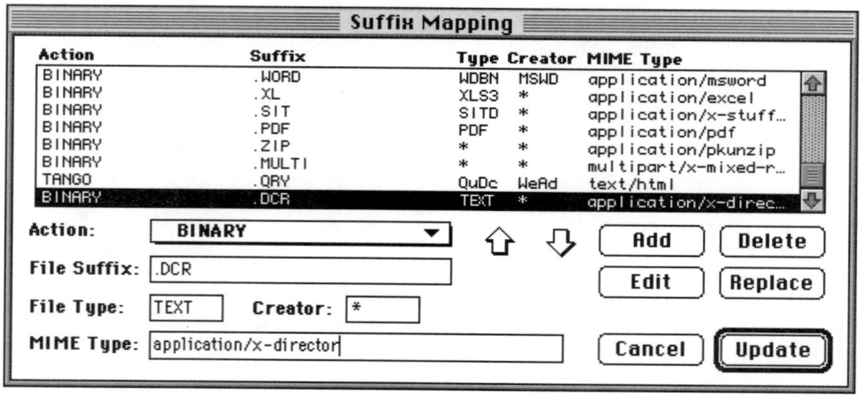

Figure F-1: *WebSTAR's suffix mapping controls.*

Index

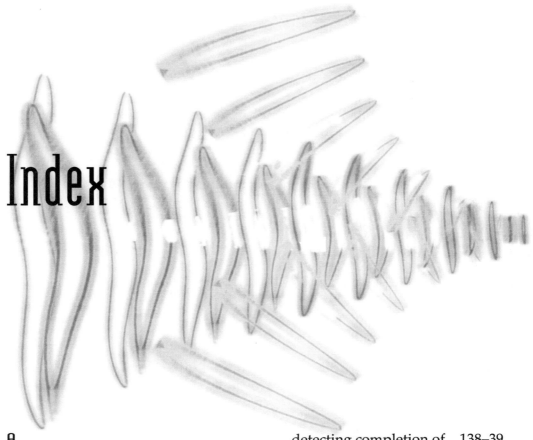

Don't Miss Your Connection!

Location: http://www.vmedia.com/

What's New? | What's Cool? | Handbook | Net Search | Net Directory | Software

Are you sure you have the latest software?
Want to stay up-to-date but don't know how?

Ventana Online helps Net surfers link up to the latest Internet innovations and keep up with popular Internet tools.

- **Save money by ordering electronically** from our complete, annotated online library.

- **Explore Ventana's** *Online Companions*™—regularly updated "cybersupplements" to our books, offering hyperlinked listings and current versions of related free software, shareware and other resources.

- **Visit the hottest sites on the Web!** Ventana's "Nifty Site of the Week" features the newest, most interesting and most innovative online resources.

So check in often to Ventana Online. We're just a URL away!
http://www.vmedia.com

Internet Resources

Internet Business 500

$29.95, 488 pages, illustrated, part #: 287-9

This authoritative list of the most useful, most valuable
online resources for business is also the most current list,
linked to a regularly updated *Online Companion* on the
Internet. The companion CD-ROM features the latest
version of *Netscape Navigator*, plus a hyperlinked version
of the entire text of the book.

Walking the World Wide Web, Second Edition

$39.95, 800 pages, illustrated, part #: 298-4

More than 30% new, this book now features 500 listings
and an extensive index of servers, expanded and
arranged by subject. This groundbreaking bestseller
includes a CD-ROM enhanced with Ventana's WebWalker
technology; updated online components that make it the
richest resource available for Web travelers; and the latest
version of Netscape Navigator along with a full
hyperlinked version of the text.

Quicken 5 on the Internet

$24.95, 472 pages, illustrated, part #: 448-0

Get your finances under control with *Quicken 5 on the
Internet.* Quicken 5 helps make banker's hours a thing of
the past—by incorporating Internet access and linking you
directly to institutions that see a future in 24-hour services.
Quicken 5 on the Internet provides complete guidelines to
Quicken to aid your offline mastery and help you take
advantage of online opportunities.

Windows 95 Revealed!

Windows 95 Power Toolkit

$49.95, 500 pages, illustrated, part #: 319-0

If Windows 95 includes everything but the kitchen sink, get ready to get your hands wet! Maximize the customizing capabilities of Windows 95 with ready-to-use tools, applications and tutorials, including a guide to VBA. The CD-ROM features the complete toolkit, plus additional graphics, sounds and applications. An *Online Companion* includes updated versions of software, hyper-linked listings and links to helpful resources on the Internet.

The Windows 95 Book

$39.95, 1232 pages, illustrated, part #: 154-6

The anxiously awaited revamp of Windows is finally here—which means new working styles for PC users.
This new handbook offers an insider's look at the all-new interface—arming users with tips and techniques for file management, desktop design, optimizing and much more. A must-have for moving to 95! The companion CD-ROM features tutorials, demos, previews and online help plus utilities, screen savers, wallpaper and sounds.

Internet Guide for Windows 95

$24.95, 552 pages, illustrated, part #: 260-7

The *Internet Guide for Windows 95* shows how to use Windows 95's built-in communications tools to access and navigate the Net. Whether you're using The Microsoft Network or an independent Internet provider and Microsoft *Plus!*, this easy-to-read guide helps you started quickly and easily. Learn how to e-mail, download files, and navigate the World Wide Web and take a tour of top sites. An *Online Companion* on Ventana Online features hypertext links to top sites listed in the book.

 Books marked with this logo include a free Internet *Online Companion*™, featuring archives of free utilities plus a software archive and links to other Internet resources.

Web Pages Enhanced

The Web Server Book

$49.95, 680 pages, illustrated, part #: 234-8

The cornerstone of Internet publishing is a set of UNIX tools, which transform a computer into a "server" that can be accessed by networked "clients." This step-by-step in-depth guide to the tools also features a look at key issues—including content development, services and security. The companion CD-ROM contains Linux™, Netscape Navigator™, ready-to-run server software and more.

Java Programming for the Internet

$49.95, 500 pages, illustrated, part #: 355-7

Create dynamic, interactive Internet applications with Java Programming for the Internet. Expand the scope of your online development with this comprehensive, step-by-step guide to creating Java applets. Includes four real-world, start-to-finish tutorials. The CD-ROM has all the programs, samples and applets from the book, plus shareware. Continual updates on Ventana's *Online Companion* will keep this information on the cutting edge.

Exploring Moving Worlds

$24.99, 300 pages, illustrated, part #:467-7

Moving Worlds—a newly accepted programming standard that uses Java and JavaScript for animating objects in three dimensions—is billed as the next-generation implementation of VRML. *Exploring Moving Worlds* includes an overview of the Moving Worlds standard, detailed specifications on design and architecture, and software examples to help advanced Web developers create live content, animation and full motion on the Web.

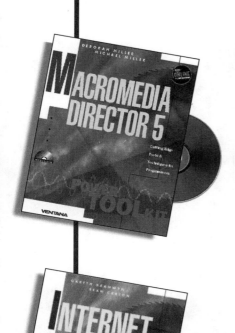

Macromedia Director 5 Power Toolkit

$49.95, 800 pages, illustrated, part #: 289-5

Macromedia Director 5 Power Toolkit views the industry's hottest multimedia authoring environment from the inside out. Features tools, tips and professional tricks for producing power-packed projects for CD-ROM and Internet distribution. Dozens of exercises detail the principles behind successful multimedia presentations and the steps to achieve professional results. The companion CD-ROM includes utilities, sample presentations, animations, scripts and files.

Internet Power Toolkit

$49.95, 700 pages, illustrated, part #: 329-8

Plunge deeper into cyberspace with *Internet Power Toolkit*, the advanced guide to Internet tools, techniques and possibilities. Channel its array of Internet utilities and advice into increased productivity and profitability on the Internet. The CD-ROM features an extensive set of TCP/IP tools including Web USENET, e-mail, IRC, MUD and MOO, and more.

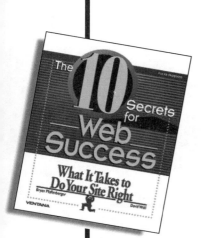

The 10 Secrets for Web Success

$19.95, 350 pages, illustrated, part #: 370-0

Create a winning Web site—by discovering what the visionaries behind some of the hottest sites on the Web know instinctively. Meet the people behind Yahoo, IUMA, Word and more, and learn the 10 key principles that set their sites apart from the masses. Discover a whole new way of thinking that will inspire and enhance your own efforts as a Web publisher.

 Books marked with this logo include a free Internet *Online Companion*™, featuring archives of free utilities plus a software archive and links to other Internet resources.

TO ORDER ANY VENTANA TITLE, COMPLETE THIS ORDER FORM AND MAIL OR FAX IT TO US, WITH PAYMENT, FOR QUICK SHIPMENT.

TITLE	PART #	QTY	PRICE	TOTAL

SHIPPING

For all standard orders, please ADD $4.50/first book, $1.35/each additional.
For software kit orders, ADD $6.50/first kit, $2.00/each additional.
For "two-day air," ADD $8.25/first book, $2.25/each additional.
For "two-day air" on the kits, ADD $10.50/first kit, $4.00/each additional.
For orders to Canada, ADD $6.50/book.
For orders sent C.O.D., ADD $4.50 to your shipping rate.
North Carolina residents must ADD 6% sales tax.
International orders require additional shipping charges.

SUBTOTAL = $ _____

SHIPPING = $ _____

TOTAL = $ _____

Name _____

E-mail _____ Daytime phone _____

Company _____

Address (No PO Box) _____

City_____ State_____ Zip_____

Payment enclosed ___VISA ___MC ___ Acc't # _____ Exp. date_____

Signature _____ Exact name on card _____

Mail to: Ventana • PO Box 13964 • Research Triangle Park, NC 27709-3964 ☎ 800/743-5369 • Fax 919/544-9472

Check your local bookstore or software retailer for these and other bestselling titles, or call toll free:

800/743-5369